"a metaphysical pseudo ...

Lee Martin

with John F McDonald

HEY KIM
MUCH LOVE!

London

Published by Gatecrasher Books
London – England

Copyright © 2016 Lee Martin & John F McDonald

This is a pseudo-biography. Some names have been changed for privacy reasons and some of the characters are fictional.

'All I Really Want To Do'
Lyrics & Music by Bob Dylan
© 1992 Special Rider Music
Reproduced by permission of International Music Publications Ltd

The authors and publisher have made all reasonable efforts to contact copyright-holders for permission, and apologies for any omissions or errors in the form of credits given – corrections may be made to future printings.

ISBN: 978-0-9929731-3-1 (pbk)
ISBN: 978-0-9929731-4-8 (ebk)

Cover image: © BenG.Photography
Book and cover design: www.shakspeareeditorial.org

For Nooly, Daffy, The Barons of Ridley, Nicki, DRP, Nate and Jack G
for Geordy, Weasel, The Crows, Strutts, Big Steve and Big Rich
for Stephen Murray, Caroline and Jake "Pooshtee Boy" Denton

For Beck, Jimmy, Matilda and all my family

and for anyone who wants to break free from the banality of convention

PROLOGUE

This is a book on two levels.

First, it's a history of the hippie phenomenon, from its origins in the Beat Generation of the 1950s, through to its survival today in the form of new-agers and post new-agers, environmentalists, alternative lifestyle enthusiasts and spiritualists. It traces the life of one particular Hippie on a journey from the Haight-Ashbury area of San Francisco in the 1960s to New York during the Summer of Love and then to Woodstock in 1969.

The biography comes back to England at the end of that decade and the story resumes in the UK of the 1970s and 1980s. It narrates the history of the free festivals like Windsor and Stonehenge and the brutality hippies faced from the establishment and a rabid tabloid press. The book touches on Greenham Common and the Peace Movement, before taking to the Hippie Trail and trekking to India and Nepal. The pseudo-biographer suffers personal loss on the way back and experiments within a commune as a way to deal with this trauma. He eventually goes back on the road in a horse-drawn vardo before organising his own music festival in Gloucestershire.

On a second level, the book delves into the metaphysical philosophy of the hippie culture, at first using hallucinogenic drugs, but eventually experiencing enlightenment through understanding. This element of the story may be difficult for non-hippie readers to grasp – but here's a simple step-by-step guide to its meaning.

If you get this, you'll get the essence of it:

∞ What's your view on life – do you think it's got meaning, or is it just a random one-off?

∞ If it's got meaning, do you believe in "god", or a more Buddhist concept – like a universal entity that we're all part of?

∞ If you take the wider view, do you think becoming part of that universal entity can be achieved in one life or does it take many?

∞ If it takes many lives, you obviously believe in some form of reincarnation.

OK

∞ Do you think it's fair that some people are born rich, healthy, intelligent, with access to education and opportunity to become enlightened, while other people are born into poverty, have terrible physical handicaps, suffer mental problems, die as infants, etc.?

∞ If you think it's unfair, is it because this universal entity that we aspire to be part of is essentially unfair? Is it flawed? Can it be flawed?

∞ If it can't be flawed, what would make it fair – so that everybody had the same opportunities to achieve it – to get there?

∞ Maybe through a series of lives (reincarnations)? But no two series of lives could be the same – they'd have to be identical to be utterly fair, wouldn't they?

∞ How could that be? How could every individual experience an identical series of lives?

Answer: By experiencing EVERY LIFE!

So, logically, we are everybody who ever lived and who ever will live. When we look at somebody, we see ourselves in a separate perception of the universal entity. When we help someone, we help ourselves. When we hurt someone, ... !

It's what Jesus Christ taught.

The author of *Hippie* was born with the realisation of this line of logic. He tries to follow it. But human nature is human nature and he can't get past his human emotions – love, hate, greed, violence, envy, etc. Even though he realises that doing bad things to, or wishing bad things on, others is merely hurting himself in a separate perception of the universal oneness.

However, in the beginning, the author has the ability to tap into those other perceptions with the help of mind-altering drugs – he can "become" the people he actually is in a different universal perception.

He can do it without the drugs by the end of the book.

Give it some thought –

it's easy to understand –

no big mystery.

I ain't lookin' to compete with you
Beat or cheat or mistreat you
Simplify you, classify you
Deny, defy or crucify you
All I really wanna do
Is [maybe] be friends with you.

Bob Dylan

Contents

1
The Beat In My Blood

*There is no present. As soon as the future becomes the present,
it immediately becomes the past. It never actually exists as the
present. A moment? – second? – split-second? – nanosecond?
– zeptosecond? – chronon? – plancktime? Unless you realise
that time is continuous, indivisible. If you realise that, you'll
realise everything.*

I come from fairground people originally – booth boxers and animal
circuses and gaff-lads and stilt-walkers and the like. But this book
ain't about fairgrounds nor fire-eaters nor street jugglers – it's about
Hippies. I think I was born around 1948, but that ain't important
either, because I ain't got an age – at least, not in the way you think
of age. I'm every age, if you really want to know – new born to ninety-
nine, and even older. As old as the hills, like they say in Shropshire. I
was five years old when my mother ran off to America with a railroad
drifter – and took me with her. When I say "ran off", it wasn't like
she could've stayed, like she had a choice or anything. I'm not certain
about the detail, but there was some scandal with a married man. Not
my father – he was never married to my mother – some other married
man. We travelled over on a big boat called the *Carinthia* – me and
my mother and the railroad man, who had a thick black moustache
and wore a hat with a round, narrow brim and knew a lot about freight
trains. He knew nothing about women – otherwise he would've picked
someone other than my mother to run off with.

My mother was a witch. Not a real witch in the wart-nosed sense
of the word, not a black witch, nor a white witch for that matter –
she was a wicce-witch and she came from the New Forest region of
Wiltshire. She practised her own kind of magic and she believed in the
Wiccan Rede and travelled round to festivals and Sabbats. She met
the American at the horse fair in Stow-on-the-Wold and hypnotised
him into taking her and me to America. My father wasn't around to

stop her and that's because he wandered away when I was conceived and I never knew who he was – my mother told me he was an animal-handler with a travelling circus. I don't know what the American was doing at a horse fair in Gloucestershire but, by the time he recovered from the spell my mother put on him, we were in North Platte, Nebraska, and it was too late.

You might think that was all there was to it and we lived out our lives in the middle of nowhere, singing Glen Campbell songs. But my mother was a restless soul and couldn't breathe easy in the dust-dry railroad town, and she left the man with the thick moustache and the pork-pie hat one night when he was sleeping, and me and her rode a boxcar all the way across the mountains on our way to California. It wasn't a single boxcar, it was many boxcars – first out of North Platte from the big Bailey Yard and west across the Nebraska state line into Wyoming. So, apart from travelling from fair to fair in Britain when I was but a small chavvie, I also travelled from state to state in America, and you can see I was a traveller from the very day I was born. Nobody'd heard tell of the word Hippie in those days and it was mostly the Indians who wore their hair long and plaited, with feathers.

We travelled across the Wyoming cattle-country with my mother doing the fortune-telling, or dukkering like she called it, and the farmers' wives loved her New Forest accent, and they paid money for her lies and they gave us grub and buttermilk and moonshine, and it wasn't such a bad life. We didn't stay long enough in any one place for the authorities to try to make me go to school and my mother taught me herself how to read and write, after her own fashion. She also taught me about the stars and the seasons and dreams and fetiches and all sorts of wicce-witch things. But I didn't want to be like her, I wanted to be a rock 'n' roller like Frankie Avalon and Chuck Berry and Elvis Presley, and I didn't know then that I actually was all of those people, and everyone else besides.

By the time we got to Reno in Nevada, it was 1960 and the greatest decade in the history of mankind was just about to begin. Las Vegas was taking over from Reno as the gambling capital of America, but the city still attracted crowds from the San Francisco Bay Area – to stuff like motorbike rallies and cook-offs and bowling tournaments and air shows. People I met told me about this group in Frisco called the Beat Generation who were experimenting with drugs and free love and eastern religion, and were rejecting the world of the freight-yarders and farmers and city-slickers and god-fearers. It sounded like something else to a young guy like me and I wanted to go live with them and be one of them, but my witch mother wouldn't let me. So I started reading books like *Howl* and *On The Road* and *Naked Lunch*, and it was different to the stuff my mother was teaching me. I hid them away from her because the wicce part of her wouldn't agree with all this free-thinking and I believed she lived for the most part in a time that was pagan and past. I didn't know then that the stuff she taught me about the summerland and reincarnation and all being one and one being all was actually true!

But I was young and new to the world and I wanted the new things and set little value on the old. I let stuff into my head that the generations before me didn't know much about and I knew it'd change me forever, and it'd only be a matter of time before I got to cross the state line from Reno into northern California and down the valley to the city of poets and cool non-conformists. Something was in the air – in the music and the sexiness and the style of life and even the sun on my face felt different. I could sense it in the dry mountain air of northwest Nevada, and maybe that was something I inherited from my mother, that sixth-sense thing. Maybe she gave me something useful in my short life with her. My mother was doing the dukkering and she liked Reno – it was a town with money to spend and she wasn't getting no younger. She said she'd had enough of the road and wanted to find a rich man and stop moving. She forgot about going to California.

But I didn't.

She never did find Mister Right and spent most of her time with hustlers and gamblers and shysters and riggers, and we lived in a trailer park on the edge of town, out near Hidden Valley. Because my mother decided to stop moving, I had to go to school – and I hated it. I hated being stuck in a classroom all day, learning crap like history and math, and I day-dreamed about being in the back of a pick-up, bouncing down to San Francisco with the wind in my hair. My grades weren't good and I missed class a lot and was always in trouble with the stupid teachers. They sent reports to my mother, which she never read, and threatened a few times to throw me out, but they never did. After a while I went to high school and it wasn't so bad there. Some of the pupils were with it, and I got in with a crowd who smoked some weed and we went skinny-dipping in Virginia Lake and hung round the bars and the clubs in the gambling district, and I was getting used to being in one place – calling someplace home, instead of always moving on. But the thing was inside me, the wanderlust, and it just wouldn't let me be.

I got to be a teenager in '61 and puberty brought an even deeper longing inside me to get away from the seediness of my life in Reno. I started learning to play the violin at school and music was the only subject I was truly interested in. I didn't have a fiddle of my own, but the music teacher let me use the school's scratchy old maple-wood that was made in Salt Lake City. Most of the other kids wanted to learn guitar, but I liked the lonesome sound of the fiddle and I found I had a talent for it too. Me and a few others formed up into a kinda folksy-skiffle group and we'd hang out together and play stuff by The Weavers and The Kingston Trio and Joan Baez and Trini Lopez. We'd mostly smoke grass or resin and take amphetamine – but then something else came along.

One of the guys we hung with, who was a bit older and whose dad was in the army, came by these sugar cubes. He said some stuff called acid was soaked into the cubes, but we didn't believe him. There was about half-a-dozen of us bad kids playing music and just drifting on the day, so we took the sugar cubes and let them melt onto our tongues.

I didn't know then if what happened next was real or just a dream, but I do now. It was part of what my wicce-witch mother was teaching me and was true forever in the past and forever in the future and was part of the all-ness of rocks and grass and mountains and sky and water and air and atoms and protons – and people!

We all split and went our separate ways and I was heading back to the trailer park on my own. I used to take a short cut along a narrow road with a high growth of wild lilac and flannel bushes and black oak on either side. There were fields behind the tall bushes and the trailer park was at the other end of the road. It was bright and sunny when I went into the road but, as I walked, it got darker and darker and quieter and quieter. It was like something had scared all the birds away and was lurking somewhere in the shadows, ready to jump out and swallow me up. I started to run – not quick, just a kinda half-jog. The road seemed to go on forever and I didn't remember it being so long before. As well as that, a misty fog was falling and it was getting difficult to see more than a couple of feet in front.

I was gonna go back, but it was really dark now and there was something weird in the air and I thought I'd reach the trailer park any second. Then I seen this vague, flickering light up ahead and some kinda shadowy creature coming hump-backed outa the gloom towards me and I held my fiddle at the ready to whack whatever it was. A soft rain started to fall, running down my face like little tears and cooling my nervy heart. I stopped being scared and started to feel reassured and even kinda optimistic, upbeat – like when you're taking speed and your heart's beating all-a-flutter and the blood's racing through your veins. The figure came closer and I seen it was a young boy with brown skin and long black hair. The boy turned round when he drew alongside me and started walking back in the direction I was heading.

'You from the trailer park?'

But he didn't answer. He was holding an old-style lantern that lit the road for a few yards in front of us and threw shadows behind that followed us like ghosts – until we came to a wooden gate, set back in the high bushes on the right side of the road. I'd never seen that gate before and I'd been up that road a thousand times. There was a faerie ring on the ground – I knew it was a faerie ring, because that was one of the old wicce things my mother taught me when I was little, back in England. I knew I'd have to step into the ring to get through the gate and I didn't want to do that, because I might never be able to get back out again.

The boy was already gone through and waiting for me on the other side, holding his lantern high so I could see in the heavy mist. I decided to keep going towards the trailer park but there was nothing ahead of me but a high barrier of pine and hemlock and the road seemed to have come to a dead end, even though I knew that couldn't be possible. I reckoned this was too weird for me and I turned round to go back the way I came, rather than cross through the faerie ring. But I found more bushes looming high behind me, blocking the way I'd just come. There was only one option left to me – to go through the gate after the boy with the lantern. I was scared again, but there was nothing else I could do. I couldn't stay standing in the road, in the cold and the mist, with the soft rain falling forever on my cheeks. So I stepped across.

It was bright on the other side of the gate, just like it was when I came into the road after being with my friends earlier. The sun was shining and the birds were singing again and flowers were blooming and the grass was high and sweet-smelling. I found myself in a kinda encampment, with small makeshift huts and teepees and a bunch of people milling around.

There was horses grazing close by and fire-smoke rising into a scudding sky. The women had reddish-black hair, cropped to their shoulders, and wore beads round their necks and headbands. The men were bare-chested and wearing leather leggings and their heads were shaved up the sides, with a top-knot and a long plait hanging down the back. The top-knots were braided with feathers of all shapes and sizes. Dirty-faced kids played in and out of the tents and teepees and dogs barked, and it looked like one of the redskin camps I'd seen in the movies, but not exactly the same. This was different from the black-and-white cowboy-and-injun Hollywood stuff. It was more colourful, more real, more true. I thought to myself, "this is a scene outa the past … these people don't exist no-more in the 1960s". I thought I musta made it home and was dreaming in my bed in the trailer and my mother was somewhere close by and everything'd be fine and dandy and back to normal again when I woke up.

But it seemed so real and I wondered if it was maybe a passing fair or circus or something, and I couldn't figure it out. How come it was bright and warm on this side of the gate, while it was dark and cold on the other side? The boy moved away from me, into the camp, and I started to follow him. We made our way through the low spread of small wood-and-mud huts and animal-skin tents and carts with bright yellow-spoked wheels and woven baskets of spring flowers hanging from the shafts. The people stopped what they was doing to stare at me as I traipsed after the boy. Faces peered out from the gloom inside the teepees and dogs growled at me from the recesses between the huts. The air was full of strange words and a fire burned down at the end of a grassy track, with some young guys standing round it. The boy brought me to the group of youths, who were maybe a few years older than me – maybe fifteen or sixteen – then he disappeared into the bustle of the encampment. The youths studied me with glowing eyes and I remembered some of the stories my mother used to tell me when I was little, about far-off times that were gone now and would never come back again, except to a few, who'd see them on bright spring days in remote areas for an instant, a moment, a brief second, before they disappeared again.

The youths round the fire wore very little, just short britches made of animal hides and their hair wasn't shaved like the men, but plaited at the sides – and they wore headbands, but no feathers like the older guys. They were bare-footed and they looked at me for a long time, like they was trying to see inside me, to see what was in my heart. I stretched out my hand in greeting for them to shake it, but they stepped back like I was threatening them. Then the youngest smiled and offered me some liquid from a pot that was brewing on the fire. It tasted like tea, but it wasn't – it was something else, something I'd never drank before. But it was hot and good and it warmed my bones after the dark dismal road outside the gate. This gesture seemed to spark up the others and they all smiled at me and came back close to the fire and laughed to themselves in their sing-song language.

Suddenly, this tall guy with hair like jet and deep blue eyes came from behind one of the tents, leading a coloured horse. He came close up to the group of youths and spoke to them and they bowed their heads to him like he was their king or their leader or their father or something. He was obviously an expert horseman, because he swung up onto the coloured stallion and rode it off at speed, coming back at the gallop and stopping inches short of me.

But I wasn't scared and I didn't jump outa the way – I knew somehow he wouldn't let the horse trample me – he was just showing everybody what he could do, even if they knew already, all except me. And I knew now. He spoke to the youths again and they repeated the word Telihu and I guessed it must be his name – the horseman's.

The group of youths started to drift away, following this Telihu guy up along a sloping hill, away from the encampment, to a stretch of level ground about a half-mile in the opposite direction to the dark road where I first seen the boy with the lantern. I felt light-headed and kinda mercurial, like I was becoming part of something again, something that I once was and had forgot how to be. I thought it might be the effect of the hot liquid I'd been given to drink and maybe it had some herb or alcohol or something in it. And I thought, maybe it might be better to be in the bright springtime with these strangers than outside on the lonely road or in the trailer park with my mother and the shysters. Telihu looked down at me from his horse and a small feather drifted from his headband – a brownish red feather from some bird. Then he was gone, racing away to a starting point at one end of the level stretch, where a bunch of other horsemen were lined up for a race.

The land around was teeming with people – men and women and children. I could hear the growing din of their voices as I came closer, bargaining and bantering and betting on their favourite horse and rider. Trinkets of gold and silver and beads and bracelets of teeth and claws changed hands, and kids and dogs ran between the legs of the adults and horses, with honey-balls and corn-cakes in their hands. I could see all sorts – plains people and river inhabitants and cave dwellers and mountain trekkers – and I knew what they were, even though there was no way I could've known. Telihu lined up with the other horses and riders, about twenty altogether, all serious-faced and the excited steeds rearing and bucking and the crowd yelling. I had a dollar in my pocket and I tried to place a bet on Telihu, but the bet-takers looked at the paper money and laughed – they had no use for the stuff.

Then the race was off! They all seemed to be neck-and-neck for a while, maybe half a mile, then Telihu started to get a little in front, maybe just an inch or so. It was hard to see with the crowd jumping up and down and yelling in my ears. The riders who hadn't slipped off their bare-backed horses turned at a given point and began to race back to the start, where I was still standing. I could see them approaching, like in slow-motion – the shoeless hooves flying and the nostrils flaring and the riders trying to force each other off the level track and a pack of dogs and kids and youths running behind them. Telihu was up there with the front runners and I could hear my own voice screaming with the others.

'Telihu! Telihu! Telihu!'

About a furlong out, I seen him lean over his horse's neck and whisper something into the animal's ear, and the two seemed to me to be one – horse and rider. For a split second Telihu became the horse and the horse became Telihu, blended together like one entity in time and space. The people around me cleared back outa the way, to let the racers fly across the finish line and they passed me in a flash and I couldn't see who'd won. Then Telihu was taken from his horse and carried shoulder-high by the crowd. The bet-takers paid out medallions and amulets and other stuff and some of the people were happy and others weren't so much.

Suddenly, there was a high-pitched shout from the middle of the crowd. It was the young boy with the lantern who'd guided me to this place. He pointed to the horizon and everybody turned to look. I could see a dark cloud of dust that seemed to be approaching quickly, like smoke from an engine or forest fire or something, except there was no forest. It seemed to fill the whole skyline and it was heading our way fast. The people panicked and started to run in all directions. Horses were rearing and churning up chaos all around me. I was confused and scared again and didn't know what to do – all alone in a swirling maelstrom of turbulence and commotion and fear and noise. Then I got shoved hard by something like the flank of a horse and I fell face down onto the ground.

When I raised my head back up, my hair was wet, even though the ground wasn't. I was kneeling in the road with the high flannel bushes and black oak and wild lilac on either side. Moonlight was slicing through the branches and the way ahead was open now, with no tall hemlock or pine blocking my path. The gate and the faerie ring were gone and I could see the lights of the trailer park up ahead. I walked on, believing I imagined it and for sure I was tripping on that sugar-cube stuff. My mother was waiting for me when I got inside and she asked me where I'd been. It was real late and she was worried about me. She'd called my friends and they said I left them hours ago and headed into the short-cut. She went down and searched the road and couldn't find no sight nor sign of me and she was about to call the cops. I put my hand into my pocket to see if I still had my dollar. It was there alright and I pulled it out to make sure – and along with it came a small brownish-red feather from some bird. My mother took it from my hand and looked at it, then she looked at me, straight into my eyes. She asked me where I got the feather and I told her I found it, because I didn't want her to know I was tripping on that acid stuff.

My mother said it was strange, because the feather belonged to a passenger pigeon. I asked how she knew that and she said she just knew, it didn't matter how. So I asked what difference it made and she said none, except that passenger pigeons had been extinct in America for at least a hundred years.

Like I said, it's just a story and it happened the way I just told it, but whether it really happened – you'll have to make up your own minds. I didn't see no more of that stuff the kid called acid until I'd run away from Reno and was living in San Francisco, two years later.

2
On The Road

I feel the urge to go somewhere else – to be someone else. I'm beginning to understand – beginning to know what is. No north or south – left or right – black or white – wrong or right. Only a fundamental strangeness. Dreamlike. Uncertain. And it crosses over and interacts with the everyday world.

———————

Back when I was with my mother, I taught myself how to look into the future, as well as the past. The present was a vague kinda thing – if it existed at all. I was thinking all kinds of crazy things that nobody else I knew thought. I reckoned I could see stuff. Like everything. I told my mother, but she said I was wrong – even she couldn't see everything and she was a witch. But I knew I could, even though I knew that was impossible. My mother told me I'd have to see through all the eyes on earth to be able to see everything. I told her I was all the eyes on earth – all the eyes in the universe. She didn't understand. I didn't really understand myself back then in 1963, because I was only fifteen, but I knew I knew something strange, different. I just didn't know exactly what, or exactly how.

It was like I'd fell through a gateway. Accidentally. Inadvertently. I'd stepped over a threshold and found myself there, on the other side. In a strange place that looked familiar. It was like I was able to by-pass a filter in my brain that was blocking out reality – real reality – and only letting through enough for me to function as a kinda pseudo-animal. I knew the real story of life and death and being everybody at the same time, because it was really only a kinda fragmented ego that stopped the seeing of this stuff before. I was capable at any moment of seeing all and being all, if you get my meaning. It was only my brain and nervous system that were blocking it. Selecting stuff. Sifting stuff. To keep me sane. I had to find an escape mechanism from the small world and make my way to where I could be what I knew I could be.

Me, I was real small as I was – kinda insignificant against the backdrop of everything!

Then I met Florica.

Florica's people were a mixture of Cerhara tent dwellers and Chlara carpet traders and they travelled south from Romania and camped by the shores of the Van Gölü, near the border between Turkey and Iran. At least, that's what she told me when I came across her on a piece of wasteland out past the trailer park near Hidden Valley. She was camped there with her horse and a bow-top wagon that she called a vardo, and she gave me a cup of coffee brewed over an open campfire. She said how she crossed the Mediterranean and lived with the Gitana Espagñola for a while, then travelled to England, where I first came from, before crossing the ocean to America. She played a musical instrument called a zurna and I played my scratchy old fiddle and we sang songs that neither of us knew and laughed together and, even though I was only fifteen and she musta been ten years older, it seemed like we was the same age.

And, of course, we were.

So, when she moved out in her vardo Florica didn't know I'd hitched a ride and was hiding under some old blankets in the back. She didn't discover me until we reached Lake Tahoe, travelling down the back roads and ravines and it was too late by then to turn around and take me back. She wanted to put me in a boxcar or on a greyhound to Reno, but I told her I wouldn't go. I said I'd run away again and next time I might not be so lucky to find a woman like her. But she made me call my mother from a payphone and I told her not to worry, I was with someone who'd take care of me until I could do it for myself. She sobbed on the other end of the line, but she knew she couldn't keep me with her no longer. She knew it was time for me to go, so she said goodbye in Gaelic and told me to look in and see her if I ever passed that way again. 'Course, she didn't need to say nothing because I was her and she was me, and although she didn't know that – I did.

We crossed the mountains, heading west into California and keeping to the rural areas and away from towns. We camped near

Placerville for a day or two to rest the horse, then moved down the valleys towards San Francisco and my dream of a new life. It was autumn and there was plenty of casual work to be had on the cattle ranches and nut orchards and prune farms of that part of the country. And we moved on from place to place until we ended up in the Stanislaus Forest, about two hundred miles east of San Francisco. By this time I'd turned sixteen and was getting impatient. The trekking and the chaotic poetry and weird prophesy inside me were making me hyper. I wanted to go on, but Florica wanted to get settled down somewhere for the winter. The place we found ourselves in wasn't private owned, so we didn't have to get permission from anyone to be there. And Florica followed one of the old horse trails to a remote, secluded area, away from the public and police, and she set up camp. We had enough money from working through the autumn to buy food from local stores and we found fuel in the forest and there was plenty of good grazing for the gry, like Florica called her horse.

Then, one night, a backpacker stumbled into the camp. He'd been badly whacked about by rednecks in a brawl in a hicksville bar. It took him a week to recover and Florica and I looked after him all the time, giving him water and small amounts of food until his strength returned and he was well and fit again. His name was Mirabeau Molke and he was a little older than me, but younger than Florica – maybe twenty or twenty-one. He told us the story of what happened to him, but I kinda already knew – because I was him in that time, in that moment that was part of all the other moments in the universe. But I listened to him talking and I felt the pain he felt. I was reminded of it by his words. It was there, in the air all around us, his pain and my pain and all the pain that'd ever been inflicted or endured.

He was trekking down through the Sierras, hoping to do some eagle spotting, when he decided to make a final stop-off at a remote diner called The Bischwind, somewhere between Emerald Bay and San Andreas. He wanted to have a last civilised meal before completely losing himself for a couple of months. The place was empty, except for a bunch of hunters drinking beer and talking with loud voices. Mirabeau sat at a secluded table and ordered coffee and asparagus salad. The hunters were getting louder the more beer they drank and waving their guns in the air and taking simulated shots through the window. It became clear to Mirabeau that one of the group was a woman and he got pissed off listening to them and wanted to stand up and leave. But he thought to himself, why should he? That's the problem sometimes, he thought, people get intimidated by intimidation and they leave. Or they look away. Or apologise for something they ain't even done.

One of the men at the beer table saw Mirabeau glancing over.

'What you looking at, dude?'

'You.'

'Looking at me or chewing a brick, either way you'll lose your teeth.'

The rest laughed and turned away from Mirabeau.

The hunters ordered more beer, spilling it over the table and onto the floor when it arrived and giving the waitress a hard time. The girl was trying to clean up the spilled beer and Mirabeau went across to help her. He was bending down to wipe the floor when the man with the loudest voice pushed him over with his foot. Mirabeau got to his feet and the man rose from his seat.

'What's with you, dude?'

'I don't know.'

'You don't know? You don't know what?'

'What's with me, but I'm thinking about it.'

'You're a real moonraker sonofabitch.'

Mirabeau escorted the waitress over to the bar and then went back to his seat to finish his meal. The hunter woman kept looking at him and he decided maybe it was best to leave after all. He'd come up here to get away from people and he didn't want to get into no trouble with no-one. He was just about to get to his feet when the woman crossed to his table.

'What's your name, honey?'

15

'Mirabeau.'

'Wow, that's a weird name. Where'd you git it?'

'From my mother.'

'What's it mean?'

'She was an admirer of the French revolutionary politician and orator, Honoré Gabriel Riqueti Mirabeau, who lived so recklessly and profligately that he was imprisoned several times and was once sentenced to death, but the sentence was later annulled. He wrote *essai sur le despotisme* and *erotica biblion* and his political sagacity made him a great gubernatorial force, while his audacity and volcanic eloquence endeared him to the masses.'

'Wow! You speak real cute.'

'Git away from that moonraker, Jessie.'

Jessie took no notice of the big-voice and that made the guy mad. He crossed the room and grabbed her by the arm, obviously hurting her, because she let out a little squeal.

'Leave her alone.'

'How'd it be if I knocked some of your teeth out, moonraker?'

'You could try.'

Mirabeau stood up as big-voice took a swing at him. He side-stepped the blow and returned a punch straight into the man's guts. Big-voice was surprised. He didn't know that Mirabeau Molke's mother was worried for her son when he was young, having to live on the mean streets of New York – even if it was the Upper East Side. So she sent him to O'Brien's Gym and Boxing Emporium on East 96th Street, where he got good at the noble art – to the extent that O'Brien reckoned he could easily become professional. But Mirabeau wasn't interested in hurting people – except when they tried to hurt him.

Big-voice swung again. The shot was so wide and slow that Mirabeau easily ducked it and returned a right-hander to the guy's jaw. He fell to the floor and didn't get up. The rest of the hunters were on their feet by now, but none of them were too eager to take the backpacker on. They had their rifles in their hands and levelled at Mirabeau. He looked them straight in their nervous eyes.

'You people going to shoot me?'

There was no reply.

'I didn't think so.'

Mirabeau grabbed his rucksack and left the diner, pushing the barrels of the guns to one side as he passed.

I listened to him and his voice was lush. I never before heard anyone talk the way he did. The words that came from his mouth were like a kinda music – his accent was half English and half French and half sun and half moon. He carried on, telling me and Florica what happened after that, and we listened without saying a word, with our eyes wide open, even though I knew what he was gonna say. I'd heard the words already. Not, like, as sentences, strings of words. And I didn't hear them, I knew them – as a complete thing. The complete meaning of them in the same split second, not in the ham-handed focus of separate sound-symbols – but a complete picture. Concept. Understanding of what was meant to be communicated by them. I said them myself to a strange couple I met in the forest with a horse and a bow-top wagon and they helped me when I was hurt. And I knew I'd make love to the woman – and I'd take her with me when I went.

Take her away from the boy.

Mirabeau told us the year was growing older and he'd been away from San Francisco for many months. But he wanted to see the eagles before he went back to the city – hoped the solitude and spirituality would set things right in his head. He knew eagle spotting should really be done on guided field trips with the Eagle Institute, from the regulated roadside blinds. But there was too many dopes with binoculars, yelling to each other and slamming car doors and honking horns and flapping their arms and crashing about like a bunch of hyperactive bears, so no eagle would come anywhere near them. And, anyway, he was hoping the eagles would be a catalyst and they couldn't be a catalyst unless he was alone. Really and truly alone. So, the backpacker kept on trekking along the Tahoe Rim Trail and eventually moved off the regular route altogether. He was drawn south into the backcountry, kept company by hawks and little towhees and moving parallel to the backdrop of high sierra, the colours of a kaleidoscope all around him, filling his heart with a sense of hope and anticipation that he hadn't felt for a long time.

Mirabeau erected his own observation blind and set up his spotting scope and waited, lying in the quiet of the forest and the comfort of his own company. He was uncommon restless one night, waking from a fretful sleep at every sudden animal sound and feeling feverish, like he'd caught a cold or some kind of chill. It was about 2:00am when he woke again for the fifth time. Only now he thought he was hallucinating, because there was someone standing over him with a gun. The face came slowly into focus and it was the ugly mug of big-voice from the Bischwind diner. The other hunters were behind him, shining flashlights into the blind and grinning all over their sneering snouts. Mirabeau immediately tried to unzip his sleeping-bag, but it was fixed fast with wire at the top of the zipper and he couldn't undo it. Big-voice grinned down at him.

'Well, well … if it ain't the moonraker.'

'What do you want?'

'Want? Nothing from you. We was just following some old bear that Mike here winged. The sonofabitch goes crashing off into the undergrowth and we had to follow him. You'd agree with that, wouldn't you moonraker? Can't let a wounded animal suffer?'

Mirabeau struggled again, trying to get himself out of the sleeping-bag.

'I bet you're sorry you socked me in that diner, ain't you?'

'I'm not sorry at all.'

'Well, you will be. OK guys, let's send moonraker here on a little trip.'

There was a ravine close to the eagle blind and the hunters carried Mirabeau in his sleeping-bag to the edge. Jessie tried to stop them, but big-voice pushed her away.

'You'll kill him. Don't do it!'

'We won't kill him, it ain't that deep. Just teach him a goddamn lesson.'

'You don't know how deep it is. Just leave him.'

'He knocked me out, now I'm gonna knock him out. OK guys?'

The hunters swung the sleeping-bag. One. Two. Three. Then they let go. Mirabeau felt himself flying through the air, then landing with a breath-blasting thump on the steep side of the ravine. He started to roll. Over and over and over and over, bouncing off boulders and young saplings, and crashing through thorns and poison-ivy and all sorts of undergrowth. He seemed to roll forever. And ever. And ever. Until he finally blacked out and everything faded into feathery darkness. I could feel every bump and bounce and I saw the unconsciousness coming like a cloud.

Mirabeau Molke told us he didn't know how long he was out cold. But when he opened his eyes, he couldn't see nothing, just a kind of whiteness. He could move one of his arms and he wiped the thick covering of snow from his face. It was day, with a blizzard falling so hard that he couldn't make out the boundary between land and sky and couldn't see further than a couple of feet. He could've been there for a day or a week – the snow was deep, so he guessed it must have been some time. There was a searing pain in his head and he put his hand up to find congealed blood on his right temple. The sleeping-bag was ripped to pieces in the fall and so were his clothes. He tried to stand, which he was able to do only after several shaky attempts and he was relieved to find that, as far as he could tell, no bones were broken. But he was real disorientated, still feverish and shaking from head to toe – not knowing how far he was from a trail or which direction to start walking in. He knew he wouldn't last long with no boots and his clothes in tatters and the ravine wall was too steep to climb back up for the rest of his gear. He couldn't see the sky, to know which was east or west or north or south. But he took a chance, as he started to move off slowly, that he was heading towards a road of some kind.

I stumbled along over rough terrain and my feet were cold and bleeding. It started to grow dark and Mirabeau realised that night was approaching fast. I swallowed some snow to slake my dried-up and blood-encrusted mouth. Although he was an experienced backpacker and had survived in some of the roughest terrain in the world, this wasn't good. Without clothes and without a sense of direction and without food, I was just not gonna make it. The night, when it came, would surely finish him. If only I hadn't come so deep into this remote area. Darkness fell, along with the snow. Mirabeau decided it was no use to keep stumbling about in the night. I was trying to find some shelter when I saw, through a break in the blizzard, what seemed to be a column of smoke rising up into the grey-black sky from a secluded campfire, deep in the dark woodland.

There was a gypsy woman and a boy.

When Mirabeau recovered, he and Florica went to find the eagle hide and his gear. We shared our food with him and let him camp down close to the vardo for some company. Florica told him why she left her homeland and how she travelled across Europe and how she met me, and Mirabeau told her he was intending to go back to New York City, where he came from, before heading on down to the docks – maybe stow away on some old steamship and end up in Indonesia or Tamil Nadu or Phuket or southern Sri Lanka.

Then one evening he came to her, like I knew he would. I wasn't there – maybe gone to get provisions or out gathering mushrooms and berries or taking the horse down to the stream to water it. Or maybe I was just staying away because I knew what was gonna happen.

The inside of the caravan was ornate, baroque even. Rococo and chinoiserie and filigreed and champlené, without being gaudy or ostentatious. I never knew fancy words like that, but Mirabeau Molke did. They're the words he was thinking. I hesitated when I entered. There was a small fire burning in an epergne stove, yet the interior was cool – not cool, exactly – *tranquille*, *reposant*, spiritual even.

It was a milieu I hadn't experienced before and I was a little unnerved by it, even though I tried not to show it. There wasn't much light in the caravan, except for that coming through the small windows and from the dancing red shadows of the fire. A scent of celandine was in the air and the sound of violin music came from somewhere in the background. I think it might've been the "allegro non troppo" from the "Symphonie Espagñole", or the "Fandango Asturiano" from the "capriccio", or even "Scena e Canto Gitano". Or it could have been something I'd never heard before – I couldn't be sure.

This wasn't what I expected. I don't know what I expected, but it wasn't this. And, although this might've seemed to someone outside my head like a thoroughly instinctual, spontaneous excursion and not something I'd normally do, the subliminal force that called me in there was real powerful. It expected something of me. It was waiting. But I didn't really know what I was doing there or what I was expected to – or maybe I did.

The emanation seemed to be coming from the gypsy woman. And, while it was distant before – vague, ethereal, somewhere remote inside my head – now it was close up and personal. I didn't know whether or not it had something to do with god, or if it was a completely different entity, outside my scope of experience. Outside my traditional christological and trinitarian position. How could that be? How could that be? But there was no time to think about it right now. The woman stood across the room, watching me. She knew I was nervous – unsure of my surroundings and even myself. Yet it seemed so perfectly right to be there. It seemed in accordance with the poetry of nature – inside the wagon, with the shadows and dusky twilight and strangely-hued chiaroscuros and dancing silhouettes.

It was as it was.

And there were three ways of knowing a flame – to be told of it, to see it, and to be burned by it.

Blood-red light leaks from the embers inside the epergne stove. I look up into the beautiful angelic face of the backpacker, smiling softly at me. His body's fit and strong and his skin's so translucent I can see beyond it, into his soul. I whisper some gypsy words that he cannot understand and has no need to. And I am god at that moment, there in the fireglow, as my fingers comb through his hair and little bubbles of perspiration appear on the satin skin above his cheekbones. In the end, the sybaritism of his true nature overpowers his propriety and he grabs my shoulders in his moment of crisis. Blood drains down from his head and his muscles tense over his arching back. I can feel his excitement, which heightens my own.

Breath comes in short spasms from our mouths, as I lean my head back and my black hair spreads out from my face. Savage animals howl in the woods outside, trying to get in – to join the ritual of –

The union of dorjes and ghantas.

The synthesis of light and dark.

And we come together in a rebirth of soft insubstantiality. Hearts beating. Lungs snatching at blood-red air.

Then calmness comes creeping and sanity slowly, slowly slips back.

We lie together in the giaour fireglow.

After that, I guess it was time for Florica and Mirabeau Molke to leave. I didn't want them to go, but I knew they had to. I shook hands with Mirabeau, who gave me his backpack, saying he wouldn't need it no more, and I kissed Florica on the forehead. Then they drove the horse on and the vardo was lost into the surrounding woodland.

And I was sorry for their going.

3
Haight-Ashbury

Thought is a function of being, not doing. And all the thoughts are already there, to be tuned into and made real. And a thought, once created from the quantum wave, is as real as an electron – or a stone.

———

After Florica and Mirabeau Molke left me alone in the woods in wintertime, I wasn't sure what to do. I was still only sixteen and, though I'd been travelling with my mother since I was born, my survival skills weren't good and I was scared of getting lost or maybe getting shot by the hunters who attacked Mirabeau. I was still a long way from San Francisco, so I packed up the gear they left me and started trekking back to civilisation. I started out early and, by the time it was getting dark, I found myself on a country road. There was no traffic to speak of and I thought I'd have to pitch camp for the night. Then I seen a set of headlights coming towards me. It was a farmer, driving an old 3100-series Chevy pickup truck. The truck stank of pig-shit and offal, but I was glad of the lift, as it was getting cold. He told me his name was Cyrus Perkins and asked where I'd come from. I told him Reno. He asked if I was on the run.

'No. I got family in Frisco. I'm visiting them.'

'They hipsters?'

It was the first time I'd heard the name hipster and I wasn't sure what it meant.

'They're Methodists.'

He laughed.

We bounced our way through New Hogan and skirted Lodi to the south and got on the highway at Antioch. It was a bumpy six-hour ride and Cyrus Perkins dropped me off at Wildcat Canyon at two in the morning. I slept in the park until it got light, then hitched another ride in a Pontiac Tempest, down through Berkeley and Oakland and across the Bay to the Embarcadero. South Beach was a working-class area back then and I wandered round the streets not really knowing where to go or what I was looking for. I went into a diner on Bryant Street and had a hamburger and fries and a cup of coffee. I asked the waitress if she knew where I'd find the beatniks.

'You mean hipsters.'

'No, beatniks.'

'Beatniks are all gone, fella. It's hipsters, over in Haight-Ashbury.'

She told me how to get there. It was an area surrounding Haight Street with a lot of Victorian houses with steps, situated round the storefront streets. When I got there they were protesting against the building of a freeway through the area and lots of people were out on the streets chanting. So I joined in. The group I was with were mostly young people and they were louder than the rest. It wasn't long before they attracted the attention of the cops.

The police didn't like beatniks, or hipsters either, and it soon got confrontational. One cop hit the guy in front of me with his night-stick and some woman hit the cop with her placard and it turned into a brawl. I tried to get outa there, but I fell over something and ended up on the ground, with my camping gear on top of me. Last thing I remember was a boot coming straight for my head. Then blackness. I woke up in a holding cell in Park Station with six or seven others. Anyone who could pay the ten-dollar fine for disturbing the peace got let out without charge. So that's what I did.

It was late by then, with night coming on, and I had nowhere to go. So I set up camp in Buena Vista Park. It was cold and it took me a while to get to sleep. When I did, it was fretful, constantly disturbed by the sounds of the city night and shadows creeping past me in the noisy half-light. I don't know how long I'd been sleeping when I was woke by a hand shaking my shoulder. It was a teenage boy, about the same age as myself. He was short, with dark matted hair and weather-rough brown skin, dirty like an old shoe and wearing a coat that was too big for him. He asked me for money.

'D'you think I'd be here if I had money?'

He smiled and told me it was dangerous for me to be sleeping here, I could be picked up by the cops. I didn't want that, having just got clear of the police station.

'You should come with me.'

So I did.

His name was Lennon and it was just beginning to get light when I followed him to Waller Street in the southwest of Haight-Ashbury with "painted lady" houses all in a row, like tarts teasing. We climbed the steps to the front door and he made a secret knock. After a few minutes, a girl opened the door sleepily and let us in. It was a big house, with about twenty people sleeping on the floors. A pungent-sweet smell filled the place and I could hear music playing somewhere – not loud, just kinda beating in the background. Lennon told me to stow my gear wherever I could find a space and, when I turned back to him, he was gone – absorbed into the ambience of the place.

I took myself on a tour of the house. It had four stories and at least a dozen rooms. Most of the people were still asleep. Some were coupled up together and others were on their own. They were mostly young, not older than twenty, but one or two were probably closer to thirty – especially one dude, who was dressed in a black dress thing that covered him from head to toe. But I could see his face through a hole in the headpiece. He had a beard and an eyepatch and a diamond set into one of his teeth. I was hungry, so I left the house and found a deli down on Masonic Avenue. I was worried in case someone might steal my gear when I was gone, but I decided to risk it rather than lug the stuff around with me. I was sat there eating some bacon and eggs when the weird guy from the house came in. He was dressed in the black dress thing and his face was covered now, with only his eyes showing.

But I knew it was him. He looked round and then came and sat opposite me in the booth. He sized me up and down.

'What's your name, kid?'

'Aaron.'

I lied.

'How old are you?'

'Eighteen.'

They obviously knew this crazy guy in the diner, because the waitress brought him over some coffee and he opened the flap in the headpiece to drink it.

'I'm Selcraig.'

He offered me his hand and I shook it.

'You're new ... in the squat, I mean.'

I guessed he was talking about the house on Waller, so I said yeah and told him I seen him asleep down there earlier.

'Why're you wearing that dress?'

'This ain't a dress, it's a burqa.'

He said he was a sailor and he stole the full-length black burqa from an Iranian woman while on leave in the port of Bandar-e'Abbás on the northern shore of the Strait of Hormuz. He liked to sleep in it because he found the total envelopment and security of the coarse cloth reassuring, like some kids find a favourite blanket reassuring, or a man has an old pair of slippers or a comfortable chair.

Once he got started talking, I couldn't stop him. His insecurity harked back to when Selcraig was young – a rating aboard the *SS Scleroderma* – and missing his mother. He was always a bit of a loner and didn't mix well with the other sailors, which made things real difficult in the close confines of an Arleigh Burke-class destroyer. In the absence of friends to confide in, Selcraig retreated into the security of his own world – real and imaginary. It might've been different if he'd had the guidance of a father-figure, but the ships' officers didn't know what to make of him, especially after his left eye got taken by a wild parrot during an exercise drill on the remote South Atlantic island of Tristan da Cunha, and he began to wear a black eye-patch and had a diamond inserted into one of his front teeth by a tattoo-artist in Zanzibar. Selcraig said he never knew his real *père* at all – that's what he called his father, like he was French or something – the man deserted his mother when he was real young. That's what started the insecurity.

Selcraig's mother tended bar in a drum on the Vieux Carré in New Orleans. She was half Creole and half Cajun and her motto was *laissez les bon temps rouler*, and she loved her boy Selcraig more than anyone else in the entire world. And Selcraig loved her just as much, especially after his père left – even if he never much knew his père and some said it could've been any one of a dozen men. Then Selcraig's mother got herself killed in a knife-fight when he was seventeen and just out of high school. That's when he joined the navy and his emotional problems started in earnest. He talked to himself a lot, on board the variety of ships he sailed in over the years. Never staying long with any one vessel and going from the military to the merchant navies and back again. People thought Selcraig was talking to himself when, in fact, he was talking to the many paranoid voices in his head and he took to singing a lot of nautical songs and shanties, which nearly drove his shipmates as insane as himself. Some of the shipboard officers recognised his illness – particularly the ones who was a little schizophrenic themselves – and they tried to get Selcraig some treatment. He was taken ashore and given drugs, but being away from the water made him worse than ever and he just wanted to get back to the sea.

Stuck shoreside and going crazier than he already was, Selcraig walked out of the sanatorium one day and took a job on a riverboat. They were steaming upriver past Southhaven, just approaching Memphis and south of the mouth of Wolf River. There was a thunderstorm raging and the rain was coming down hard, making visibility so poor that it was hard to see the Memphis skyline on the port side. Selcraig should've been up on the open deck, piloting. But he wasn't. He was in bed with a woman he'd just met at the roulette table and she was fascinated by his diamond tooth and his eye-patch and they were going at it good and making a lot of noise in rhythm with "Yankee Doodle Dandy" being played on the typhone horns and chimes of the steam calliope. When, outa the blue, the room door burst open and Elvis Presley crashed in. He shouted at Selcraig,

'You're dead!'

Then Elvis pulled out a derringer and tried to shoot Selcraig. The roll of the boat in rough water affected Elvis's aim and bullets were flying and ricocheting off the metal bedposts and smashing his whisky bottle as Selcraig ducked for cover under the bed. Elvis was bending down and sticking the muzzle of the gun in after him and Selcraig was kicking out at it with his bare toes, when the riverboat ran aground on Mud Island – because Selcraig wasn't where he should be, piloting on the open deck. Elvis got knocked off his feet and the derringer went flying across the floor. Selcraig made a break for it, noticing on his way through the swinging door that the lady had also left the room. Elvis was still scrambling around looking for the derringer as Selcraig grabbed a dinghy and made it over the side, into the mighty Mississippi river. Rain was driving down and the wind rotated the dinghy like a spinning-top, making Selcraig dizzy, and the lightning was flashing and the currents were so strong that, no matter how hard he tried to gain control of the dinghy, he was taken downriver in a crazy, revolving, zig-zagging, roller-coaster ride.

Selcraig Cruz was eventually washed ashore near Lake Village. He was dazed and confused and he staggered away unsteadily from the dinghy. Trouble is, he didn't realise he was stark naked and a highway patrol found him wandering along the interstate 55 freeway.

He was scaring people passing in their cars, so they took him to the psychiatric hospital at Pine Bluff, Arkansas. But he kept hallucinating about Elvis Presley trying to kill him and, after a few weeks, Selcraig walked out again and made his way to Frisco. He bought a little boat and moored it down near South Beach Harbour and lived there happily – until it sank.

Just then, Lennon came into the diner. He saw us and came across to the booth and spoke to me.

'What you doing with this crazy guy?'

'He's been telling me his life story.'

'Don't you listen to him, man. He's been telling them lies since he turned up at the squat.'

Selcraig gave Lennon the finger sign and left the diner, much to my relief. I wanted to know what a squat was, because they both said that word and I wondered if it was Frisco lingo for a house or something. I didn't like to ask, in case it made me look stupid, but it got the better of me in the end.

'What's a squat, Lennon?'

'Don't you know?'

'Nope.'

He told me squatting was taking over vacant buildings by homeless people. It wasn't just for a place to live, but also to expose inequality in housing and land issues. Trouble was, the law didn't tolerate it much and it wouldn't be long before the cops came and evicted us and we'd have to find somewhere else.

'You mean I don't have to pay no rent?'

'Nope. But there ain't no power, so we gotta cook over open fires and it gets cold this time of year.'

He told me if I couldn't get a job I could go busk downtown to make some money. Otherwise I could get a handout from the charities.

'What's busk?'

'Sing, or play a musical instrument.'

'I can play the fiddle.'

'Cool.'

Back at the painted lady, I met other people who played musical instruments. One guy called Larry played the acoustic guitar and a girl called Winona played the tambourine and some other guys played the bongos and Cajun accordion and trombone. We decided to start a band and busk for money in downtown San Francisco and we called ourselves The Methadones. We were a strange group, not really suited to any particular style of music – we weren't skiffle and we weren't jazz and we weren't rock 'n' roll. We didn't know what we were. Our music was a kinda country-folk, with a bit of blues thrown in, and we performed along California Street and outside Grace Cathedral and over in Union Square. We got moved on by the cops a lot, but people liked us and a guy called Joe Shultz came up and asked us if we'd like to play in his folk club on Fillmore. It was a converted pizza shop called the Kool Klub and it attracted a lot of alternative types who chilled on marijuana and amphetamine and LSD, which had become much more popular since I took that first sugar-cube when I was only thirteen.

We made enough money to rent a place on Clayton Street because we were sick of being hassled by the squat police and moved on here and there and everywhere. Squats were OK, up to a point, but your gear got stolen if you weren't careful and we were always worried about our musical instruments. Without them we'd have to go get a job in a tattoo parlour or a convenience store or a city park. Life was good for a while, until Marty Balin took over the club in 1965 and turned it into The Matrix. He showcased bands like Jefferson Airplane and the Butterfield Blues Band and Boz Scaggs, and the house music got known as the San Francisco Sound, which didn't suit our wild impro style.

So we left.

After that the band broke up. Winona went back to Baton Rouge and Lee joined another group called The Prairie Dogs and the others all just sorta drifted apart. I went to live with a group of Bohemians in what they called a commune, over on the edge of Haight-Ashbury, near the Kezar Pavilion. It was a big old ramshackle place that was owned by one of the group, I don't know who. But they took me in because they liked the way I played the fiddle and we hung out in the bars and cafés around the Golden Gate Park. Writers, actors, musicians, poets, who used drugs and embraced music like a spiritual force in their lives.

We mostly played tracks from Bob Dylan albums and talked about free love and eastern religions and we rejected the world of prerogatives and protocols and points of etiquette. It was attractive to a young guy like me, just coming up to eighteen, and it was great to go live with them and be one of them. I started to become an open-minded, free-thinking liberal – even though I was that already. The memories of my mother and Florica and Mirabeau Molke faded away. They lived for the most part in a time that was past. I was still young and new to the world and I wanted to experience new things instead of all the time repeating the old. I hoped someday everyone would think like I did. Which of course they would – because I was everyone. Even then.

There was an entity inside me – like a voice that told me things, even when I wasn't on the acid. Some right and some wrong – familiar and strange – coming close up then fading back into the distance.

By 1966 kids from all over the world were moving to Frisco. A journalist on the San Francisco Chronicle called Herb Caen gave them the name Hippies, which I suppose he made up from the word hipster. They were getting high on peyote and magic mushrooms and mescaline, as well as cannabis and LSD. The place was getting real crowded. The Beatles came over and played in Candlestick Park and a big psychedelic event called The Trips Festival took place at the Longshoreman's Hall. Ten thousand people turned up, with thousands more being turned away each night. The Grateful Dead and Big Brother and The Holding Company played on stage and everyone drank punch spiked with LSD and freaked out to the first light show I'd ever experienced. Selcraig the sailor was there, I seen him going schizo with a few others I knew from the old squat, but I kept away from him because he was crazy like a betsy-bug.

After that, the Avalon Ballroom and the Fillmore Auditorium started doing the full psychedelic music experience with liquid light projection. Hippies bought up all the costumes from the Fox Theatre when it went out of business and people just dressed any way their fancy took them. They danced all night, free-form and spontaneous, like at an orgy or something. It was real cool – to begin with. By June 1966, fifteen thousand hippies had moved into the Haight-Ashbury area, along with bands like Jefferson Airplane and The Grateful Dead and a guerrilla street group called The Diggers. The Diggers named themselves after some seventeenth-century English guys who had a vision of a society free from buying and selling and private property – they wanted to create a "free city" using spontaneous street theatre and art and anarchist action. I joined up with them and helped open free stores that gave away food and drugs and money. We organised free concerts and the actors performed political art. At 4:00pm every day, two hundred people turned up for free stew that was served from behind a giant yellow picture frame called the Free Frame of Reference. We made digger bread outa wholewheat baked in coffee cans in the basement of Episcopal All Saints Church on Waller Street and we had free crashpads for homeless kids.

We got the food from the stuff the stores threw out, anything that was still in a usable condition. The Frame of Reference came from the first free store, which was in a six-car garage on Page Street. The garage was full of picture frames that we tacked up the side of the building. We also opened a free clinic with volunteers from the San Francisco Medical School and threw free parties with music by all the psychedelic bands. We drove a truck full of naked belly dancers through the financial district, inviting bankers to climb on board and forget about making money – none of them did. We held a happening called The Death of Money and dressed in animal masks and carried a coffin full of fake cash down Haight Street singing "get out my life, why don't you babe" to the tune of Chopin's "Death March". We coined the phrases "do your own thing" and "today is the first day of the rest of your life" and it was a time like no other since.

Then the State of California outlawed LSD, so we got together to protest in the Golden Gate Park panhandle. We called it The Love Pageant Rally and we wanted to draw attention to the fact that, even though LSD was illegal, the people who used it weren't criminals and they weren't crazy either – except for Selcraig the sailor. But only about eight hundred people turned up to celebrate transcendental consciousness, the beauty of the universe, the full experience of being. Trouble is, a lot of the kids coming in were just playing at being hippies. They had rich parents and were just looking for a "happening" before going off to college at Berkeley or Yale or Princeton and turning themselves into lawyers or bankers. Then the salesmen and the media cottoned on to the fact that these kids had money to spend and it all got commercialised. Nothing was real anymore. These guys weren't born to be wild, they were born to be mild.

It was time for me to leave Frisco!

4
Schizophrenia

There are many windows in the wall. Some see love and some see hate and some see life and some see death. Every man chases his own dragon – and every woman too. And that's all it is – an illusion. To transcend the world for even a few minutes is a longing of the soul. People don't chase their dragon because they want to be bad – they do it because they want to escape. Sanity and sobriety will only take you so far – after that it must be religion, or violence. And god is the worst killer of all.

I decided to head for the east coast – maybe things were more authentic in New York or Philadelphia or Atlantic City. I didn't have much money, so I decided to hitchhike. I was down on the Frisco Bay Trail, having a last look round before trying to get a lift across the bridge, when I seen Selcraig the sailor. He was just standing there, staring sadly out over the water. I tried not to let him see me, but I was too late.

'Aaron! Hey, Aaron!'

He came over.

'What's happening, man?'

'I'm moving on, Selcraig.'

'Where to, man?'

'I dunno ... east.'

'I'd go with you, but that's too much land for me. I gotta stay near water.'

I was glad to hear that, I didn't want him coming with me. The guy looked spaced and I guessed he was on the acid. He started talking about his boat sinking out in the Bay or some crap and I was finding it hard to understand what he was talking about. I had time to spare so I decided to be sociable and listen to him for a while. He gave me some stuff that I didn't recognise and I took it – can't remember if I smoked it or swallowed it, one or the other. Then I thought it'd be better if I could see this dude from the inside – like, know what he was really about. Maybe I'd learn something.

Maybe not.

So I look inside him while he's talking and all I can see is an upturned sailboat drifting further and further away from him and he's cursing the thing for sinking on him. He seems to be on some little piece of land and I guess it must be Angel Island or one of the Marins or Red Rock. His tooth-diamond stops glistening in the sun when he finally closes his mouth and I start to become him – I see what he sees – I am him.

For a while.

I consider trying to swim for it, but I know the distance is too great and I'd almost certainly drown. Still, I wonder if that might not be better than whatever fate has in store for me on this strange, psychedelic island. Before I can weigh up my options, there's a rustling sound in the undergrowth behind me. I stand real still, not wanting to turn round. Beads of sweat appear on my forehead and start to trickle slowly down my face. The rustling sound stops and I wait for what seems like a lifetime before looking over my shoulder. When I do, I trip out.

There's an alien standing behind me – a short black alien, wearing a tuxedo and a white dress-shirt. It's a disguise, I reckon. The alien's shape-changed into a penguin. I wonder what it's doing, here in the middle of San Francisco Bay. My guess is maybe it's designing some mind-bending communications system to annihilate the intelligence of the entire population of America – maybe call it Phlox News – so that the greatest country on earth can be recolonised by the lowest common-denomination of creature.

'I come in peace ...'

I reckon the best course of action for now is to humour it. The alien don't reply and I'm scared it may have mastered the art of telepathy and is reading my mind at this very moment.

I try to jumble its thoughts – confuse it. I think of the sea shanties my mother used to sing to me back in New Orleans.

> *Was you never down the Congo river,*
> *Blow, boys, blow;*
> *Where the fever makes the white man shiver*
> *Blow, me bully boys, blow.*
> *Oh, what does the crew eat for dinner?*
> *Blow, boys, blow;*
> *A monkey's arse and a sandfly's liver*
> *Blow, me bully boys, blow ...*

No good.

> *When I was just a lad, my mother always told me,*
> *If I didn't kiss the girls, my lips would grow all mouldy*
> *Away, haul away; I'll sing to you of Nancy.*
> *Away, haul away; she's just my style and fancy ...*

But none of it works.

I gotta escape, make a run for it. Otherwise I'm done for. I edge closer to the treeline. The alien follows. As soon as I'm close enough, I dive headlong into the foliage and scramble away as quick as the wet burqa I'm wearing will allow. The island's lush with vegetation and I crash through it in blind panic, until I'm exhausted and can't go no further. I collapse to the ground, panting heavily. After a while, I realise I've lost the black-and-white alien. I've escaped – musta run for miles. Miles! How big is this island anyway, I ask myself, but get no answer.

Whatever.

I reckon the alien will never find me now.

Then I remember – telepathy. The thing'll follow my thought waves.

I put my hands up to my head and roll my eyes.

'Stop thinking. Stop thinking, you goddamn gobby!'

But my brain won't turn off. I put my head down onto the ground and cover it with leaves and twigs and grass and earth. I stay real still.

Then I fall into an exhausted sleep.

Night covers the island.

It's dark.

Pitch black.

And quiet.

Real quiet.

No moon or stars show in the deserted sky and no sound of night animals or even insects. Selcraig the sailor stays in the same position. Still asleep. A snoring black mound, now dreaming about a girl he once knew in the port of Cayenne in French Guiana, called Michelle. He mumbles to himself in his desire-drenched slumber.

> 'Ma chère Michelle ... j'ai le goût des homards ... savent les secrets de la mer.'

While Selcraig the sailor's in this state of self-induced trauma, the alien disguised like a penguin comes outa the dark undergrowth and stands behind him.

> 'Quel parfum utilisez-vous? Ça sent le pingouin.'

There's complete silence. Selcraig's real still – so's the alien.

'Penguin?'

Slowly, real slowly, I start to take my head out from under the vegetation. I look up and see the black eyes of the alien looking back at me.

'Abandon ship!'

I disappear into the trees again, running on all fours, which ain't too easy in the burqa, until I'm some distance away. Then sprinting on two legs as fast as my feet will fly. Branches whip at me and thorns rip at me and nettles and poison ivy sting me and roots trip me and I don't care – I keep going and going and going, until I can't go no further.

Dawn's breaking when I finally lean my back up against a tree and wonder how long I've escaped for this time and know I gotta get off the island. There's gotta be a way, but I don't know where or how. I've run and run and run so much I could be anywhere by now. Lost, gone away from the water and my sinking boat. Just then, I see this sign, half hidden in the undergrowth. The sign reads:

DIS WAY TO DA PALACE OF DA KING

The King? I didn't know there was natives on this island. Probably being forced by the aliens to work on their communications system. It could be dangerous, but it's worth a shot. If I can get to the palace. Make contact with the King.

I start walking in the direction the signpost said and, after a couple of hundred yards, I come upon another. This one reads:

C'MON EVERYBODY DONCHA BE NO SQUARE

I'm a bit freaked out by this 'cos Elvis Presley tried to kill me once. I'm scared it might be a trap, but I got no other choice. No other way out. I keep moving. The sun's high in a late morning sky when I stumble onto a road. The road's well surfaced and I follow it to its termination – at the entrance of a large cave. There's little vegetation here and more signposts. The first one reads:

DIS IS DA PLACE

and:

KEEP OFFA DA BLUE SUEDE GRASS

I move inside – real slow – keeping my back pressed up to the cave wall in case of ambush. I'm hoping the King's home, that'd be fine. But where's the goddamn aliens? The interior's dark and I can see less and less the further in I move. I think about yelling out to the King.

Maybe not.

This is all real strange to me, as Selcraig the sailor. But then, most things that happen on land are strange. The sea's different, you know where you are when you're at sea. You know your ship – and the rest's wind and water. Darker and darker, the further into the cave I go. Until it's pitch black and I can't see nothing at all. This reminds me of something. It won't come to me for a while – and then I remember. It reminds me of before I was born – waiting to be born. The anticipation, fear, uncertainty, darkness. And I remember what came after and that makes me even more scared. Since it happened – being born – I reckon I've spent my whole life trying to get back to where I came from.

And now.

There's a sudden ear-shattering screech of "Jailhouse Rock", being sung by Elvis Presley. Along with the sound of an engine revving and a car horn blasting. I race back for the entrance to the cave, tripping over the tattered hem of the burqa in blind panic. I see daylight and emerge at flying speed from the burrow-hole and dive for cover behind a boulder. Straight on my heels comes a 1958 pink convertible Coupe DeVille Cadillac, model 58J-62. Elvis Presley's driving. He's black now and wearing a glittering, sequined outfit and a huge quiffed-up wig. The alien's standing on the back seat. The Cadillac speeds past and disappears round a bend in the road. Selcraig the sailor's crapping himself behind the boulder. This is the way it was before – when he was flung out into the world, followed by a hideous pink thing. He shook then and he's shaking now.

Uncontrollably.

I crouch behind the boulder for a long time.

An hour?

Shaking.

Two hours?

Eventually the spasms subside and I start to focus again on my surroundings. I ain't noticed the day growing dark and the dropping of the sun's let the island cool. I shiver. It's hard to stand because my legs are gone to sleep from being in the crouched position for so long and they buckle with numbness. I rub my thighs and calves until they tingle and the blood starts to flow again. I reckon I'll freeze out here, but I don't want to go back into the cave neither. The cold makes me move real cautious-like towards the opening. Again, I keep my back to the wall as I move inside the warren – deeper and deeper. I can't see nothing, but I sense I'm in a bigger part of the cave. Then my hand touches a switch and the whole place lights up. I stifle a scream and stand rigid against the wall with my eyes shut – waiting for the worst.

Nothing happens.

I gradually open my eyes and look round. The tunnelled cave entrance has opened out into a large vaulted area, with picture posters of Elvis Presley when he was white, pinned up around the walls. It's my worst psychedelic nightmare since the guy tried to shoot me and I'm crapping myself now in case he comes back. Guitars and other crazy stuff hang from the ceiling and a big dressing-table, with a mirror surrounded by coloured lights, sits in the corner. There's a pink leather couch and some other pieces of art-deco furniture – a low glass table with some glossy showbiz mags and an unfinished drink. A kitsch cocktail bar's built into the opposite wall and I don't see a scary assortment of different coloured wigs on a special stand full of tailor-dummy heads. There's rugs and cushions scattered all over the floor, with the face of the white Elvis and the colours of the confederacy.

Selcraig the sailor wants to run – but where? He wonders how Elvis Presley turned himself black, but that could be the aliens' doing, because they're black as well. I guess they're all in this together – a plan to take over America and maybe even the world. Unless, like, it's all an illusion, a mirage, a psychedelic somnambulism induced by the taking of the shit he gave me. Or it could be a trick, created by the alien-penguin-creature to confuse me. They might be watching me on hidden scanners right now and I try to make myself as inconspicuous as possible.

Slowly, I make my way round the cavern – my back to the wall at all times. I come into contact with the wig-stand and accidentally put my hand on one of them, vivid purple, glowing. I freeze in my tracks and stay in that position for what seems like a year until, real slow, I bring my hand into vision, still holding the hairpiece. I jump back in horror, flinging the wig into the air.

41

'Shit ... it's a goddamn scalp!'

I'm really freaked out now. I gotta get away and, in my hurry, accidentally trip a concealed switch. Now the coloured lights round the dressing-table mirror start to flash and "Hound Dog" blares out from four large speakers, high up on the walls of the cave. I search frantically for the switch, telling myself this ain't real – but what if it is?

I eventually find the trigger and the music and flashing lights stop.

I'm exhausted by now and I flop down onto the couch and wipe sweat from my face. I know I gotta compose myself, pull myself together, or I'll never get outa this. There's some cigarettes on the glass table. I light one up and swallow the half-finished drink. Then I sit back, telling myself to relax. Selcraig the sailor's been in more difficult situations than this. Ain't he?

In the end, fatigue overcomes fear and he falls asleep.

A sudden loud burst of "All Shook Up" and the sound of an engine approaching wakes Selcraig the sailor from his schizophrenic sleep. I dive behind the pink-leather couch, just as the Cadillac 58J-62 roars into the cavern and screeches to a skidding halt. The black Elvis turns down the music and climbs outa the car.

The alien follows him.

Elvis jives round to the boot and unloads a crate of beer.

'Hey there, Nashville. Did we, I say, did we leave the lights on?'

I peer over the back of the couch and notice the half-smoked cigarette in the ashtray and the empty glass on the coffee table. I know the alien'll notice them too.

Bound to.

'Let's jive, I say, let's jive this booze to the boudoir, Nashville.'

The black Elvis Presley moves away to another part of the cave and the alien follows him. I take this opportunity to crawl from behind the couch and grab the cigarette from the ashtray. I look round for something to half-fill the glass with.

At that precise moment, the black Elvis comes back, followed closely by the alien. I duck down behind the bar and watch as Elvis moves across to the glass table. He's looking for his half-empty glass. He scratches his head, which makes his hair move, and turns towards the bar. I panic and, in my crazy confusion, suddenly stand up and hand the glass to the black man, smiling as I do so and showing my tooth-diamond. The black Elvis looks at Selcraig the sailor, takes the glass and looks down at it in his hand. Then back at Selcraig again.

'Zip-a-dee-doo-dah!!!!!'

The black Elvis Presley throws the glass into the air and runs from the cave. The alien stays put. I look at the alien. The alien looks back with cold black eyes.

'OK, you got me this time, you sonofabitch. Get it over with.'

I close my eyes and wait for the worst.

I wait.

Nothing happens.

I open my eyes again and the alien's gone. I'm nervy. Jingly-jangly. Suspicious.

Something's going on here and I don't know what it is. Should I move, make a break for it? Maybe the place is booby trapped. Can't just stay where I am either. I don't get a chance to decide, because Elvis reappears, sticking his head round the tunnelled entrance. He steps into the room, real slow, staying well away from the cocktail bar.

'Who, I say, who're you, baby? You some kinda transvestite nun or sometin'?'

'You're Elvis Presley!'

'Course I ain't Elvis, man.'

'The alien ... where is he?'

I'm trying to keep my voice to a whisper. The black Elvis looks round in alarm.

'What you talkin' about, man?'

'He hypnotised you? Brainwashed you?'

The black Elvis moves closer to Selcraig the sailor. Slow.

Real slow.

'Listen, man … I don't dig, I say, I don't dig this crazy jive. Why don't you cool it and have a drink? I ain't, I say, I ain't got no money worth talkin' about or no valuables … just some beer an' ol' Betsy.'

I'm guessing Betsy must be the queen of the island. But I can't figure out why this guy's dressed like Elvis Presley if he ain't Elvis Presley. Must be something to do with the aliens – reading Selcraig the sailor's mind and finding his greatest fear. I realise I've gotta communicate somehow with this guy, tell him I'm a friend, come in peace. And if we co-operate, there's a good chance we may come outa this alive. The black Elvis crosses to the automobile and pats it on the hood. I ask the question.

'Betsy?'

'That's right, man. Course there's Nashville there. You kin have him if you're a mind to. He ain't, I say, he ain't nothin' but a pest anyhows.'

'Nashville?'

The black Elvis points his finger and I turn to find the alien standing behind me. And I knew right then I had to get outa this guy's skin, before I went as crazy as him. But I couldn't – the schizophrenic stranglehold was too strong. The black Elvis is holding out a can of Old Milwaukee. I take it reluctantly. He shouts at the alien.

'Git on there, Nashville. Go git yourself outside, boy. You got, I say, you got this dude all in a stew now.'

44

To Selcraig the sailor's amazement, the black Elvis chases the alien from the cave, then beckons for me to sit down and drink his beer, as it ain't often he gets folks visiting. Selcraig the sailor thinks, careful.

Careful.

This could be a clever trick. But he decides to humour the guy for now and wait his chance.

Wait his chance.

'Nice place you got here, mister ... ?'

'Nite's the name, baby. You kin call me Saturday.'

'Saturday Night?'

'Nite. Nite! Cool, eh? What's your handle?'

The black Elvis laughs when I tell him and the sailor wonders why. He laughs along with the guy, just to be polite. I could feel myself coming back. I could see Selcraig the sailor on the Frisco Bay Trail, staring sadly out over the water and talking to himself. It was time for me to go, but I could still hear the voices in my head.

'I like you, Selcraig baby. I like you. Why you wearin' that crazy dress?'

'It's a burqa.'

The manic visions started to fade and the voices drifted off into the distance. Hazily – vaguely, like in a dream – I seen the penguin coming back into the cave and Selcraig the sailor shrinking away from it. The voices swam across the water towards Oakland.

'The little critter just won't stay outside. He must think you're a female penguin in that crazy black thing.'

I walked away from Selcraig the sailor and he didn't even see me go – still trying to figure out if it was all an illusion. Difficult for him to tell what was real and what was surreal any more – had been for some time. And stuff like that could drive a man completely crazy. He'd have to be careful if he wanted to keep his sanity. Careful.

Real careful.

'You live here alone, Saturday?'

'That's right, Selcraig baby. This here's my summer resort. I go back to the city for the winter.'

'Your car, what's it run on?'

'Gasoline, baby. What else?'

'Where d'you get it from?'

'The gas station.'

Selcraig the sailor and the black Elvis Presley continued their conversation, long after I was gone. One of them was definitely crazy, that's for sure.

5
Crossing America

The bread I eat is only mine when nobody else wants it.
Everything that's heard is the static of want. Want – want
– want – want. All the time is spent wanting, listening to the
want static. What you want is only good when you don't have
it. As soon as you get it, it immediately loses its value and you
want something else.

———

I hitched a ride outa Frisco in a Cadillac Fleetwood-Brougham bein'
driven by a couple in wedding clothes, on their way to get married
in Reno. They said they wanted to tie the knot in the Cosmo Casino
where Tuli Kupferberg from The Fugs got hitched. I wasn't sure that
Kupferberg was ever in Reno, but I didn't disillusion them. It was
September and 1966 was coming to a close and I wanted to go where
things were more real. The nuptial couple dropped me outside the city
because I didn't want to run the risk of meeting my mother – if she
was still alive, which I knew she was. It was three years since I ran
off and I wanted to keep moving forwards, not backwards in time. I'd
turned eighteen that summer and felt like I was grown up now, no
longer a kid. People my age were on the move all over the country,
trying to find the meaning – what it was all about. But I already knew
the answer to "what", I was looking for the answer to "why".

I picked up another ride on the outskirts of Reno, this time with
a group of Mormons in a Chevvy Greenbriar. They were heading for
Salt Lake City and they tried to convert me on the way. These guys
called themselves elders, although they weren't much older than me.
They said it was part of their mission to bring people into the Mormon
Church and they prayed in the back of the Chevvy and preached the
doctrine and told me to accept Jesus. They wanted to baptise me in
the Humboldt River and take ten percent of everything I earned,
which was nothing right then, and I'd be reborn. It took us two days
to make the trip and I thought about it along the way. Maybe I kinda

needed something to love because I didn't have my mother or Florica, and maybe Jesus was as good as anything else. For a while I felt like maybe being a child of their god, like belonging with them, being part of them. But I really wasn't. I was outside them, thinking my own thoughts and dreaming my own dreams and believing my own truths and imaginings. The feeling went when they told me they didn't drink beer or smoke weed. I thanked them for the ride and politely declined their invitation.

It was night when we pulled into Salt Lake City and I got myself a two-dollar room in a flophouse on Gladiola Street. Next morning I ate a hamburger and fries in a diner on Ninegret Drive before taking a look round the place. I wondered if there might be anything to keep me here – maybe something spiritual that was more all-embracing than the Mormons and didn't discriminate against people who needed a little something to get them through the day. But it wasn't what I was looking for. It was kinda conservative and family orientated and lots of sweet-looking couples with sweet-looking kids. I played the fiddle in Modesto Park for a while and they threw me a few dollars, but didn't hang around to listen to the music. Then I packed up and moved on.

I trekked a ways outa Salt Lake City, but nobody picked me up as I made my way east. After a long day's walking, I found myself on the edge of the Ashley National Forest and decided to camp for the night. I came across a friendly site and built a fire and cooked some beans and hotdogs and brewed up some coffee. There weren't many other people about this late in the year and the place was quiet. About two o'clock in the morning I was woke by a rustling noise outside my tent. I hoped it wasn't a bear or a wolf or some kinda killer.

Then I heard a female voice.

'Hello ...'

I didn't answer.

'Hello!'

I unzipped the tent flap and looked out. It was a girl about my age. She was wearing a buckskin dress trimmed with a fringe and she had a feather in her hair. I thought I was hallucinating again, like when I was thirteen and I took that sugar-cube.

'You for real?'

'Sure I'm for real.'

'What you want?'

'Ain't you gonna invite me in?'

I held back the flap and she slipped inside. She was pretty, with a smile full of white teeth and skin the colour of honey. Her voice was light and sing-songy.

'I seen you when you arrived.'

'You did?'

'Yeah. Thought I'd come over and say hello.'

'At two in the morning?'

'I waited till the others fell asleep.'

I didn't ask who the others were. She sat down close to me – close as a lover. I could feel her breath on my face, hear her heart beating.

'You got anything?'

'Anything?'

'You know ...'

I had an eight of resin, so I heated it up on a spoon and flaked it into some hand-rolling tobacco and skinned it. We smoked a couple of joints together and laughed out loud at nothing much and talked some bullshit. Then she slipped her buckskin dress off – and she was wearing nothing underneath. Her breasts squeezed themselves against my chest and we fell backwards onto my sleeping bag, still laughing at nothing.

We lie close together on the cool ground and the cannabis makes it like the whole tent's undulating, moving up and down. The brand new smell of this girl breaking on my brain like a wave. My tongue and lips caress over her smoothness and she responds with a touch that's

49

pure skill, man. And, as we bob about on our imaginary ocean, I want to take out my heart and fling it overboard. At the moment of crisis, she produces a rubber from somewhere and slips it on almost without me knowing. Her cool eyes are burning into mine and it feels like I'm weightless in the palpitating tent.

We come together in a rolling ball of soft sweat and sighs.

When I woke the next morning she was lying beside me. I nudged her awake, in case she gotta get back to the others – whoever they might be. Maybe one of them was her beau, or her husband, and was on the way over with a gun in his hand. She smiled and stretched, like a cat does.

'What's your name?'

'Aaron.'

I lied again. I thought it was the best thing to do, under the circumstances.

'I'm Angel.'

And she was. I told her I was hitching my way east, to find some reality. She said I could get a ride with them as far as Colorado if I wanted. They were going there to spend some time on a Native American reservation in the northeast of the state. Maybe I'd get to find some reality there.

The others were cooking breakfast and she invited me over. There was six of them altogether, including Angel, and they were a country/ folk band calling themselves Tom-Tom. When I told them I played the fiddle, they were happy for me to join them, even after spending the night with Angel. That didn't seem to matter none – they were into free love and sharing everything and the commune spirit. They all had these cool names like Rainbow and Wolf and Raine and Starlight and Buffalo. They said Aaron didn't fit in with their existentialist persona, so they called me Hillock. I didn't realise it at the time but, when I came back to England three years later, I found out about the word pillock, which comes from the Norwegian word *pillicock* and means a complete dick. I don't know if there was a connection or if it was because I screwed Angel and they weren't as open-minded as they made themselves out to be. Right then it was OK for them to call me whatever they wanted.

After a vegetarian breakfast of beans and greens, we set off to cross the Rockies in their bus. It was an old yellow-framed GMC school bus and it looked like it was ready to fall apart. We came outa the Ashley National Forest at Vernal and headed north into Wyoming. We joined Interstate 80 at Rock Springs and turned east towards the Rocky Mountains. The old bus struggled to make the steep climbs and Buffalo, who was driving, had to back down on his speed and use the gears to build more torque, climbing the grades slow and steady. There were times I thought he wasn't gonna make it and we'd slip backwards and end up at the bottom of a gulley somewhere. But we kept our cool and crossed through the Medicine Bow and Laramie Hills and pulled into Cheyenne just as the first snow of winter was starting to fall.

We ate at a diner and the others frowned at me for ordering a hamburger with my salad. That night we slept in the bus and smoked hemp and Angel screwed Raine and Rainbow screwed Wolf and Starlight screwed Buffalo and the waitress from the diner screwed me. Next day, we drove on down into Colorado and the Native American camp on the Pawnee National Grassland to the north of Sterling. The first thing I noticed was, the place didn't look anything like the encampment I seen in my crazy acid dream when I was thirteen. OK, there were a few teepees dotted about, but it was mostly Volkswagens and Winnebagos and customised truck-campers and bow-tents like the one I was packing. The people didn't look like Pawnee either, or Cheyenne or Ute or any other tribe of American Indians. Some wore feathers and fringed buckskin like Angel, but they spoke with accents that came from Pennsylvania and Vermont and upstate Illinois.

We set up camp with the others and, that night, we all drank mescal and chewed peyote and played music round the campfire. Some of them danced like they were demented and Buffalo told me they were doing the Grass Dance or the Sioux Ghost Dance or something, but it looked more like a cross between the Mashed Potato and the Watusi to me. My head hurt next day when I finally woke underneath the chassis of the bus. It took me a while to get my mouth open to drink some water and the girl beside me had been sick in my hair. I washed in the cold water of Crow Creek and dressed as fast as I could. The Tom-Toms were eating grass or leaves or some other kinda green stuff when I got back to camp, but I just had coffee. It was all I could stomach. I knew this wasn't the place for me, so I decided to move out. I don't think the band were sad to see me go – they gave me a coat made of elk or the skin of some other animal, which I thought was ironic. But it was cold and I had no hard-weather gear, coming from the summer climate of San Francisco.

I kissed Angel goodbye and shook some hands and headed down to the highway on foot. It wasn't long before I got a ride with a trucker driving a ten-wheel rig east along Interstate 76. He took me across the great plains of Nebraska – to the sound of Jim Reeves and Eddy Arnold and Buck Owens and the Buckaroos – through North Platte and Lexington and Kearney, as far as Lincoln.

I was down in Vine Street Fields, looking round for a place to stay, when I heard this chanting coming from R Street. It wasn't long before a group of about a hundred students from the University of Nebraska came into view, carrying placards and shouting slogans about the war that was going on over in Vietnam. Up to now I hadn't given much thought to this war. I'd just turned eighteen and never registered with the Selective Service Agency, so there's no way I was getting drafted. America had military advisors out there even when the French were in control and it was called Indo-China. When the French got kicked out the US started to ship in troops to keep the Communists at bay. In 1964 an American destroyer clashed with a North Vietnamese attack craft and that escalated things – it was called the Gulf of Tonkin Incident.

After that, in 1965, regular US combat units were deployed – now the bombing was starting and it was getting outa hand. Earlier in 1966 people in Hollywood built a sixty-foot tower of protest on Sunset Boulevard and there was demonstrations in New York and Boston and Washington and Chicago and San Francisco. People started burning their draft cards and the boxer Cassius Clay refused to go to war, saying the Viet Cong never called him a nigger and he wouldn't go ten thousand miles to kill for the white slave masters. Now the demonstrations were spreading to university campuses and young people were refusing to get involved in an imperialist conflict.

The demonstration came closer and I thought maybe I should march with them. I remembered what happened when I joined the freeway protest in Frisco and ended up with a cut head and had to pay ten dollars to get outa the holding cell – but, hell, you gotta stand up for what you believe in, don't you? Some guy handed me one end of a banner that said

WE WON'T FIGHT ANOTHER RICH MAN'S WAR

and I held it up as high as I could. Next thing I knew, the street in front of us was blocked by dozens of stick-wielding cops. The demo stopped and there was confrontation. The students wanted to keep on to city hall to make their opposition to war heard, the cops were determined to keep them on campus. It was a standoff. Someone in the crowd shouted 'PIGS' and the chant went up, 'PIGS! PIGS! PIGS!'. The demo started moving forward again.

The cops taunted the demonstrators continuously and encouraged them to come at them.

'FAGS! HIPPIES! FAGS! HIPPIES!'

I could hear them screaming in their thick Nebraskan accents that grated on my nerves and I wanted to break all their teeth. But I wasn't a fighter in that sense of the word and I knew I'd get badly hurt if I tried. The whole thing was getting outa hand. The demo organisers couldn't control the crowd. I could feel the pounding in my chest. Heartbeat! Heartbeat! Heartbeat! By now the no-man's-land between the cops and students had disintegrated and the people in the front were the first to be struck with the night-sticks – blood splattered the sidewalks. The demonstrators were trying to defend themselves, punching and kicking and gauging and biting and, in return, being whacked to the ground by the cops. I was pushed closer and closer to the front line by them behind me. I tried to move back, but got pushed forward again. Bodies lay on the ground and were stepped on by others. Blood streamed down the screaming faces of girls and the area around me became a scene of crimson carnage.

I picked up a broken piece of wood from one of the banners and tried to force my way towards the edge of the melée, lashing out at the cops who were trying to keep me corralled. The panic-stricken crowd parted for just a couple of seconds, but it was enough to get me through – then it closed again behind me. I found myself being carried along by a bunch of people running away, back down R Street and onto the campus. I ducked into a drugstore and hid in the washroom until things quietened down. When I came back out, it was all over.

That was enough of Nebraska for me. I was looking for something real and I found it. But it was too real, I was too young, I wasn't ready for that kinda brutality yet – the kind I'd see in the Beanfield and at Stonehenge when I got back to England. I caught a greyhound from the Lincoln Bus Depot on Superior Street and was soon heading east along the Iowa-Missouri border. I got off at Peoria in Illinois and found a hostel full of travellers like myself, mostly young people with middle-class families who were taking a sabbatical from college. They'd had an adventure on the road, exploring America, and were now making their way back to mom and dad for Thanksgiving and the winter, before the spring semesters started. I slept well after the terror of Nebraska, and set out on the road again next morning after a cheap breakfast of waffles and eggs.

It took me a while to get a lift and October was moving on into November, bringing a cold wind with it down from the Great Lakes that cut like a knife into my elk-skin coat. A pick-up truck took me as far as Fort Wayne in Indiana, where my cash finally ran out. I busked for a while on East Beach Street, near The Heights, but it was too cold and I didn't make much money. So I got a job as a dishwasher in a short-order joint called Red Barn Burgers and one day this guy called Kyle came in who recognised me from busking. He asked if I'd play fiddle with his hillbilly group. They called themselves The Black-Eye Peas and performed at a club called Pierre's in the downtown area every evening. It was in a converted textile factory and it mostly attracted rednecks and crackers in denim overalls, but I didn't mind. I knew I wouldn't be staying long. We played stuff like "Pinetree Boogie" and "Makin' Moonshine" and "Ham Beats All Meat" and, between the two jobs, I had enough money to move on by early December.

I checked outa the fleabag hotel I was staying in and made the short hop from Fort Wayne to Cleveland Ohio, on Lake Eerie. By now it was cold as a witch's tit and I wanted to keep moving through Pennsylvania and into New York City, my final destination – so I thought. Everything would be in New York from what I heard. It was the place to be for guys like me, who wanted authenticity instead of play-acting. Cleveland was the scene of vicious race riots during the summer of '66. Four black people were shot dead and thirty others critically injured. The city still hadn't recovered and things were tense. I was treading carefully, because I didn't want to get involved in more mayhem. The Civil Rights Movement in America was giving the establishment major headaches and J Edgar Hoover was trying to paint the organisation red. This guy Martin Luther King won the Nobel Peace prize back in '64 and things were gathering momentum. Phil Ochs and Joan Baez and Pete Seeger were singing protest songs and it felt like something was really happening.

Anyway, I was having a beer in a place called Charlie's Bar on Huron Road East. It was happy hour and the place was crowded. This guy came in wearing a crown and sat on the stool beside me. I tried to ignore him because I didn't want to get involved with no weirdos after the crazy sailor in Frisco, but he kept looking at me like he knew me.

'You're British, ain't you.'

'I was born in Wiltshire.'

'I knew it!'

'But I've lived here in the States since I was a kid.'

'Don't matter, blood's blood.'

I turned back to my beer, hoping the guy'd start talking to whoever was sitting on the other side of him. But he didn't.

'I'm British too ... well, kinda.'

'Oh yeah? What part?'

'New York.'

That was enough for me. I was getting off my stool to go, but he bought me another beer and I had to stay and drink it. He told me his name was Thomas Shelbourne and he was born in St. Matilda's Maternity Mission on East 150th Street, New York City. His mother's name was Rhonda, a sixteen-year-old Puerto Rican girl from the South Bronx, and his father was long gone. Rhonda was drunk when she conceived and she couldn't even remember the auspicious occasion. She'd have had an abortion, but her strict Catholic family wouldn't allow it. She did vaguely remember a guy who was passing through, doing some political survey or something and he wasn't the kid's father or anything, but he was real sweet and well-educated and his last name was Shelbourne. And surely that was good enough for the birth certificate?

Rhonda walked outa St. Matilda's Maternity Mission without her baby and Thomas was sent to the Olla-Podrida Orphanage in Hoboken. He didn't remember much about the early years of his life and he was never permanently adopted by anyone, because he didn't look all that cute. As he got older Thomas was fostered out to a bunch of good-doing, right-thinking, Christian families who said they didn't really need the money they were making for taking him in and it was their god-fearing duty to help those less fortunate than themselves. And they told him he must love Jesus and hate all the heathens, because Jesus loved him and hated all the heathens – and by heathens they meant all the fags and niggers and abortionists and arabs and commies and stem-cell researchers and white-trash and drug addicts and welfare blood-suckers and smart-ass women's liberation dykes and gypsies and people who thought too much.

Thomas listened to all this and it made a mark on his young mind and he got to believing he was better than all those low-life scumbags Jesus hated – that there was something special about him. He promised himself he'd make a lot of money when he grew up and he'd change the world for the better – get rid of all the hateful people for Jesus, cleanse the world of them, create a new Garden of Eden here on earth. Then some of his god-fearing foster-parents started to abuse him and he realised Jesus didn't love him after all.

When he was younger, he couldn't do much about this treatment but, as the years went by, Thomas worked out ways to get back at his born-again foster-parents and asshole foster-siblings. Things like urinating in their soup and dusting their beds with itching powder. A favourite was placing dog crap covered with dry leaves on the front porch, setting fire to the leaves, knocking the door and then running off. After that he got serious – dusted the beds with fibreglass needles, put mercury in the soup and, instead of setting fire to the leaves, he set fire to the porch.

When Thomas turned sixteen, he learnt to drive, stole fifty bucks and his current grotesque and abusive foster-father's car and never came back. He got himself a cheap room and a job as a taxi driver with the Cromagnon Cab Company in Harlem. But he didn't like the long unsociable hours and the crap-heads that crawled into the back of his cab in the early hours of the morning, so he became a chauffeur, working freelance through the Albigenses Agency on the Upper West Side.

But Thomas still believed he was something special. Some of the old holier-than-thou brainwashing got stuck inside his skull, despite all the disillusionment, and he wanted more than the short-term chauffeuring contracts. He wanted something better – something with a future. He wanted to be somebody.

Thomas also wanted to know who his father was.

So he used his paychecks to trace the name Shelbourne. It started off as pure curiosity, just trying to find out something about his father, and he reckoned the guy must've been some kinda heel to dump him in the Olla-Podrida Orphanage out in Hoboken and just beat it – never show up for his birthdays or nothing – and Thomas just wanted to confirm this and he thought he wouldn't want to know anything else after that. It was impossible to trace his mother, because she didn't leave no surname at the Maternity Mission on East 150th Street and there was no records or nothing to go on. But he had the name Shelbourne from his father and the more he looked, the more he found and the name went right back to the Revolutionary War.

The earliest Shelbourne he could trace, with the same spelling of the name, was a guy called Armistead Shelbourne. This dude was a British colonial master carpenter, who petitioned against the Stamp Act in 1766 and was one of the activists who succeeded in having the Townshend Acts repealed. Armistead Shelbourne also dressed up like a Mohawk Indian and helped dump the tea into Boston Harbour. But, although he was against direct taxation by the British and was pissed off by the Intolerable Acts they devised to punish Massachusetts for the Tea Party, he just wanted to make a point and was still a loyal subject of George III – and no revolutionary.

Thomas was fascinated by all this stuff and kept digging and digging. He found out that old George III seen the writing on the wall, as far as the colonies were concerned, and decided he had to appease the colonials or lose everything. He knew, if revolution came, the backbone of that revolution'd be made up of ordinary farmers and tradesmen, many of them loyalists at heart, just like Armistead Shelbourne, but who reckoned they weren't getting a fair shake from direct rule. So, he had a brilliant idea. He decided to give them their own king, one who'd prove he had the interests of the colonies at heart, but who'd still be loyal to the old country and the old monarchy.

Thomas read all these dusty old documents about how most political thinkers of the time weren't convinced that revolution was the right way to go and they doubted if republicanism could survive in such a huge land and many favoured a monarchy, supported by a parliament and modelled on the British system. But George III was crafty, even if he was a little crazy, and he knew the ordinary farmers and tradesmen'd never accept one of the old order of aristocrats as their king, someone they'd recognise as an obvious stooge. No, it needed to be a man with the right credentials, someone on their side. So he hunkered down with some guys called Cornwallis and Clinton and North and decided, after a deal of table-thumping and hollering and wig-throwing, to give the Americans one of their very own. A man who'd spoken out against injustice and who'd nailed his colours to the common mast and who they could trust and accept, yet one who was still loyal to the British throne.

Armistead Shelbourne.

Consequently, though he was never to be recognised as such, Armistead Shelbourne was the first King of America.

And, by birthright, Thomas Shelbourne discovered that he should now be the present King of America.

6
Summer Of Love

Truth isn't absolute – it's multiple and contradictory – either known or not known. I was trying to see the point, but could only see the glare – without shadow or relief, ubiquitous and implacable.

———————

I pulled into New York City on Christmas Eve 1966 in the middle of a snowstorm, with the King of America. He was on his way home when I met him in Cleveland and he told me he knew people in the Big Apple and could help me get set up there. We came in through Pennsylvania and New Jersey in Thomas Shelbourne's beat up old Pontiac station wagon – past Newark and Jersey City and through the Holland Tunnel into Manhattan. We were lucky to get that far. Snow started falling as we came through the Allegheny Mountains and the forecast on the car radio said the entire northeast was in for a blizzard. Thunder and lightning came with the snow and the King of America said it was a sign. God was on his side! He got chains on the wheels just in time and the storm was in full swing by the time it got dark. It made for heavy going on the final few miles and New York was at a standstill by the time we got to his apartment in the South Bronx.

The apartment was a two-room craphole in a tenement building – definitely not a palace fit for a king. But it was somewhere to get in outa the freezing weather until the storm passed over. By Christmas morning the snow'd stopped and people were out with their shovels and ploughs. Shelbourne cooked breakfast of beans and coffee and we went for a drink to a bar called Finnerty's on Williamsbridge Road. It was an Irish shebeen and I wondered what the King of America would be doing in a place like this – especially if the Micks found out he was really English and me too. But they didn't.

I woke up in 1967 with a hangover the size of Central Park and a note pinned to my shirt. It was from Thomas Shelbourne:

Hey Aaron,

I gotta split to go get my birthright. I owe four month's rent on this apartment and I hope you're gone by the time the landlord comes round. His name's Paulie Gambino and he's a capo in the Cosa Nostra. If you're still here and you got the money, it'll be OK. If not, there's a paraplegic clinic on Pelham Parkway. See ya when the sun comes up.

His serene highness, King Thomas I

I could hear heavy footsteps coming up the stairs, so I grabbed my gear and climbed out the window onto the fire escape, just as the door got kicked in. Down on East 169th Street, I zig-zagged as fast as my pounding head would tolerate to the nearest subway. I jumped on a train and emerged at Times Square in the downtown area.

Manhattan was a mad, bad crazy place. I'd never been there before, but I knew all about it. Didn't everybody? It was a dreamscape. The ubiquitous image in everyone's eye. That indefinable thing that made people want to go take a look. This city was everything that was off in the world – and everything that was on. A schizophrenic city. Diseased. Genetically flawed. But still strangely beautiful. Everything that was good-bad and bad-good. I felt a surge of adrenaline at finally being here.

I made my way over to Madison Avenue in Midtown, the area of the city that's kinda unmistakably the New York of everyone's imagination. Skyscrapers reeled and traffic cops rolled and yellow cabs clicked and clacked and honked and swore and people swarmed like insects and vents belched steam from ancient underground heating systems – just like in the movies. Madison was sandwiched between Fifth and Park and didn't quite have the same sense of glamour as its more famous neighbours. But it was still impressive, with coffee bars and delis and big strutting buildings and mucho self-assurance.

I needed a temporary place to stay until I found my feet. Morgan's Hotel was self-consciously chic. A place inhabited by has-beens and wannabees and handsome resting-actor staff in designer uniforms and an air of low profile about the whole place. I seen it was the kinda hotel that could be slipped into and out of without too much attention being paid to whatever it was you were doing. A mixture of multiplex and art deco, just a little past its bedtime, with lizards lounging and girls calling. But my room was big and clean and had some kinda spa bath and a coffee bar and two hundred complementary Camel cigarettes. After stowing my gear in the room, I tried to watch TV for a while and smoked a couple of the Camels. But I was shook up after the near miss with the Mafia and decided to go do a bit of sightseeing. I took the elevator from the fourteenth floor and sneaked across the lobby and out into the city's early January afternoon.

I stood on the sidewalk for a moment, wondering where to go and trying to keep outa the crazy crowd's way. I decided to head south for a while and then right, into West 55th Street. There was plenty of bars and bistros and super stores and fashion shops. Car horns honked and sirens shrieked and everything moved at a fast pace – much faster even than Frisco. After half an hour or so, I got tired of being pushed around by the city crowds and I slipped into a place called Shorty's on Fifth Avenue and looked at the mind-blowing list of cocktails on the menu. I ordered a Manhattan, which seemed appropriate, and found a quiet corner table with its back to the wall.

It was mid-afternoon and happy hour crowds were yet to pour in from the shops and offices. One or two other customers sat along the bar and an odd couple held a serious and psychologically demanding conversation with some arm waving and shoulder shrugging and feigned oblivion to the rest of the world. I stared out through the curtained window at the street scene – a colourful melting-pot of sights, sounds and smells. I could feel the ambiance, sense it, touch it, taste it. The rich vein of electricity that ran through this place. I reckoned it might suit me, more than anywhere else I'd been. It could be my soul-space. I believed back then I could feel something in the air and hear it in the street music and smell it in the unique perfume of possibility.

I slipped into a kinda trance thinking about what I could do here. First of all, I'd have to get a job and somewhere permanent to live.

Then I'd look round for a venue to play my music at – either solo or with a group. I wanted to get away from folk and jazz and hillbilly and get involved in something progressive. Things were getting interesting with The Doors and The Stone Poneys and The Youngbloods and I wanted to get in on the new scene here in NY. Thinking about all this stuff, I didn't notice that Shorty's was beginning to get crowded as happy hour approached. The place was filling with accents from Bronx and Brooklyn and hookers from Harlem and freethinkers from Flatbush and queens from Queens and sharks from Staten Island. Martinis got mixed and Wild Turkey poured over rocks. Dubonnets stirred with sours and the staff served up bottles of Budweiser and Rolling Rock and Molsons and Dos Equis and pitchers of Anchor Steam and Samuel Adams.

The noise of conversation swirled all around me, but I stayed quiet, alone on my little island in this sea of pseudo-sophistication. Until a black guy pushed his way in through the crowd outside on 5th Avenue and sat on a chair just opposite me.

'What you drinkin'?'

'Are you talking to me?'

'Sure I'm talkin' to you. Ain't takin' to no one else.'

'I'm OK.'

'I know you OK. I didn't ask if you be OK. I asked what you drinkin.'

I hoped this guy wasn't the black Elvis who crazy Selcraig ran into on his schizophrenic island. I tried to get up from the table. The guy put a hand on my arm.

'You better let go of me.'

'Or what?'

'Or ... I'll punch you in the eye.'

The black guy looked at me with a frown – a long frown. He pushed his coat back and I could see the handle of a revolver sticking out of his waistband. Then he started to laugh – loudly. He took his hand off my arm and the frown returned for a couple of seconds and he looked like he was gonna say something. Then he laughed again – even louder than before. I left the bar, holding my head.

Hunger kicked in that evening and I decided to go get a bite to eat somewhere. I didn't want to go back to 5th Avenue, so I headed into Central Park and found the Tavern on the Green, near West 66th Street on the Upper West Side. I liked the view and I was glad to be outa the hotel room for a while. I ordered a cheeseburger and fries and a cup of coffee and looked out at the footpaths wandering like snail trails through the trees. It was getting dark and the lamps gave the place a still, quiet feel, even though I reckoned it was full of gunmen and gaylords. A few horse-drawn buggies ignored the danger and carried romantic couples for a view of the night-time skyline – to the music of Manhattan.

All the joggers and roller skaters and street performers were gone home, in case someone stole everything from them. Everything they had in the whole world, and even maybe their very souls as well – snook up and took them at knifepoint when they were enjoying themselves and at their most vulnerable. One or two brave locals walked fierce looking hounds out among the ponds and pavilions, while the sounds of zoo animals drifted across on the still air above the noise of the peripheral traffic. The Carousel was quiet, its organ safely locked away for the night and the statues of Robert Burns and Sir Walter Scott and Hans Christian Andersen and Alice and The-Angel-of-the-Waters closed their eyes to the rapes and robberies and their ears to the screams of the innocent and naive. Away to the north, the reservoir hid the grinning skulls of them wearing concrete boots and Latino locals fished the Meer. And, around it all, the clear star-filled sky was a canopy of crystal hope that'd never again become black and lifeless.

The next morning was bright and unseasonably warm. I had breakfast in the hotel restaurant, while smells of the street drifted in and mingled with the deli odours of sausage and eggs and waffles and pancakes and maple syrup and coffee. I had eggs over easy with toast, just for appearance's sake. I stared at the food without touching it and sipped a cup of Colombian, not sure about what to do now. The smell was becoming overpowering – the smell of New York at this time of the morning. A just-woke-up smell of staleness from the night before, covered over with a blanket of breakfast. It was beginning to get to me as I waited, wondering where to go and what to do. Eventually, I took the subway south into the Village. The quaintness there seemed genuine enough, although the bohemians looked passé to the point of being trippers – nothing like they were in Frisco. Brownstones and camp copywriters passed me by on my way into Soho, with its continentals and cast-iron buildings. I was getting close to Little Italy and I hoped Paulie Gambino wouldn't be on the lookout for me – break my legs for Thomas Shelbourne's rent. But, despite the pretentiousness, I liked the area. I thought I should get a place here, or sleep on the street – eat off it, become absorbed by it, part of it. Flesh and blood and concrete and sinew and steel.

I trawled the neighbourhoods until a found a room to rent over a Chinese takeaway in Mott Street. It was two hundred dollars a month, which was a bit steep by my reckoning, but this was New York and it was in the right area. So I took it. I had some money from working in Fort Wayne, but it wouldn't last long. I took a job as a dishwasher in the Chung Wah Chinese joint underneath my room and started cruising the clubs in the East Village and Soho and Tribeca. I met a girl called Sonia Starr, who was looking for musicians to play in a club called The Hobo, down on Delancy. She was really looking for a bass guitarist, but she was intrigued when I told her I played the fiddle. She gave me a try out in the club, but the sound wasn't quite what she was looking for.

'You ever played an electric fiddle, Aaron?'

'No, but it can't be much different from playing acoustic.'

So I bought a 1959 Fender with the last of my cash and practised until I got the hang of it. Sonia was real happy because the sound was just what she was looking for. She teamed me up with a group of people calling themselves the Village Idiots and we played in The Hobo and other clubs through the spring of 1967 and into summer. The group was a loose association of sounds and people came and went all the time. We played stuff that was popular, but mostly we improvised and you never knew what was gonna happen on-stage. The crowds loved us and we soon built up a fan base in Lower Manhattan.

Then the summer of '67 happened.

They called it the Summer of Love, but I thought it oughta have been called the Summer of Protest. In the spring, gatherings called Be-Ins were organised in San Francisco and New York, protesting about all kinds of stuff. The first one in Frisco in January was touted on the cover of the San Francisco Oracle as "A Gathering of Tribes for a Human Be-In". It was a direct response to the banning of LSD and one of the main speakers was Timothy Leary who told the crowd to 'turn on, tune in and drop out'. Allen Ginsberg was there too and Gary Snyder and Michael McLure. Music came from Jefferson Airplane, The Grateful Dead, Big Brother and the Holding Company and Quicksilver Messenger Service.

The Hell's Angels kept order and underground chemist Owsley Stanley gave out massive amounts of white lightning LSD to the thirty thousand people who turned up. It was a bringing together of the militant Berkeley radicals and the non-political Haight-Ashbury Hippies, to let off steam about drugs and the Vietnam war.

The New York Be-In happened at Easter when ten thousand people turned up at the Sheep Meadow in Central Park – most of them were hippies, including me. We wore carnation petals and paper stars and little mirrors on our foreheads and the New York Times described us as "poets from the Bronx, dropouts from the East Vill , painters from the East Side, teachers from the West Side and teenyboppers from Long Island". We were escorte by cop and we covered their black-and-whites with flowers. At one point, five uniforms approached a couple of naked hippies, but they got surrounded by the crowd chanting 'we lov cops' and 'turn on cops'. Later that night, they beamed lights on us and used bullhorns to yell at us to disperse. There was a standoff but, in the end, they let us carry on.

Later the same month another art   Be-In started in Central Park, then marched to the United Nations building. There was an estimated four hundred   d of us and it was the biggest rally of all time up to then. As well as us hippies, there was Sioux Indians from South Dakota and African Americans from Washington DC and the people held signs saying MAKE PEACE, NOT WAR. At the UN, Benjamin Spock, James Bevel and Martin Luther King made speeches against the war and demonstrators burned their draft cards. In May the cops forced us to move from Tompkins Square to Central Park for a concert where various bands, including The Grateful Dead, performed. The young people came in their bare feet and danced around crazily to the music.

So, these were the kind of events that led up to the Summer of Love. It started when around one hundred thousand young people converged on Haight-Ashbury in Frisco. I was glad I was outa there by then. Hippies also gathered in New York, Los Angeles, Chicago, Atlanta and across Europe. But San Francisco was the centre of it all. It was a melting pot of music, psychedelic drugs, free love, artistic expression and alternative politics. It got to be the defining period of the 1960s, as the hippie counterculture came into the mainstream. But it was a popularised version of the hippie experience and not the real thing. They gave out free food, free drugs and free love in Golden Gate Park and set up a free clinic for them who overdosed on any or all three. The Frisco authorities were overwhelmed by the ever-increasing number of youths making the pilgrimage to Haight-Ashbury – they did nothing to help the residents who couldn't cope. Haight community leaders formed the Council of the Summer of Love, giving the phenomenon an official name. The mainstream media's coverage of the hippie lifestyle in Haight-Ashbury drew youth from all over America. Reports appeared daily in the newspapers and Hunter S Thompson labelled the district Hashbury.

The Monterey Pop Festival was held in June and an estimated sixty thousand people gathered there for the music. The song "San Francisco" was written by John Phillips of the Mamas and Papas to promote Monterey – it was sung by Scott McKenzie and got to be an instant hit. It transcended its original purpose and popularised an idealised image of San Francisco.

If you're going to San Francisco
be sure to wear some flowers in your hair
If you're going to San Francisco
summertime will be a love-in there.

Large numbers of hippies who attended Monterey then headed to San Francisco to hear bands like The Jimi Hendrix Experience, Otis Redding, The Byrds, The Who and Janis Joplin – swelling the ranks of the hippies even further.

In New York, the Summer of Love was less spectacular and less commercialised. July and August were hot, with temperatures up in the thirties centigrade. Problem was, New Yorkers couldn't quite figure out the best way to be young. They were full of college politics and opinions about what was good and bad taste and pushy put-downs about voguey stuff. Big Apple longhairs were more obnoxious than California hippies and now it was all happening out west – New York City wasn't the centre of the universe after all. What was happening was a happening – and the slickers had to deal with it the best way they could.

They had to figure out how to be New York freaks, on a different level to Frisco freaks. They had the chic and the shifty but, over there, they had the acid and the naked girls. Some New Yorkers couldn't resist going out to San Francisco – not to would've been to ignore a generational phenomenon. But I'd been there during the best of times – at the beginning – when it was real. I'd seen the redwoods and the dreamscape and the cosmic coastline. I'd experienced narcotic nirvana.

In '67 they were all clean and white and blonde and dumb – clones of each other.

You had to look like a hippie to be a hippie. We did our best to match the San Francisco Summer of Love here in New York, but how could you stay mellow in the rush-hour or after being busted at a Smiler's Deli for stealing a gladioli to wear in your hair. Everyday shit intruded on the barefooted. In California they were given free food along with the free love and they didn't have to work. Here, steam billowed from manhole covers and rust fell from the overhead trains and even mainlining jazz musicians had day jobs. The dark, dampness of the Port Authority bus terminal couldn't compete with the wide open spaces out west.

The thing is, by the autumn everything had gone sour in Haight-Ashbury, just like I knew it would. A dark side distorted the hippie hopeful philosophy. The movement had become a commercialised media spectacle – and a big mess. The realities of "dropping out" hit home – "free love" was used to excuse rape and thousands suffered from serious drug addiction and mental problems, or became homeless. San Francisco was overrun with dealers and teenage runaways, and the Haight-Ashbury scene deteriorated through overcrowding, homelessness and crime. Most of the founders of the scene moved elsewhere. They realised that peace and love couldn't sustain them forever. Most of the pseudo-hippies had to go back to university or get a job, although the real ones found ways to keep with their alternative lifestyles. For most, though, the utopian dream had come to an end. On 6 October 1967 them who were still in the Haight staged a mock funeral, The Death of the Hippie Ceremony, to signal the end of the played-out scene.

By then, I was sharing a ground-floor apartment with a girl called Tulip over on Avenue B. We weren't lovers or nothing like that, it was purely an economic arrangement. She was into the new computer stuff that I didn't think would ever take off, but it paid well and she earned more than I did and she was hardly ever home. I was working as a flunky for the Port Authority, riding a hand truck through the monoxide-choked bus terminal by day, and doing gigs in the Village clubs by night. I'd learnt to play the guitar by then and I could switch from that to the fiddle, which made me more versatile and employable.

But the summer of '67 wasn't all about love. In June there was race riots in Atlanta and Boston and Cincinnati, as well as Buffalo and Tampa, Florida. In July, the unrest continued in Birmingham, Chicago, Milwaukee, Minneapolis and Connecticut, and the Twelfth Street riot in Detroit, Michigan. So, it wasn't a summer of love for everybody.

There was hate as well.

In the end, 1967 became 1968 and I turned twenty, bringing to an end my teenage years. By then I was getting disillusioned with New York. I hadn't found whatever it was I was looking for and I'd come as far east as I could.

Next stop had to be back to Britain, where my mother took me from all those years ago.

7
Woodstock

A single silhouette against a black universe. Isolated.
Invested with absoluteness. Alone in the eternal namelessness
and formlessness, which is the very substance of everything.
Being intensely and absolutely there!

I didn't have enough money to get me back to Britain. The job and the music didn't pay that well and I spent all I earned on food and rent and weed. Early in 1969 Tulip told me about some happening in upstate New York later that year. She said it was called The Woodstock Music and Art Fair and the company she worked for had links to some guy called Michael Lang, who was a music promoter from Brooklyn. She said she could get me a backstage pass if I wanted it, but I was a bit disillusioned with all the protest Be-Ins from '67 and I didn't want to go. Tulip said it wouldn't be like that, it was purely a music-fest and no politics. They were hoping to get bands like The Rolling Stones and The Who and it might do my music career good to mix with those kinda people. As far as I was concerned, The Stones and The Who were far too mainstream, but they were British and, who knew, they might have a vacant seat on a plane going back there.

Lang organised the Miami Pop Festival in '68 and twenty-five thousand people turned up to listen to Jimi Hendrix, Chuck Berry, John Lee Hooker and The Mothers of Invention. It was supposed to be a two-day event, but it got rained out on the Sunday. Thing was, Tulip told me the organisers were having trouble attracting the big names bands and it looked like the Woodstock fest wouldn't take place after all. Then, in April '69, Creedence Clearwater Revival signed and the others came after that – The Who and The Grateful Dead and Mountain and Santana. The line-up for the three days is legend now, Richie Havens, Arlo Guthrie, Joan Baez, Janis Joplin, Joe Cocker, Hendrix and so many others. It was billed as "An Aquarian Exposition: 3 Days of Peace and Music" and it was called Woodstock because the original plan was for it to take place in Woodstock, New York State. But local residents objected and the organisers found another site in the town of Wallkill – town officials were assured that no more than fifty thousand would attend. But, again, the residents objected and the concert was banned on the grounds that portable toilets wouldn't meet requirements. The ban turned out to be a publicity bonus for the festival because it got reported and people were pissed off about it. They finally found Max Yasgur's farm, a natural valley sloping down to Filippini Pond, close to the town of Bethel.

Woodstock was actually about forty miles away.

The organisers repeated to the Bethel authorities that no more than fifty thousand people'd turn up. The residents objected again, making up signs saying "Stop Max's Hippy Music Festival", but permits were approved and the event was scheduled to run from Friday 15 to Monday 18 August, with the music kicking off at 5:00pm on Friday and finishing at around 11:00am on Monday.

I can't remember now how Tulip's company was connected – I think it was advertising or PR or marketing or something, but I can't be sure. She gave me a preview of the schedule when her people got it from Woodstock Ventures. They'd booked thirty-two acts altogether. Sweetwater would be first up on Friday afternoon and they'd be followed by the Incredible String Band, Bert Sommer, Tim Hardin, Richie Havans, Ravi Shankar, Melanie Sofka and Arlo Guthrie. Joan Baez'd bring the first day to a close at about 2:00am.

Saturday's music was scheduled to start in the evening, with Quill kicking things off at around 5:00pm. Country Joe McDonald would be followed by Santana and Iron Butterfly, then The Keef Harley Band, Canned Heat, Mountain, Grateful Dead, Creedence Clearwater Revival, Janis Joplin and Sly and the Family Stone. With The Who and Jefferson Airplane to wrap things up at 10:00am the following morning. Seventeen solid hours of music.

Sunday'd see Joe Cocker on stage first at 2:00pm, then Country Joe and the Fish, Ten Years After, The Band, Johnny Winter, Blood Sweat and Tears, Crosby Stills Nash and Young, Paul Butterfield Blues

Band, Sha Na Na and Hendrix to bring the whole thing to a close at 11:30am on Monday morning.

Sounded cool to me.

Woodstock was supposed to be a profit-making venture. Tickets cost eighteen dollars in advance and twenty-four dollars on the gate. You could only buy the tickets at record stores in the greater New York City area, or by mail from a post office box at Radio City in Midtown Manhattan. Tulip told me they sold about one hundred and eighty-five thousand advance tickets and they reckoned around two hundred thousand people'd turn up. It didn't matter to me, I had my free pass.

The late change in venue didn't give the organisers enough time to prepare. With only a couple of days to go, they had two options: finish the fencing and ticket booths, or finish the stage. If they didn't finish the stage, the people who paid would be mad and there could be trouble. If they didn't finish the fencing, the promoters'd lose their shirts. When the hippies started arriving in tens of thousands, the decision was made for them. The fences at Woodstock became a joke and the stage gave birth to a legend. Half a million people turned up and Woodstock got to be a "free concert" as well as a pivotal moment for the counterculture generation.

The crowds caused massive traffic jams and some bands had to be flown in by helicopter. Television and radio news stations reported chaos on the roads. I was OK, because I'd come up early with my ticket that Tulip gave me and I was one of the first to arrive on the Thursday. Final stage construction and sound system setup were still underway and about fifty thousand people had already arrived and set up camp.

Sound for the concert was engineered by a guy called Bill Hanley, who I met backstage. He built special speaker columns on the hills and had sixteen loudspeaker arrays in a square platform going up to the hill on seventy-foot towers. He set it up for a hundred and fifty to two hundred thousand people, but five hundred thousand showed up – Altec-designed marine-plywood cabinets that weighed half a ton apiece and stood six feet tall, almost four feet deep and three feet wide. Each of these enclosures carried four fifteen-inch JBL

D140 loudspeakers. The tweeters consisted of 4×2-cell and 2×10-cell Altec Horns. Behind the stage were three transformers providing two thousand amperes of current to power the amplification setup. For many years after, this system'd be called The Woodstock Bins.

Residents of Bethel were mad as hell that town officials were allowing the "swarm of hippies" to descend on them like locusts. They formed human roadblocks across the only entrance to Max Yasgur's farm, but the people just parked up and walked the rest of the way. I pitched my tent in a good spot and waited for the action. My backstage pass gave me access to the crews and roadies and I mingled with them and even played some improv jamming sessions on my fiddle with some of the backing musicians.

The Stones never made it to Woodstock because Jagger was in Australia filming "Ned Kelly", but other British bands were there – Keef Hartley and The Who and Joe Cocker and Ten Years After – and I mainly hung out with their crews. Nobody had a spare plane ticket back to the old country, but a guy called Digby, with a big handlebar moustache, said I could get a working passage on a ship called The Queen Elizabeth 2. He'd done it himself a couple of times on other ships, before he got a job as a roadie with Ten Years After. The ship had made her maiden voyage across the Atlantic in May and she'd be sailing outa New York for Southampton at the end of August.

Off-duty cops were banned from providing security, so a New Mexico commune known as the Hog Farm were hired to form a Please Force. The Hog Farmers were led by Wavy Gravy, a toothless former beatnik comic, who put on a Smokey-the-Bear suit and warned troublemakers they'd be doused in fizzy water or hit with custard pies. As well as forming the Please Force, the Hog Farmers were in charge of catering, ordering in bushels of brown rice, buying one hundred and sixty thousand paper plates, forks, knives and spoons and thirty thousand paper cups. They fed between one hundred and sixty and one hundred and ninety thousand people at the Hog Farm Free Kitchen, five thousand at a time.

The large food-vending outfits that handled ball games and other arenas didn't want to take on Woodstock. Nobody'd ever handled food services for an event that size. Nathan's Hot Dogs, from Coney Island, stepped in, but they pulled out again after the site was moved from Woodstock to Sullivan County. In the end, the organisers hired Food For Love who had very little experience in the catering business. But the concession stands weren't finished when the concert got under way and there was fist fights between the vendors. Food For Love were quickly outa their depth. Queues were long and supplies were short and then they decided to jack up the price of a hot dog from twenty-five cents to a dollar. People saw this as capitalist exploitation and burned down the stands. Wavy Gravy tried to calm the situation and announced to the crowd,

> 'There's a guy up there, some hamburger guy, that had his stand burned down last night. But he's still got a little stuff left, and for you people that still believe capitalism ain't that weird, you might help him out and buy a couple of hamburgers.'

The Friday line-up was supposed to start with Sweetwater, a psychedelic rock band. But they got stuck in traffic and the crowd was entertained by one of the Hog Farmers, who led them through a series of yoga exercises. With the festival start-time running over by several hours, there was panic to find a performer ready. Tim Hardin, who later died of a heroin overdose, was too stoned, so Richie Havens went on. When Havens finished his set he kept trying to leave but was told to do more encores as the next band wasn't ready. His song "Freedom" was improvised and got to be a worldwide hit. Some eastern guy called Swami Satchidananda gave a speech and then Sweetwater finally turned up and did ten songs in their flute and bongo style.

Bert Sommer came on next with his acoustic voice, then Tim Hardin sang a few ballads and, with storm clouds on the horizon, the crowd started chanting 'No Rain! No Rain! No Rain!' The chorus of voices didn't manage to stop the deluge and, in three hours, five inches of rain fell and it became a mud-fest. Ravi Shankar played Indian music on his sitar and he said later it was real scary, the crowds and the mud reminded him of wallowing water buffalos at home in India.

Even the rain couldn't dampen the crowd's spirit and the mood was crazy by the time Melanie Safka came on. Her dressing room was a small teepee and when Joan Baez heard her coughing, she sent over a pot of herbal tea. Safka never had a performer's pass and had to sing for the security guys before they'd let her onstage. When she did get on, it was in front of five hundred thousand people and she was an unknown nineteen-year-old folk singer. No one could have predicted that the fragile, dry-mouthed girl, shaking with nerves, would become the festival icon. She sang seven songs in that unique and high-throaty voice of hers – "Mr Tambourine Man" to the jingle-jangle people and "Beautiful People" to the beautiful people. She said later,

> 'I had no experience, I just wanted to sing. Something clicked and by the time I came offstage, I was a celebrity. It was unbelievable.'

Arlo Guthrie announced from the stage that the New York Thruway was closed – he and Joan Baez took us into the early hours. Baez told the crowd how her husband, David Harris, was arrested and imprisoned for three years because he didn't follow his draft notice. The rain started to drizzle during her performance and it was a thunderstorm by the time she finished. I managed to get back to my tent and slept through the rain that night until about 10:00am on Saturday.

People kept coming to Woodstock, it was like everyone in America was here. For the lost and confused there was two wooden signposts nailed to a tree. Chalked on one was "Groovy Way" with arrows in opposite directions. On the other was "Gentle Path" and underneath was "High Way" pointing to the left. Rain made the roads and fields a slurry and there wasn't enough sanitation or food or first aid. A medical tent was set up to treat bare feet cut by broken glass and metal can lids that littered the site, bad acid trips, and burned retinas when their stoned owners lay down and stared direct at the sun. One guy, asleep in a trash-strewn field, hidden under his sleeping bag for protection from the rain, died when he was accidentally run over by a tractor hauling away sewage from the site's portable toilets.

Saturday's performances were originally scheduled to start in the evening, but they began shortly after noon so the crowd wouldn't get restless and become unruly. Bands were asked to lengthen their sets and, throughout the day, rain and technical delays wreaked havoc with the schedule. Quill started things off at around midday. Technical problems prevented their performance from being included in the documentary film that was being made, which caused Atlantic Records to drop them later.

Country Joe McDonald was scared to death and had to be pushed onstage for his solo performance. Iron Butterfly were scheduled to follow him, but they got stuck at the airport and didn't make it because the helicopter booked to ferry them to the site didn't arrive. Someone spotted John B Sebastian of the Lovin' Spoonful backstage and got him to come on instead. Sebastian had smoked a couple of joints and taken LSD and started shouting,

'Far out! Far up! Far down! Far around!'

His performance was shambolic. Nobody noticed much and he shouted to the crowd,

'You're really amazing, you're a whole city.'

And we were – we were the third biggest city in New York State at that moment in time.

By now, half a million people were at the festival and another million had to turn back because of traffic congestion. Santana got the crowd dancing with their unique blend of Latin rock and Soul Sacrifice contrasted with the other music played so far. But the beat was electric and they were a hard act for the Keef Harley Band to follow. Canned Heat were the essential hippie blues band, with "Goin' Up The Country" and six other numbers, including "On The Road Again". Mountain were mind-blowing and played an hour-long gig of eleven numbers. Electrical problems and ankle-deep water on stage caused Grateful Dead to get a shock when they touched their microphones and electric guitar strings.

The people of Sullivan County, hearing reports of food shortages, gathered thousands of food donations to be airlifted to the site, including about ten thousand sandwiches, water, fruit and canned goods. A Jewish community centre made sandwiches with two hundred loaves of bread, forty pounds of meat cuts and two gallons of pickles, which were distributed by nuns. Wavy Gravy's Hog Farmers passed out thousands of cups of granola to people who didn't want to lose their place near the stage and who hadn't eaten in two days. They served brown rice and vegetables to free food lines.

Wavy Gravy announced to the crowd,

'What we have in mind is breakfast in bed for four hundred thousand! Now it's gonna be good food and we're going to get it to you. We're all feedin' each other.'

But despite all that, and despite the festival mood being anti-war, things might've turned bad without the grub and medicine airlifted by the army. The message was loudspeakered from the stage,

'They're with us man, they're not against us. Forty-five doctors are here without pay because they dig what this is into.'

The revolving stage was designed to minimise wait times, turning when one act finished with the equipment in place for the next one. But it couldn't support the weight of so many people on the side of the stage watching the performances and the wheels fell off. Grace Slick and Janis Joplin and me and a lot of others were standing on it and you couldn't just sweep us off with a broom. When it wasn't raining, people were skinny-dipping in the pond and sliding on the mud and making love in the fields. And, as the day and night moved on, the music kept coming.

Creedence Clearwater Revival came on at 3:30am on Sunday morning. John Fogerty said,

'We were ready to rock out and we waited and waited and finally it was our turn ... there were half a million people asleep. These people were out. It was sort of like a painting of a Dante scene, just bodies from hell, all entwined and asleep, covered with mud. And this is the moment I will never forget as long as I live: A quarter mile away in the darkness, on the other edge of this bowl, there was some guy flicking his Bic and in the night I hear,

"Don't worry about it, John. We're with you". I played the rest of the show for that guy'.'

Creedence were followed by Janis Joplin and Sly and the Family Stone. The Who performed an unprecedented twenty-three numbers and left Jefferson Airplane to wrap things up at 10:00am with "The House at Pooneil Corners". Twenty-two hours of music.

On Sunday, the crowd issue was becoming critical and the Governor of New York was gonna deploy ten thousand national guard troops, but the organisers talked him out of it. I reckon it would've accelerated the problems and led to confrontation and violence. Luckily, he had enough sense to realise this. Sullivan County declared a state of emergency and people from the nearby Stewart Air Force Base helped out and made sure essentials were able to get in. Joe Cocker was first on stage at 2:00pm, with more storm clouds looming. After Cocker's set, there was a two-hour thunderstorm delay.

There were two deaths from drug overdoses and four births – three at a makeshift clinic that'd been set up by an area hospital in a school just off the festival grounds, the fourth at a motel in nearby Bethel, which was the first place the new father could find when his wife went into labour. And four miscarriages.

Country Joe and the Fish came on when things got going again, but it kept on raining. During the downpour there were fears some artists'd get electrocuted. It was so humid that Ten Years After couldn't keep their guitar strings in tune and Alvin Lee was warned of the risk, as it was still raining when they came on. He replied,

'Oh come on, if I get electrocuted at Woodstock we'll sell lots of records.'

The Band played without Bob Dylan – there was different reports on why he didn't turn up. Then Johnny Winter, Blood Sweat and Tears and Crosby Stills Nash and Young. Neil Young only performed two songs in the band's acoustic set and refused to be filmed during their electric set, complaining that the cameras were too distracting.

A mass exodus began when a thunderstorm delayed the proceedings again at about 5:00pm. But thousands still stayed on through Sunday night and into Monday morning to hear the Butterfield Blues Band and Sha Na Na. Hendrix came on about 9:00am on Monday to bring the whole thing to a close. By then, most of the crowd had dispersed and about thirty-five thousand were left, including me. Hendrix and his band were introduced as The Experience, but they were really called Gypsy Sun and Rainbows. Everybody thinks he brought the show to a close with his psychedelic national anthem, but this really happened about three-quarter way through the set and it morphed into "Purple Haze".

Woodstock was remarkably peaceful, given the number of people and the conditions involved. There was a sense of social harmony and that, along with the quality of the music, made it one of the enduring events of the 1960s. Many artists who thought they were too good to perform there deeply regretted that decision afterwards when it was said, 'If you weren't at Woodstock, you weren't in the '60's'. After the concert Max Yasgur, the farmer who owned the site, said it was a victory of peace and love. Half a million people thrown together like that was reckoned as a recipe for riot, looting, catastrophe and disaster. Instead, it was three days of peace and music. The farmer told the general public of America,

> 'If we join the Hippies, we can turn those adversities that are the problems of America today into a hope for a brighter and more peaceful future.'

Sadly, they didn't listen.

Rolling Stone magazine said it was "one of the moments that changed the history of rock and roll". The event was recorded in an Academy Award-winning documentary movie called "Woodstock". The accompanying soundtrack album and Joni Mitchell's song "Woodstock", which commemorated the event, both got to be major hits. Time magazine called it "The greatest peaceful event in history".

I hung round for as long as I could, not wanting to go back to New York. I was one of the last ones to leave, hitching a ride with a group of hippies in a painted Volkswagen Kombi. The first thing I did when I got back to the city was to head down to the docks, but the QE2 had already sailed on 15 August. I didn't want to wait for it to come back again so I found a merchant ship that was making a transatlantic crossing to Cobh, in Southern Ireland. The captain took me on as a deckhand, I could work my passage for food and a berth, no wages.

I packed up my gear, kissed Tulip goodbye and left America.

8
Coming Home

Life isn't sacred at all – it's quick and ignominious and brutal
and misunderstood. Yet it has to be lived. Learn to take
only what's needed – not what's wanted. Learn to identify
need. It takes discipline – mind control – to control desire.
Distinguish it from want. Create it. Shape it. Like a child
discovering something for the first time.

———————

Crossing the Atlantic in early September was tense. It was storm season and we just missed Hurricane Debbie that travelled up the east coast at the end of August. I was hoping we wouldn't be hit by high winds, as I wasn't sure of my sea legs. It was a long time since I came across the ocean with my mother and the railroad man, back in the 1950s. Maybe I should've called Selcraig the sailor and asked him to come with me – help me get over my fear of water. But then, he had a fear of land and couldn't cross the continent. He'd have to have gone down the west coast and through the Panama Canal and back up the east coast.

Take him two years.

The freighter was called *Iphigenia* and it was Greek, with ochre stripes of rust running down from the anchor like huge tearstains. I was given a berth and stowed my gear and we set sail. It was dark when we left the lights of New York harbour and headed east along the line of forty degrees latitude. The night was warm and humid, with a blood-red moon shining through layers of mist and dust. This spectre-light faded the further out we sailed and soon the colours of the night turned to silver and black. The purser who took me on told me it'd take nearly two weeks to get to Cobh. The distance was three thousand one hundred and fifty-five nautical miles and we'd be sailing at a rate of ten knots a day. Given contingency for delays, it'd take fourteen days. A few miles out we turned north towards Nova Scotia and the temperature cooled. We continued to sail northeast, up past Newfoundland, then due east, along the line of fifty degrees latitude.

I was called a workaway, or a freighter bum, as opposed to a deckboy who got wages. There were two crews, the engine-room crew and the deck crew. I was part of the deck crew. My job was to clean and maintain the non-engine parts of the ship – painting the hull and hosing the decks to keep the corrosive salt spray from building up too much.

Most of the sailors didn't like being at sea, they was only there because they could earn more than they could on land. When I was off duty, I could go to the mess to eat or have a beer with the boys. There were all nationalities on board – Greek and Russian and African and Asian. I was the only American – which I wasn't, of course, because I was English, but they thought I was.

Once we got out into the open sea the ship started tossing about on the waves and the remains of Hurricane Gerda was blowing up from the Caribbean, with nothing in its way but water. I was no sailor – my guts churned and my mouth was dry with salt and sea air. At night the crew played cards and drank rum and black vodka, or slept in crude canvas bunks fixed to the side of the sweating hull. Them on watch were quiet, and appeared or disappeared like ghostly silhouettes – like the phosphorescence that shimmered in the widening luminescent trail of water left behind in the ship's wake.

I couldn't sleep that first night. So I went up on deck and stared down at darting flashes in the water. It was like lightning flickering beneath the waves, where fish turned and twisted in the turbulence of the *Iphigenia*'s passage. Back in the berth I eventually drifted off in my swinging hammock and was woke again by the dawn noises of the ship's cook – and the smell of food turned my stomach. Seabirds screeched and wheeled overhead and the captain announced that a depression had formed and was moving our way. He started to bark orders at the sailors – everything loose was lashed down or stowed away. Before I realised what was happening the sky grew dark like the previous night. Rain came. It pelted crazily down and ran in sheets across the deck. Waves crashed over the sides like foam from the mouths of a million mad dogs. Flashes of lightning lit up the grim faces of the sailors as the ship pitched wildly in the angry water – like a crazy animal, tethered against its will. I tried to get to somewhere safe, but my bare feet slipped on the wet deck. I fell over and started sliding towards the side, thrashing about wildly for something to hold onto, a rope, a railing to stop myself from being washed overboard. A sailor grabbed my arm and dragged me below. I vomited over his boots, even though there was nothing in my stomach and the effort of it hurt like a knife being turned in my guts.

The storm rolled on for what seemed like a few hours. I was too sick to know, lying on the floor of my berth and holding on for my life. I cursed the day I decided to sail back to Britain. I cursed my mother for bringing me to America in the first place. I cursed the railroad man she ran away with and wished him haemorrhoids and eternal diarrhoea. Then, just as quick as it came, the storm left and the sky overhead turned blue.

The rest of the trip was eventless and, after a few days, I got used to the swell of the sea. I managed to eat something that stayed down and I started to feel a lot better. The sailors found out I was a musician and, in the evenings, we drank rum and I played the fiddle for them. Very few of them could speak English, but that didn't matter. They'd start off a sea-shanty and I'd get the rhythm of it. I played and they sang.

And so the days and nights went by, until we sailed parallel to the south coast of Ireland. We turned north between the lines of 8° and 9° longitude and came into the deep water quay in the Port of Cobh harbour after thirteen and a half days at sea. The *Iphigenia* was set to refuel and sail on, down the west coast of Africa to Dakar, so this is where I got off. It took me a while to get used to the ground not moving under my feet, but I was glad to get back on dry land again. I had some dollars that I'd earned working for the New York Port Authority and gigging in Greenwich Village at night. So I booked myself into a bed and breakfast place called O'Rourke's Óstán and relaxed. I reckoned I'd hitch-hike to Rosslare and cross on the ferry to Fishguard in Wales, then make my way back to where I came from – in Wiltshire.

Some guy called Larry in the B&B told me about this beer festival that was happening in a town called Kilkenny, about a hundred miles northeast of Cobh, so I thought I'd go take a look. Kilkenny was classed as a city, but it was really just a big town. I got there on Friday night and the centre of the place was turned into a pedestrian precinct, due to the crowds of people. There were all sorts – bikers and beatniks and students and streetwalkers. Buskers played on the kerbsides and there was even a German oompah band. Beer flowed like water and all the bars were open and tents pitched on every spare piece of grass. I found a vacant spot not far from the river and set up the tent I'd been carrying with me ever since Mirabeau Molke gave it to me in the Stanislaus Forest. For the next two days I played my fiddle on the streets of Kilkenny and drank in the multitude of bars and danced on tables with the students. Things got rough on the Sunday, when a pack of bikers from Dublin decided to break the place up. The cops came in and mayhem ensued.

I packed up and left on foot for Rosslare.

I was picked up on the road south by a trucker with a lorryload of sheep. He asked me what part of America I came from and I told him nowhere in particular. He said he had family in Wyoming and asked if I'd ever been there and I told him I'd passed through it a couple of times.

'Maybe you met my sister, her name's Lizzy Malone.'

'It's a big place.'

'Bigger than Ireland?'

'Maybe.'

The trucker dropped me off in Rosslare and I walked to the ferry port. It was a roll-on, roll-off car ferry without much in the way of amenities. There was a bar, of course, and it was filled with people drinking at duty-free prices. The weather was calm so, after some grub, I just got my head down and slept for the four-hour crossing, as I didn't get much rest the night before.

We arrived in Wales in the afternoon and I disembarked from the ferry and took a look around. Fishguard was a bleak enough place – "Moby Dick", starring Gregory Peck, was filmed there in 1955 and it looked much the same in 1969. I wanted to go to Wiltshire, where I was born, even though I had no family there. I was young when my mother took me away and I couldn't remember what the place was like. The New Forest, where we came from, was in the southeast of the county and it was about two hundred miles away, across the Bristol Channel. My mother told me she was born in a field, close to a place called Nomansland, and that's where I reckoned to go. My British birth certificate said my name was Lee Martin, but I didn't know if this was my mother's name or not. I remembered people calling her Zelda when I was young, but never by a surname.

The surname Martin is a derivative of Mars, the Roman god of war. The English version comes from the Normans, who invaded the country in 1066, they were called Fitzmartin, which was shortened to Martin. It's a common surname, with variations all around the world, and maybe that's why my mother gave it to me, because she didn't know who my father was and Martin was as good a surname as any – a bit like Thomas Shelbourne back in New York. Or it could have come from the local region round the New Forest, in Hampshire – for the settlement by the lake, *mær* for lake and *tun* for settlement. Who knew?

It was wet in this part of the world and I wanted to get outa Fishguard as soon as I could, so I took a bus to Swansea on the Welsh south coast. It was getting late by the time I arrived, so I grabbed some fish and chips and checked into a hostel.

Next morning I moved on, catching another bus from Swansea in Wales to Bristol in England, crossing the famous Severn Bridge on the way. I had a bit of money, but not a lot, and I wanted to save as much of it as I could – I didn't know how long it'd take me to get settled in Wiltshire, if at all. So I decided to hitchhike the rest of the way. September was at an end and October was waiting in the wings. It was about sixty miles from Bristol to Nomansland and I got a lift to Salisbury in the back of a Bedford J1 pickup, sitting on bales of hay.

My final destination was only a few miles from Salisbury, so I decided to walk the rest of the way and take in the local scenery.

Nomansland wasn't even a village, just a few fields with farm buildings dotted here and there. It was a place that went back to the sixteenth century, when it was listed in a survey of the number of trees felled in the New Forest. Nobody actually lived there until the eighteenth century, when squatters arrived and started enclosing it. These people had names like King and Dibden and Batten and Winter – one of them, called Shergold, was evicted but the others were left where they were. Maybe nobody else wanted the land? The first reference to an actual name for the area in a parish register wasn't until 1796, when the children of the squatters started recording their place of birth as Nomansland in the national census of that year. When I got there, at the end of 1969, the population was no more than a couple of hundred.

There was no hostel or B&B or hotel or anywhere else for me to stay, and it was raining again. So I found a secluded spot at the edge of a field, sheltered by a tall hedge, and pitched my tent. When I woke the next morning, horses were grazing round me and I could see other tents and vardo wagons in the field. For a minute or two, I thought I was back on the Pawnee National Grassland in Colorado. I closed my eyes and rubbed them, in case I was tripping, even though I hadn't taken anything – but when I opened them again, the tents and horses was still there. A woman approached as I came outa my tent. She was mid-twenties and was leading a big horse with feathered hooves.

'Hi, I'm Serena.'

'I'm Aaron. No, sorry ... I'm Lee.'

'Which, Aaron or Lee?'

'Lee. Lee.'

'You travelling, Lee?'

'Have been. Just stopped.'

I asked her where I could get something to eat round here. There was no restaurant or café but, just like Angel in the Ashley National Forest, she said I could join her group.

Unlike the vegetarians, they were frying up black pudding in a pan, along with bread in dripping and wild mushrooms. I sat and ate with them and they told me their story. They were from London, left over from the Family Squatting Movement that tried to mobilise people to take over empty buildings and use them to house homeless families. Their leader was a guy called Paddy Roy Bates who called himself His Royal Highness Prince Roy. In 1965 he occupied Knock John Tower, a sea fort built in the Thames Estuary during the Second World War for defence purposes. He used an old leftover US Air Force radio beacon to broadcast his radio station, called Radio Essex, and got to be the first pirate radio station to broadcast twenty-four-hour music. He was convicted of violating section one of the wireless telegraphy act and fined a hundred pounds, but he kept on broadcasting. The station went off the air on Christmas Day 1966, due to insufficient funds. In 1967 Bates established the Principality of Sealand on Fort Roughs, a sea fort off the coast of Suffolk. It existed as an unrecognised micro-nation and had its own constitution and flag.

Other people in the field belonged to the London Street Commune, who squatted a mansion in Piccadilly in Central London, but were evicted. They went to Eel Pie Island, in the river Thames at Twickenham, the site of the legendary Eel Pie Island Hotel. People who performed at the hotel over the years up to 1967 included Long John Baldry's Hoochie Koochie Men and John Mayall's Bluesbreakers and The Yardbirds. The hotel closed in 1967, but reopened for a short while as Colonel Barefoot's Rock Garden, with bands like Black Sabbath, Genesis, Deep Purple, Free, Spooky Tooth, King Crimson, Wishbone Ash and Mott the Hoople. There were two stages, the headliners on the big stage and the support on the small stage with a light show projectionist above it. There was a bar doing Colonel Barefoot's Killer Punch – cider, cooking brandy and cinnamon – and they gave it away along with beer in half-pint plastic disposable cups. They had rows with the fire department as the emergency exits were chained shut to stop people sneaking in. Eventually, after a raid by the fire chief, it closed down. In 1969 the anarchists moved in and it got to be the UK's largest hippie commune.

This group had become disillusioned with the traditional way of living and had taken to the road to live an alternative lifestyle. They were like gypsies, but they weren't gypsies. They called themselves new-age travellers, but to me they were hippies. The hippie culture in America might've died with Woodstock, but it was alive and well here in Britain. Later that day I looked around Nomansland, but there wasn't much to see. So I decided to tag along with these people – it was as good as anything else. The only problem was, I didn't have a horse or a caravan. They sold me a spoke-wheeled handcart for five pounds and I became a walking gypsy. I painted the spokes yellow, to remind me of my acid experience close to the trailer park in Reno. During the day I walked with the new-age travellers through the New Forest and into Hampshire.

The New Forest was created by William I in 1079 for hunting purposes. It was first recorded as "Nova Foresta" in the Domesday Book in 1086, between lands of the King's Thanes and the town of Southampton. Before the Normans came the forest was known as Ytene, meaning Jute. The Jutes were one of the early Anglo-Saxon tribes who colonised the area and the word ytene is also a local word for giant – maybe the old Jutes were big guys. Who knows? They said William created the forest by evicting the inhabitants of thirty-six parishes, reducing a flourishing district to a wilderness, and two of his sons died there – Prince Richard in 1081 and William Rufus in 1100. It's supposed to be as punishment for the crimes William committed when he created the forest. Some guy called Richard Blome wrote about it in the seventeenth century:

> *In this county of Hantshire is New-Forest, formerly called*
> *Ytene, being about 30 miles in compass; in which said*
> *tract William the Conqueror, for the making of the said*
> *forest a harbour for wild beasts for his game, caused 36*
> *parish churches, with all the houses thereto belonging, to*
> *be pulled down, and the poor inhabitants left succourless*

of house or home. But this wicked act did not long go unpunished, for his sons felt the smart thereof; Richard being blasted with a pestilent air; Rufus shot through with an arrow; and Henry his grandchild, by Robert his eldest son, as he pursued his game, was hanged among the boughs, and so dyed.

We passed the spot where Rufus died and it was marked with a stone known as The Rufus Stone. The inscription read:

Here stood the oak tree, on which an arrow shot by Sir Walter Tyrrell at a stag, glanced and struck King William the Second, surnamed Rufus, on the breast, of which he instantly died, on the second day of August, anno 1100. King William the Second, surnamed Rufus being slain, as before related, was laid in a cart, belonging to one Purkis, and drawn from hence, to Winchester, and buried in the Cathedral Church of that city.

Others said the poor soil wasn't able to support agriculture and the area was probably always uninhabited. Forest laws were enacted to preserve the New Forest as a location for royal deer hunting and interference with the king's deer and its forage was punished severely. But the local inhabitants had pre-existing rights of common, to turn horses and cattle out to graze, to gather wood and cut peat for fuel, to dig clay and to gather bracken for litter. At a certain time of year pigs were allowed out to eat acorns, which could be poisonous to ponies and cattle. It was called pannage and the verderers decided when it started each year.

At other times the pigs must be taken in and kept on the owner's land, with the exception that pregnant sows, known as privileged sows, are always allowed out providing they are not a nuisance and return to the commoner's holding at night, they must be levant and couchant there.

Common rights were set out by statute in 1698. We believed that meant we had a right to be there and could travel and camp where we liked – the historic right of commoners rather than the crown.

By day I walked and, by night, the handcart became a bed, with saplings bent in barrel fashion across the top and a tarpaulin thrown across to make a bender. The new-agers showed me how to make cannabis cakes, which I sold in the towns and villages we passed through, and I wondered if the local yokels knew why they were so happy after we passed them by. I played my fiddle with other musicians in the group and we busked our way through the countryside – wandering minstrels we, ha ha. Winter was on the way and we set up camp close to the Beaulieu river and spent Christmas with the robins and the wrens, and New Year 1970 with the wild ponies and the ancient trees.

9
The Free Festivals

I was the creator of my own time and I wore it like a ball and chain – measured it and carried it around with me. But it was an illusion. An illusion. Stumbling round in a dark age, mutilating myself and others, mentally and physically and emotionally.

The man thinks all alternative-lifestyle people are just a bunch of aged hippies from the '60s, but they ain't. The new-age travellers I went on the road with came from all sorts of backgrounds – gearheads, long-haired flower children, punks, heavy metal freaks, folksy types, religious nutters, you name it. They all came together in the '70s to travel the roads of Britain. By then I'd given up on being a peacenick and a flower-child – I became an anarchist. And I didn't much like the name new-age traveller neither. We were all just travellers and the media called us new-age to distinguish us from real gypsies, most of who were done travelling by then, or only went on the road in summer, otherwise they lived on designated sites provided by local councils – and we wasn't welcome there. I was in my twenties then and a different person to who I was when I was younger and more naive. That don't mean the boy in me wasn't around no more, he was – still there, trapped in time, in human physical time – and I could go back to being him if I wanted to. But, for now, I wasn't Aaron no more – I was Lee, and I was a man.

The name new-age came about when one girl on the television got asked,

'So you're not an old-time traveller?'

And she answered,

'No, we're new-age travellers.'

It stuck. When I came back to Britain I knew I wouldn't be able to fit into the mainstream, so I stuck with the travellers. Following the little free festivals and finding a kind of solidarity with the people who were disillusioned and making their own mobile communities. It ain't like there wasn't a tradition of travelling culture in the UK – there was itinerant journeymen and tradesmen and gypsies and seasonal workers going back hundreds of years.

I busked with these people from town to town, with my tent and trappings on my handcart and playing at the side of the road and outside the pubs and market places. The money I earned wasn't much and I made it up to a living by doing odd jobs and making cannabis cakes. The women made pegs and posies and tussie-mussies, like the old gypsy people used to do. And I liked being with the erstwhile London commune dwellers who were trying to set up a music festival like Woodstock here in Britain. I told them I was there and it was mind-blowing, man. And I wanted to experience it again. Even if something like that only happens once in a lifetime – but I was in another lifetime now and maybe it'd happen one more time.

The Windsor Free Festival started up in 1972 and it was organised by us – the travellers and London Commune Dwellers. We called the first one "Rent Strike – The People's Free Festival" and the Queen's back garden was an anti-monarchist choice of location. In any case, Windsor Great Park was common land that was stolen from the people by the monarchy for hunting. We were just claiming it back for a few days. We didn't get the half-million they got at Woodstock, only about seven hundred in that first year. But it was a start. The numbers rose to eight thousand the following year and the bands that played there in 1973 included Void, Hawkwind, Reverend Mother, Chief Whip & The Mayor of Wapping, Heavy Water, Wandering Spirit and plenty more. Fifteen thousand people came in 1974 – they listened to bands like Highway, Hungry Joe, Witches Brew, Global Village Trucking Company and Night-Angel. We were getting there.

I remember trudging across Windsor Great Park, pushing my handcart through a great encampment of tents and teepees and thousands of colourful people. Beyond them the bands were gathered

– the White Panthers and Divine Light Mission and Children of God. It was kinda chaos, without anyone in control and everyone doing their own thing. There was a sense of danger in the air, a sense of irreverence. We were on the, so-called, Queen's private land, giving out free LSD to whoever couldn't afford to buy it and it was all about being part of it. Being there. Participating, rather than just sitting around waiting for stuff to happen.

The three Windsor festivals were the brainchild of Ubi Dwyer, who'd been deported from Australia for dealing in LSD. By 1974 the Windsor Free Festival was an alternative to Reading, which had become a boring beer-drinking hard-rock fest. Windsor was more like the '60s happenings – spontaneous. Anything could happen. And it was illegal, which added to its sense of rebelliousness.

The town of Windsor itself was overrun with police, stopping vehicles and taking them apart in drug searches. Tabloid rags like The Sun disparaged the event, while they printed topless pictures of "Hippie Chicks" on page 3. There was a heavy police presence to begin with and they only allowed camping in a small wooded area. That wasn't enough room and the tents soon spread out over the cavalry exercise ground. There was no toilets, no water, no food and everyone was tripping. The drug welfare tent was like a scene from a Hieronymus Bosch painting. Hot-dog and ice-cream vans that tried to exploit the crowd were chased from the site or had their stuff looted and distributed for free. People were encouraged to flash cans and mirrors up at the police helicopters that were hovering overhead.

Everything was happening on top of everything else. It was a festival that was inventing itself as it went along – no security guards or barriers and trees for toilets. The beautiful people had long since moved back into conformity and what was left was the hardcore – them, like me, who believed that "moving on" wasn't really moving on, it was moving back. Despite three hundred arrests and a near-riot when someone was injured by a police van, things were peaceful enough. People were just lying on the grass, going with the flow or dancing in the central glade as night fell. It felt surprising idyllic. Woodstock on a smaller scale. Nobody paid anything and nobody owed anything – they just danced without caring much. All kinds of people – crazy, naked, straight, stoned, whatever. Everyone just absorbed by that mood of oneness that's the mark of a true festival.

The 1974 festival was scheduled to last ten days but, on the sixth morning, hundreds of coppers came storming in, wielding their sticks, and laid into us left and right. Women and kids were kicked and beaten. We didn't resist or anything like that, we didn't get violent with them. But they were under orders to provoke and cause as much mayhem as possible so the newspapers could brand us as bastards. Some of us were thrown into jail and others were thrown into hospital and it was the end of the Windsor Free Festival.

There was something in the idealism of that festival, even if it was naive. In a money-obsessed society, where nothing seems possible without financial interests and celebrity egoism, the idea that people without power could organise an event like that, for nothing, seems unbelievable and beautiful and breathtaking. Even now.

We tried to get it going again a couple of times after that, but it was no dice. They just threw us back in jail and gave Ubi Dwyer two years in prison. They did give us an abandoned airfield at Watchfield in 1975, because the police were being sued and the public didn't like the strong-arm tactics and they wanted to keep us away from royal castles. But the atmosphere wasn't there and it never took off.

So we moved to Stonehenge.

Stonehenge had been going for a number of years in one way or the other. The Tibetan Mountain Troop and the Teepee People and Circus Normal and the Peace Convoy and Wallies were all there already. So we, The Free Festival Movement, joined them after Watchfield. Free Festivals were microcosmic examples of what society could be like all the time, little oases of communal awareness and escape from the grey and paranoid life inside the system. A few days of freedom from the repressive treadmill of choking consumerism. All the bands played for free at Stonehenge – Hawkwind and Gong and Wishbone Ash and Roy Harper and The Enid and my own group of travellers, called the Roadside Ruffians. They called us Hippies but, like I said, we were more than that – we were a mixture of allsorts, mostly people who didn't want to live the life of the slave, to resist the shiny stuff being sold to us by the televisions. Free thinkers and poets and musicians and crafts people and agrarians and farm-boys and a few weekend-wanderers.

And it was good for a while.

In the beginning at Stonehenge, the police left us alone. Sure, there were drugs – drugs were a part of every lifestyle, not just alternatives. The cities were clogged up with heroin and the rich kids snorted coke and the athletes took performance shit and the bankers and lawyers drank champagne and the rank-and-file drank ale – so it wasn't just us, even if we got blamed and called junkies by people who didn't even know what a junkie was. In the beginning only a token police presence hung round and we skinned up and sat on the stones and offered them our spliffs. And the hysterical tabloids were preoccupied with the IRA and slagging off the Labour Party and grooming the fascists to be the next set of glove-puppets for the loose association of millionaires and billionaires who stood always in the shadows and never came into the light so their blood-ugly faces could be seen.

Then, in 1977, they started erecting fences around the stones and resurrected a moribund law against driving over grassland so we could be fined for coming in motorised transport. But they didn't ban us – not yet. And we turned to the sun on the solstice morning and we sang and played music and danced and painted our faces like they did back in pagan times. And we forgot about god and his priests and police and insurance salesmen and pimps and pushers and warmongers and torturers and child-killers and celebrities.

For a few days.

All that stuff's a matter of record and, if you're reading this book you probably know a bit about it. Or maybe you were there. If you were, then peace and love to you, brother or sister. What you won't know is what happened to me when I was travelling to the Tansys Golowan bonfire ceremony in Cornwall. I was fed up with walking and one of the new-agers had a wagon for sale and told me I could get a cheap horse there. I had a bit of cash from busking and stuff, but not enough to buy at one of the bigger fairs like Appleby or Epsom. I got lost on the way and ended up close to the sea, close to cliffs and rocky outcrops and deep drops down to the wild waves. On that day I was alone and travelling with a pack and my fiddle slung over my back and I met someone who knew me, even though I didn't know her and I stepped out of the fake reality and into the true reality for a brief moment – a second – split-second – nanosecond – zeptosecond.

Or maybe it was a day. Or an eternity?

Anyway, it was morning and the sun was climbing the side of the grey, wave-washed cliffs as I walked alone through the headstones in an overgrown churchyard. She watched me from the window of the old, derelict church. I was searching for some landmark – looking out seaward every so often and listening, like I could hear someone crying in the wind. She knew me from many years ago. From a different life. Before I was born to my wicce-witch mother – maybe a hundred years ago – maybe two hundred. My father took me away when I was about five years old. He took me quite sudden-like, in the middle of the night. Away from the bleak landscape and the tortured isolation for a new life on the roads and the rivers. Rumours of some treachery roamed at the time and there was a gibbet with a noose hanging from it. My father had to flee – do a moonlight flit – a bodyswerve – a runner. And he took me with him. I became a rebel, among the rabble and malcontents and mongrels of my new home. And now I'd come back – by a twist of fate. A stranger, looking for something. She knew I wouldn't find it!

The brightening sun shone through the stained glass of the old church window, and she found herself becoming part of the picture she'd been imagining for years in her mind. And she felt her insubstantiality, like I felt mine out there in the churchyard. I turned suddenly and stared straight at her. She pulled back away from the window to avoid my eyes. Instead of a half-imagined past, she could clearly see the present and, following on in a dissolving mist – the future. I moved like I was in a dream – in slow motion, with legs of lead. Coming closer and closer. She opened her arms to welcome me, out of sight behind the coloured glass, but not in an embrace – instead, there was a psychological nail for each of my hands and feet and a bloody hammer to bang them, bleeding, in.

A cold chill crossed from me into her bloodstream. Something had upset me, out there in the open. She wasn't sure what it was. Maybe a sound or a smell. A recollection? Something alien, something I couldn't understand. I started to panic. She watched me as I stumbled around in my fear, falling over the bramble and blackthorns. The sea had become psychedelic. The sky turned sanguine and the birds stopped singing in the trees. I continued to blunder about in the churchyard, bumping into the headstones like I was blind. Finally, I fell against the church door. She could hear my breath coming in short, desperate gasps.

I lay there for a long time – against the door in the overgrown grass and the gauche wildweeds and the silent air of screams. She just waited. I eventually got to my feet and pushed against the heavy wooden door. It opened slowly with a creaking sound. I stepped stealthily into the gloom of the nave. Very little light came through the high, stained-glass windows, but I could see a single candle shimmering in front of the alter. I tried to accustom my eyes to the half-shadow, still unable to see her. She remembered how my mother cried and screamed when my father took me away, cried for a long time – almost forever.

'Jesus! You gave me a fright.'

'Did I?'

'Lost my way.'

'Did you?'

I expected maybe a priest, but not a woman like her. With a face that was vaguely familiar.

'The priests have gone now ... to the new church.'

I wondered if it was her who lit the candle.

'Of course!

I wondered who she was.

'I know who you are!'

How could she know that? How?

'I knew you when you were born. Long ago, before he took you away.'

She must of been very young then, maybe just a girl?

'I was very young then … just a girl.'

'And now you're a ghost?'

Come to haunt me.

She could see the reflection of the candle in my eyes. I tried to speak some more, but wasn't able to make the words come out. I was scared now and, stumbling backwards away from her, I came against the low altar and could get no further. I noticed dark bloodstains on the grey marble. Someone had tried to wipe them away, but they were indelible – an eternal legacy of some primitive sacrifice to a pagan god. I started to hum – real softly, some long-forgot tune that came back to me now, many lifetimes later. She stood directly in front of me.

'You were looking for something.'

'What … ?'

I found my voice again.

'Out there … in the churchyard.'

Yes. A headstone – my mother's.

'I knew your mother too. I killed her.'

That couldn't be so, she died of the disease – before we left – my father and me.

'I pushed her over the cliffs.'

No!

'Many years ago.'

I didn't believe her.

I could hear my own words like they belonged to someone else – came from someone else's mouth – confused words – unsure. I wanted to get away from her, but she froze my feet to the floor with her eyes. Her mesmeric stare turned me to stone and forced me to stay motionless. I couldn't move, no matter how hard I tried, even though I was screaming silently to do so.

'That's who the candle's for. An anniversary!'

Her hands were either side of me and my back was against the cold marble of the unholy altar. Her lips drew back across her gleaming teeth in a threatening grimace and bloody saliva dripped from her mouth. She wore nothing underneath the light summer dress and she began to rub herself against me – like her whole body was assaulting mine. Then she grabbed my throat with surprising strength and pushed my head back over the altar stone.

'Let me go ... please.'

'Do you believe in heaven?'

'No.'

'What about hell?'

She relaxed her grip a little, allowing me to breathe. I was hypnotised with fear in the chill twilight. Then she let go of my throat and slowly slipped the straps of her light dress off her shoulders, until she was standing naked before me. She draped her dress across the altar and slid herself onto it, lying there like a sacrifice on the slab. The single candle flickered as her blood-red lips pouted a grotesque smile at my panic. Her eyes bored into mine and she saw my mind begin to moult. It was like we were in a time machine that started to whirl – slowly at first, but with increasing speed.

She grabbed my shirt and it ripped, sending buttons flying like bullets, as she pulled me onto the altar – onto the dress draped across the stone – onto her! While, somewhere in the distance, wild animals began to howl, their sound sending all logic fleeing from the strange and savage scene. Her voice was velvet and she spoke with little indistinguishable words, sucking my tongue from its stretching roots. Her hands pulled the hair from my head and her heavy breasts brushed against my bare chest. She sank her teeth into my shoulder, drawing blood, while her eyes rolled in their sockets. She could feel my body grow tense and rigid, trying to resist, and she laughed and held onto the shredded shirt as I tried to disengage myself from her. I finally managed to twist myself away from the altar and she drew her nails down my bare back as I retreated across the flagged floor. My lungs heaved in the silence of the church and my mouth snatched at the steamy air.

While calmness crept slowly back and sanity returned. Slowly.

Slowly.

Slowly.

She slipped her body off the altar with a deliberate action, her hair in a fury round her wild face. I was confused and only half-aware of what'd happened as I watched her come closer. Her feet made no movement and she seemed to glide towards me on a cushion of air. Half-dressed, I made a move towards the door – but it was locked. I couldn't understand how that happened, it opened alright when I came in. I turned in panic to face her.

'Why did you murder my mother?'

'I didn't murder her.'

'You said ...'

'I said I killed her.'

My hands rattled the door handle in a futile effort to escape. She stopped and watched for a moment, then started to move deliberately towards me again, leaving her dress draped across the altar. The candle flame played over her shimmering skin and it seemed like an aura of fire circled her body. She stood very close and I could smell her odour – it was the smell of death.

'You can't get out that way.'

It was the way I came in.

'That door hasn't opened in years. It's stuck fast.'

It couldn't be.

'Don't look so frightened.'

What did she want?

'I want you to remember.'

Remember what?

'Me.'

I started to hum again, the sound bounced off the walls and filled the church. She put her hands up to her ears and I stopped. I wanted her to tell me – put me out of my misery. She decided against it and kept the secret that she and my mother were once lovers. But my father came along and married one of them. It was the thing that was done in those days. The women stayed lovers – but there was always the boy between them. Eventually, the older woman wanted to stop – there was malicious talk. They quarrelled on the clifftops. The stones were loose and the tides were always strong in these parts. There was no body – no headstone. The disease story was a lie, concocted by a family who couldn't face the truth about such an *amour honteux*. But my father was suspected by a suspicious community. There was a warrant.

Now the boy had come back, who'd been the cause of such pain to both of them.

She wanted to kill me – was going to! Or maybe she wanted something else?

'How can I get out?'

'If you kiss me I'll tell you.'

'No.'

'Otherwise I'll kill you!'

Her arms went around my frightened neck and her hot breath blew in my nostrils. She laughed into my face, then pulled away and walked back to the altar. Taking the dress from the marble slab she slipped it back over her head, then silently pointed to a little half-sized door behind the chancel. I rushed through the opening and down a long corridor that led out to the coast road. As I ran, I could hear her laughter behind me – chasing me from the place and warning me never to come back.

After I was gone, she took a bloody cloth from a crevice in the altar base. There was a knife wrapped in it – the knife she used to cut her own throat after the incident on the cliffs. She came inside the church in her despair, lay on the altar and offered up her life for *l'amour*. The priests found her and kept her sacrifice quiet. Then they all moved away, as proper ceremonies couldn't be held in such a profaned place.

She replaced the knife and moved outside into the warmth of the summer day. There was a headstone in the churchyard which I could've visited – if I'd known about it. There was a grave where I could've knelt and prayed. She moved towards it while her form became increasingly gossamer, her physical being dissolving away into the very air.

The sea gradually returned to aquamarine and the sky became blue again. Up in the branches of the trees the birds resumed their capricious little lovesongs.

I went on down to the Tansys Golowan and found a horse I could afford.

I never came back.

10
Mushrooms in the Forest

The order in randomness – the context of chaos – the methodology of chance in the void before the beginning and the system of existence which must, of necessity, return to that ectopia. Understand. Understand. Understand.

———————

I liked the structureless concept of the free festivals of the 1970s. The Albion Fairs that spread through the rural landscape of Britain and went back to the ancient and mythical revivals of folklore and freedom. Barsham Faire and Bungay Horse Fair and Rougham Tree Fair and the others. Like I said, I bought a horse and wagon and travelled round to all these fairs with the Roadside Ruffians, hooking up with other groups and playing in pubs or on the side of the road, and the music was a mixture of folk and punk and heavy white reggae. We mixed with people from all walks of life – street performers and magicians and homemade jewellery sellers and druids and revolutionaries and religious nuts and free-lovers and fairground people. We moved about in convoy, like the wagon trains of the old West, and we were coming up through the Forest of Dean, in Gloucestershire, when we came across a glade where mushrooms was growing. Kem, the drummer, said he'd seen them before and you could boil them up and eat them.

So we did.

Then we got lost – seemed to be going round in circles – for hours. It got dark and the moon lit our way. I heard a sound, not like any of the forest noises. I listened – and heard it again. It was a musical note, played on a guitar string. Not a melody or a tune of any kind, just a single note. It sounded again and we followed it, trying to fathom its symmetry – its meaning. It seemed to be calling us – luring us – into its strange enchanted essence. We came out into a clearing with a ramshackle cabin, surrounded by wild flowers. It was kinda fairy-tale like, with a thatched roof and timber walls and a gabled stone chimney.

Everything was still and quiet. Otherworldly. Eternal. Time seemed to be standing still, there in the clearing. After the mushrooms, I was only half aware of what was happening, but I could see Kem going up to the door while the rest of us stayed with the wagons. An old guy with long white hair came out. He had dark skin and a white beard and he looked real fragile – like he'd break if you touched him. I could see Kem talking to him, but couldn't hear what they was saying.

Kem signalled to us and we followed the old guy into the cabin. There was a beamed ceiling, with big old cobwebs and lots of jars hanging from it. There was stuff in the jars, weird stuff. There was doors leading off somewhere – they looked like they ain't been opened in a long time and the whole structure made strange noises, like it had a life of its own. There was no furniture to speak of, except for a single wooden table. It had an earth floor and a brick fireplace full of ancient ashes. There was a hammock where he slept and an old guitar that he played for his own pleasure and no one else's.

He said he was a shaman – a faith healer who could cure sickness with natural remedies and by using the mysterious forces of spirits and ghosts. He went outside and seemed to be gone for a long time – I thought he wasn't coming back. When he did, he was carrying a big jar with a lot of green stuff inside. He put fire to the mixture and a flame shot out of it. He blew the smoke into our faces and started walking round us, chanting over us and clicking his fingers. I couldn't understand the words he was reciting, they weren't English or any other language I ever heard. When he was finished, he gave us the jar with the green liquid and we passed it round and drank from it. It was real bitter, with a taste that stayed on the tongue. I spoke to the old guy.

'We heard you playing.'

'Playing?'

'The guitar.'

'Ahh … '

He smiled wryly and sat beside us on the ground.

I don't know how long we were inside that cabin, but the next thing I knew, I was over in the trees, looking at it from the outside – from a distance. I was riding a horse and, as soon as I broke into the clearing, I dismounted and moved myself and the horse back behind the tree line. I didn't like approaching strange houses because of the danger of dogs and guns and loud voices, which were day-to-day hazards for unfamiliar strangers who'd always been outsiders and whose given name was a synonym for thieves and cheats. So I watched for a while from my cover at the edge of the woodland.

There was some bow-top wagons with horses in the clearing. A strange-looking old man with a white beard and dark skin came out from a cabin in the centre. He was followed by five people wearing coloured clothes. They didn't see me, but I could see them and they seemed to be hypnotised, apart from the old man with the beard. The people with the coloured clothes took musical instruments from the bow-tops and started to play – strange music that I'd never heard before. One of them played a fiddle and I got the feeling I knew him from somewhere. Long ago. Or maybe yet to come? I couldn't be sure. Without knowing why, I led the horse forward, out into the open. The musicians stopped playing and the man with the fiddle spoke to me.

'Who're you?'

'I'm Marid. Who are you?'

'I'm Lee.'

'Not Aaron? I knew you as Aaron.'

'You knew me?'

'I think so.'

But I couldn't be sure. All I knew was that truth was everywhere and even lies led to it.

The old bearded man offered me some green liquid to drink, but I said no. I asked the musicians if I could sing with them and they asked what songs I knew.

'I know the song of life.'

'Never heard of it.'

'It goes like this ... '

Bodyandsoul.

Singerandsong.

Beingandbecoming.

Hydrogenhuman.

Everyone I know will go

I will be left with the hostile strangers.

I will lose touch with language.

And love.

And logic.

And life

The musicians tried their best to play along with my lyrics, but they couldn't. The air was too strange for them – like nothing they'd ever heard before. I kept singing:

No more change.

No more choice.

I am aware that the present does not exist

– so it cannot be now

– it can only be then.

Whose imagination am I a figment of?

There is more I need to ask

– things that have not been explained.

But there is no time left.

It is gone!

The old bearded man smiled, like he understood, but the others didn't – except maybe for Aaron, who was trying to remember where we'd met before. After the song the band played again. They played and sang and drank more of the green liquid and the clearing in the forest started to look like a scene from *Midsummer Night's Dream* – magical – marvellous – mind-altering.

I was trying to remember where I'd seen the girl with the horse before. She said she knew me as Aaron, but I only used that name in America, we was in the middle of Gloucestershire. How could that be? Yet I got the feeling – OK, I knew she was me and I was her and all that. I knew about being part of everything and everyone. The

Oneness. But it was more than that – and I came to the conclusion I didn't know everything, like I thought I did.

So I played fiddle and we sang and danced in the clearing and it was like a scene from *Tattercoats* – macabre – moonlit – mind-blowing.

We slept there that night, in the clearing. The Roadside Ruffians, the girl called Marid and her horse, and the old shaman. In the morning, we was disturbed by a group of people who came through the trees in a Landrover. One guy was wearing a wide-brimmed hat and carrying a shotgun. He had a drooping moustache and looked like a bandit out of a Mexican movie. There was a woman in a business suit and another guy with a peaked cap and a uniform, who was driving and looked like security of some kind. The woman approached us, while the two men stood by the Landrover and looked threatening.

'I'm Renée Monroe, from the FDNPA.'

We all looked at each other, but nobody spoke. She was obviously waiting for whoever our leader was to reply to her. I guessed it was up to me.

'The FDNPA?'

'Forest of Dean National Park Authority.'

She said that like the organisation was exclusive to herself and no one else was allowed access to it. She'd come to the old gamekeeper's lodge in the middle of the forest because somebody reported gypsies there. It should've been her junior, but he was otherwise engaged in town with the housing commission. Renée didn't want to come way out here because she hated dealing with people she didn't know – especially gypsies – anything could happen.

Couldn't it? She didn't want to be there. It was a very unstable situation and there was all these hippie people.

The woman seemed to be drunk, and maybe she was – with power. An air of melancholia circled round her which escaped ordinary observation. She was scowling inside – the power drug worked instinctively, without revealing the process, and she knew she had right on her side.

'What's your name?'

She was gonna write my answer down in a notepad.

'Christopher Cruz, not that it's any ...'

'It is my business!'

She was about thirty, or forty, or maybe fifty. She could've been any age – ageless, from another time – another place. Nah, that ain't right, she was just monotone.

'You can't stay here. You got to move on.'

'What about the old guy?'

'What old guy?'

I looked round. The girl had backed away to the treeline with her horse – there was no sign of the bearded shaman. I asked the guys in the band if they'd seen him, but they shook their heads. Kem said he must be inside the cabin. We looked. He wasn't.

Renée told us no one lived in the old gamekeeper's lodge for fifty years. Or more.

Nobody. The last guy to live there was killed by some kinda wild animal – well, they assumed he was killed. He disappeared. There was a lot of blood. Some bones was found later in the forest. His name was Gerasimus and he was a hermit, by all accounts. But that, according to Renée, was neither here nor there and no reason for all kinda long-haired drifters to drop in unannounced.

'We ain't drifters, and we ain't gypsies.'

'What are you then?'

'A band.'

'Rock and rollers?'

'Not exactly.'

Christopher Cruz said this loudly, like it was some kinda vindication of his principles – exoneration of his prejudices. Exculpation. Assuagement of a conscience that had been bothering him for such a time. Final closure. 'Course, I knew his name wasn't Christopher Cruz, it was Aaron.

I heard the woman in the suit mention gypsies in a harsh tone, so I backed the horse away to the treeline. I didn't like the look of the man with the shotgun, nor the one in uniform. The woman went back over to the Landrover and pulled the cork from a bottle of something with her teeth and spat it away. She hovered unsteadily close to the man in the uniform, spilling whatever was in the bottle down his trousers. The man jumped away from her, as if he'd been set on fire.

'Jesus bloody Christ! You're a bloody alcoholic! Get away from me!'

The woman tried to calm him.

'It's alright. It's just a little accident.'

The uniform gradually regained his composure and I was glad, in case he upset the man with the gun and it accidentally got discharged in my direction.

Renée took a deep slug, losing her balance as she did so but not dropping the corkless bottle. She noticed Marid and the horse standing over near the treeline. She went across.

'Who are you?'

'Marid.'

'What are you doing here, Marid, and where did you get that horse? Is it one of ours?'

'I'm not a thief!'

'Aren't you?'

'Don't speak to me like that, you drunk.'

'Who's drunk?

Renée couldn't understand why this gypsy called her that. Why? Who was she and what did she know? Renée believed the situation had now gone from being unstable to downright dangerous and, as she sometimes had a tendency to retaliate when she was scared – a tendency which manifested itself as violence when she was drunk, she now tried to hit Marid with the bottle. Marid grabbed hold of it to stop herself getting hit and the two women began a surreal dance, round in a circle. Round and round. Slowly at first, but with growing momentum – both holding onto the bottle. The horse bolted.

The men by the Landrover came across to try to stop the crazy pas de deux.

'You're a trespasser, you bitch!'

'I am not. This is public land.'

Renée forgot the insecurity and peril all around her and the impudence of the woman facing her. The man with the wide-brimmed hat leaned his gun up against a tree and grabbed hold of Marid. The uniform grabbed Renée, trying not to get any more liquid spilled on his trousers.

Marid let go. She was angry, but she remembered a story she once heard about a nobleman who inherited a palace he'd never seen. There were in it three hundred rooms and it once belonged to a family who had, for six hundred years, collected every kind of object they could find in the wide world. The nobleman confined himself to the main rooms and learnt nothing of his inheritance, while his daughter roamed all over the house and made the most wonderful discoveries.

About herself.

I was sorry we'd come off the beaten track and got lost and found ourselves in this place with these crazy caricatures who weren't real people at all, but characters from a cartoon show that'd somehow come to life and were roaming round the heart of the forest. The Roadside Ruffians wanted to jump back onto the wagons and go. I was worried about Marid, because the wide-brimmed hat still had a hold of her.

'We can't leave her with them.'

Renée walked back across to the Landrover and took another bottle from the back seat. She sat on the ground while the two men tried to drag Marid over. I had no choice but to intervene.

'Leave her alone!'

'She's under arrest.'

'What for?'

'Assault.'

'She didn't start it and you're not policemen.'

The whole situation was trouble – and trouble like this we didn't need. It was way outside the parameters of our carefree life, playing our music and passing by. Just when I thought things were outa control, a man came from the trees, leading Marid's horse. He was a tall guy with hair like jet and deep blue eyes and I definitely seen him before somewhere. His head was shaven up the sides with a top-knot and a long plait hanging down the back. The top-knot was braided with feathers. Marid shouted out when she saw him.

'Telihu!'

The men holding her let her go when they saw this strange-looking guy and she ran to him. He picked up the shotgun that the wide-brimmed hat had left leaning up against a tree.

Nothing moved for a short time and no sound could be heard, except for the silence, which was both unnatural and appropriate for this mise en scène in the wilderness clearing, in the deep beautiful ugliness of isolated forest. We stayed where we was, even though we really needed to get the hell outa there. As fast as we could!

The Roadside Ruffians were slowly backing away to the wagons. Slowly. Not making no sudden moves. The others just faced each other in a silent standoff – wide-brim and uniform and Renée on the ground at one side of the clearing – Marid and Telihu and the horse and gun at the other side. But, even though I wanted to be gone, I felt something holding me back. Something unsaid. Something in the air around us. If I was more like Marid, more from the heart, I'd have know what it was. But I didn't and I was confused. The bearded guy's music seemed to be coming from outa the trees all around – otherworldly – eternal.

Dangerous even. Lost –

Aaron remembered a time some years ago when he heard the same sound coming from the trees in a redwood forest near San Francisco – the sound of a woman named Florica. But she left with a backpacker called some strange name he couldn't remember. Telihu and I stood like statues – we were statues, forever motionless in space and time. The horse too – and the people who faced us across the clearing. The woman with the bottle to her lips and the bandit-man and the stained trousers. All that moved in that place were the musicians, backing away slowly. Except for Aaron. I knew he'd have to move too – eventually. Not to would've been futile, he wasn't the master of his own destiny, even if he believed he was.

Time passed quickly, the whole day in a matter of minutes. It was beginning to grow dark at the centre of the forest. Noises of small animals and insects could be heard in the surrounding wildness. Still we stood motionless.

I was nervous, so far away from what was familiar and so close to eternity. I didn't want to take sides. Taking sides was dangerous, because you never knew who was gonna win. I felt myself drawing back, away from this strange tableau, even though my feet didn't seem to be moving. When I got by my wagon, I took the reins and swung myself up onto the driver's seat. I turned the horse's head towards the trail that led into the trees where the rest of the band had gone some time earlier and were now swallowed up by the foliage and the enveloping darkness. I looked back at the clearing, but there was nothing there. Just an eerie strangeness.

Dark.

Devilish.

In the pulsing heart of the forest.

As I moved through the darkening trees, trying to catch up with the rest of the band, things moved with me – either side of me in the forest. I couldn't see them, except for brief glimpses every now and then, but I knew they were there. One looked like a figure wearing a full-length black burqa – another like a lion – another like a bleeding soldier – other things I couldn't recognise – had never seen before.

Things cried out to me in their pain, begged me to help them, but I couldn't. I couldn't stop. I had to keep going. The darkness was seeping into my very soul from all sides. From all around the whole world. Covering my personal planet in a creeping blanket of black sludge. And it was difficult for me to know what was true and what was false anymore. I couldn't easily distinguish between night and day, between light and dark, and the words I heard coming from the trees turned black into white and lies into truth and I believed –

I believed –

I came out from the Forest of Dean like a crazy man. Not knowing where I was or what I was doing. A little ways up a country lane I caught up with the Roadside Ruffians making camp for the night. And they told me they didn't know where the previous day went. Away in the distance we could hear a musical note played on a guitar string. Not a melody or a tune of any kind, just a single note. It sounded again, but this time we didn't try to follow it or fathom its symmetry. Even though it seemed to be calling us back. We closed our ears to it and it fell silent.

And the whole world became motionless.

11
Stonehenge

Everything must change, in a changing universe – and consciousness is only concerned with the changing detail, ignoring the universal constant. A dimensionless quantum. A singularity. Where everything exists as possibility.

I first met Lizzie at the Isle of Wight in 1970, before the government passed the "Isle of Wight Act" in 1971 and killed the festival off. She was a wall-of-death stunt rider with a travelling carnival. We was on the outskirts of Newport and parked up and playing for the passers-by. The carnival convoy came along and threw some coins to us and I seen her looking down from the cab of one of the big trucks. She smiled at me and my heart lit up like a lantern. Later that night, we pulled into Seaclose Park where the carnival was setting up.

There was allsorts – waltzers and dodgems and a rifle range and a fortune-teller tent and hoops and floating ducks and the wall-of-death. We played for them and drank a few beers and smoked a few joints and Lizzie came and laughed with us and I got talking to her.

She was from Liverpool and her father was a man who liked to beat up his wife and kids when he came home drunk from the pubs after spending all his money on his mates. She couldn't take it no longer and ran away when she was fourteen. She was twenty when I met her and had lived in squats and refuges and been roughed up and raped a few times – before joining the fairground people. They taught her how to ride a motor bike and she was a real daredevil on the wall, not really caring if she lived or died.

That night the fairground was in full swing with lights and noise and lots of people. Even though it was summer, there was a chill in the air, like a premonition or something. Sort of threatening. It was really weird – I seen her walking towards the wall-of-death drum and, despite the crowds, everything went kinda quiet. She was real pretty and dressed in motorbike leathers and I thought I seen a tear in her eye. She walked, faltering – almost in slow motion.

She entered the drum – there was a stationary motorbike inside. I watched from the viewing area at the top as she put on her helmet. All of a sudden, the noise of the crowd came back – deafening. Lizzie revved the engine – the crowd shouted louder. She started to accelerate round the wall – the higher she rode, the louder the crowd screamed.

Higher and higher.

Faster and faster.

The faces of the viewing crowd looked grotesque and freakish and animated and violent. Lizzie took her hands off the machine and held her arms in the air. That's when the bike went flying out over the top perimeter of the drum. The crowd shrieked in horror and tried to duck outa the way.

Last thing I saw was Lizzie sailing in slow motion into the night sky.

All sound died away again and the silence was unearthly.

She was airlifted to Stoke Mandeville Hospital in Buckinghamshire and spent two years there. They thought she'd never walk again, but she did. I visited her whenever I was in that part of the country and she started to get around – with a limp, on crutches. She couldn't go back on the bikes after her accident and she learnt to play the flute while she was in hospital. She convalesced for another couple of years after she got out, then she came on the road with us. Now there was six of us – me on fiddle, Jake White on lead and acoustic guitar, Danny Bates on bass and rhythm guitar, Mick Stevens on mandolin, Kem on drums and bodhrán and Lizzie on flute.

The festival that everybody knows as Glastonbury started out as the Bath Festival of Blues and Progressive Music and was headlined by Led Zeppelin in 1970. One hundred and fifty thousand people turned up and the country lanes leading to the site got blocked up by cars and the equipment trucks couldn't get through. Donovan had to go onstage on the Sunday morning to entertain the bored crowd. He wasn't what the people had come to hear, but he asked them if they'd like him to sing while they waited for the billed acts. He ended up being onstage for two and a half hours while the equipment arrived and got set up. Led Zeppelin were rained off on the Sunday night and The Moody Blues never came on because the stage was too wet. Then the security staff stole most of the gate receipts and the organisers didn't make no profit.

Michael Eavis hosted the first Glastonbury at Worthy Farm the same year and called it the Pilton Pop Blues & Folk Festival, but it was badly organised and badly advertised and only drew a crowd of one thousand five hundred people. The headline acts were T.Rex, Quintessence, Stackridge and Al Stewart. The 1971 Glastonbury Fayre was better and attended by about eight thousand people and saw the incarnation of the Pyramid Stage. It was a replica of the Great Pyramid of Giza and made from scaffolding and metal sheeting. It was a free festival and the headline acts were David Bowie, Joan Baez, Fairport Convention, Hawkwind and the Worthy Farm Windfuckers. There was no more Glastonbury after that – not until the cops sent a convoy from Stonehenge there in 1978.

Lizzie came out of hospital late in 1973 and, after convalescing, she was on the road with us in the summer of 1976 and we went down to the Henge in June that year for the summer solstice. Trouble was, there were six stages around the site all playing at the same time and the bands polluted each other's music. A whisper went round that someone had turned up with Wally Hope's ashes. At midday, Sid Rawle said a few mystical words over a small wooden box in the middle of the Sarsen Circle and a bunch of us scattered Wally's mortal remains over the stones. I sprinkled a handful on the Heel stone, so did the other band members. If you don't know who Wally Hope was, I'll tell you –

After the first Stonehenge festival in 1974, a group of about thirty people stayed on and pitched camp in a nearby field. It was a commune, with tents and a geodesic dome covered in polythene and a psychedelic teepee. It was an open camp, with a lot of crazy notions, but mainly to find the relevance of the ancient stones by spending a lot of time there. The Department of the Environment and the National Trust wanted to evict them and, to do that in those days, you had to get a High Court injunction on named individuals. So the people in the camp all took on the name Wally and the press called them a cult. There was Kris Wally and Alan Wally and Fritz Wally and Sir Walter Wally and others and they called their camp Fort Wally. Wally Hope, whose real name was Phil Russell, wrote the promotional material for the Stonehenge festival, which was said to have been his idea in the first place. Although the Wally camp was an open and undisciplined commune, Wally Hope was its undisputed leader and wasn't scared to march round issuing orders – even if no-one paid much attention to him. He'd talk to anyone who'd listen and his favourite topics were sun worshipping and when he saw the reincarnated Jesus Christ in Cyprus.

The Wallies of Wiltshire made front-page news when they turned up at the High Court in London to defend their squatters' rights to camp at Stonehenge. A woman called Wally Egypt came in bare feet with bells on her ankles and she blew soap bubbles before kneeling to meditate. Sir Walter Wally wore an old Elizabethan doublet and Kevin Wally chain-smoked through a mask. Kris Wally climbed a lamp post dressed in a tartan blanket and bemused the tourists by shouting, 'Everyone's a Wally'. The court found in favour of the Department of the Environment, so the Wallies moved their camp six feet away to a piece of common land.

Wally Hope was arrested for possession of a small quantity of LSD while he was organising the second Stonehenge festival. He was sent to prison on remand where he refused to wear the prison uniform. He defended his use of LSD on religious grounds, so they sectioned him and sent him to a mental hospital and pumped him full of anti-psychotic drugs. As a result of this treatment, he got real ill and was diagnosed with chronic dyskinesia, which is involuntary muscle movement. After his release, Wally Hope was reported to have killed himself by taking an overdose of sleeping tablets. However, Penny Rimbaud of the punk band Crass wrote that Wally was deliberately killed by MI6 and the murder was covered up.

We went back to the Henge in '77. Hawkwind, Here and Now and the Bombay Bus Company formed the backbone that year. There was fewer acts than in '76 and the noise pollution wasn't as bad, but the acoustic players couldn't be heard due to the loud electrified acts. Richie Havens turned up unannounced and borrowed a guitar from us and then played for two hours. Outside, police were stopping vehicles and telling people not to go in because it was an illegal festival. Nobody took no notice. On site, someone was going round giving out handfuls of home-grown grass from a sack and anything inside the teepees was considered to belong to everybody – so, if you took stuff in, you had to share it round. A lot of people were shit-faced on chewies and there was the usual abundance of spliffs and bongs. But it was peaceful enough, with very little plod hassle.

At the end of the '70s, thousands of squatters were evicted from the London boroughs and they went on the road, swelling the ranks of travellers moving round the country from festival to festival. In 1978, a convoy of them heading for the Stonehenge festival was redirected by police to Worthy Farm. This had the effect of reviving Glastonbury the following year – and it's still going today. Stonehenge was kinda tolerated back then, even though it was considered to be an illegal gathering. I don't think the authorities knew what to do about it, so they let it happen and kept an eye on it. Bands who played in '78 included Hawkwind, Sphynx, Here and Now, The Mob and Catastrophe.

Music was evolving and the punk phenomenon was at its height. A lot of bands there weren't hippie at all, just straight outfits who'd never played in front of more than a handful of people. The weather was bad that year and the festival was still fairly small scale, with only a few thousand people attending. The site was usually a no-go area for the cops, but at one point in '78 a van full of them drove in to arrest somebody. It was immediately surrounded by hippies and rocked back and forth until the uniforms decided to drive back out and leave people alone.

Drugs was always a part of the Henge festivals, but it was kinda home-grown. You'd just come across little cardboard signs by the tents, "Red Leb" or "Black" or "Morphine" or "Opium" or "Orange

Barrel" or "Ying Yang". It was just individuals selling whatever they had and the plods stayed away – apart from going outside. The risk of busts was always greater near the gates.

People jammed offstage at low volume with a few instruments and anyone could sit in. Stonehenge was totally unlike going to a commercial festival like Reading. In 1979 there was a wedding and a christening in the inner circle, performed by Rick the Vic, a Church of England guy who'd dropped out and was living with the teepee people. There was public loos where you could get washed in the morning and there was the open air toilets, dug by the army – deep and dangerous wells. I never knew how nobody ever fell in, because it was a pretty risky area to be wandering round at night. Other people improvised – I remember passing some hippie, sat on a chair reading the paper – the seat was taken out and a hole dug underneath. Hey!

The festival was continuing to grow by 1979 and they paraded Wally Smith's ashes the same year. There was the ritual storming of the gates to the Stones and the people all shouting 'Wally!' Mr & Mrs Norma's Tea Party was set up near one of the smaller stages – you could get a spliff and a cup of tea for twenty-five pence – or hash cakes if you preferred. They were actually Bill Normal, an anarchist playwright, and his wife Vega. Bill also ran a gentleman's club in the back of a converted ambulance. You could become a member for a couple of quid and that entitled you to tea, slippers, a daily newspaper and a fat joint. Bill once chased a Sunday Mirror reporter off the Henge site with an axe.

Lizzie had her first hit of opium at the '79 gig. They were selling it from a jar, scooping it out with a knife onto cellophane. She didn't really know what to do with it, but someone told her she had to vaporise it. She took a biro apart and heated it on tinfoil – she said they called it chasing the dragon in Hong Kong, where she'd been once. She got a sense of supreme lightness and clear images danced across the backs of her closed eyelids. She said it was a gentle experience, not as chaotic as the acid. But I didn't like no kind of opiates – they were addictive and dangerous.

By the 1980s, Stonehenge was a major event, attracting crowds of over thirty thousand during the week and peaking at seventy thousand and more during solstice. But it was hardly mentioned in the mainstream press, except when they wanted to attack it – and the rock rags were too busy hyping crap like Adam & The Ants and Spandau Ballet and Duran Duran. With the increase in size, came an increase in hassle – facilities weren't adequate and there was a heightened police presence. The plods used the "sus law" to strip and search people. As well as that, what was essentially a hippie festival was attracting a lot of punk bands.

In 1980 a gang of middle-aged bikers went on the rampage, attacking every punk they came across and wrecking part of the site. The evening started peaceful enough, but when punk band The Epileptics took the stage, the bikers started throwing flour-bombs and cans and bottles. They stormed onstage saying they weren't gonna tolerate punks at "their" festival. The irony was, it wasn't their festival, it was our festival – the hippies. To be honest, I don't remember much about it, except what people told me after, because I scored some orange barrel and was lost in a blur of acid unreality.

Stonehenge wasn't even ours, it really belonged to the Druids, who marched there on solstice day, but we were kindred spirits – peace and love – unlike the bikers and the punks. Sometimes squaddies came over from the nearby army base on Salisbury Plain and got faceless on the rough scrumpy the local farmers sold and the festival was becoming a melting pot of allsorts. The 1981 festival had perfect weather and was said to be the best free festival in the world that year. The bands included Killerhertz, Hawkwind and Lightning Raiders and many others – they all played for free. Even though there were all these different hairstyles and trends and shapes and dispositions, the Henge was generally viewed by the wider British public as a hippie fest.

By 1982, the festival began to be threatened by hard drug dealers who wanted to use the Henge as an opportunity to sell their gear in an environment not threatened by the police. Eat Alley became Drug Alley and the central thoroughfare for hash cakes and hippie food was infested with dealers. The drugs for sale were harder than in years gone by and the acid was no longer the dreamy hallucinogen it used to be, but blotter LSD – speedy stuff that didn't suit me much.

The Henge kept growing during '83 and '84, with a lot more casual rubberneckers, as well as the usual stoners, hippies, bikers, witches and druids. So the hard core of old school hippies and travellers became a minority. That meant the original festival ideals were being lost in the crowd. They weren't there for a spiritual experience or the cosmic energy or divine synchronicity no more. And the dealers played into the hands of the authorities and gave them the excuse they needed to shut it all down in 1985. Even so, there was very few hospitalisations for overdoses and there was never an epidemic of drug abuse. The heavy drug presence did increase over the years, but this was more to do with changes in society and the nature of the crowd than anything to do with the festival itself. But hard drugs make good headlines and the tabloids went even more negative than before.

In 1984 John Pendragon was so pissed off by the way things were going that he set up an Alternative Free Festival within the festival itself. This had its own intimate stage and a dealer-free zone and it tried to recreate the spirit of the early festivals. The acid market hit crisis round about this time. You could get blue unicorns and purple OMs and love hearts for less than twenty-five pence after a massive oversupply of the psychedelics – so lots of people who weren't used to it were tripping outa their skulls and the experienced hippies had to talk them down. Snatch squads of cops hung out in the woods and busted people who went there for a shit or a shag.

But no matter what they say about it, Stonehenge was the last of the people's free festivals, riding the vibes of love and spontaneity generated by a gathering of so many high human beings.

The National Trust lobbied to ban the festival and the Tory government decided it had a mandate to deal with the national unrest created by the laying waste of the country by the moneymen. With the backing of the tabloids, they tried to show the hippie movement in the worst possible light and conditioned the British public to accept stormtrooper police actions like a regular occurrence. The trade union movement felt the brunt of this brutality in '84. Our turn would come the following year, at the Battle of the Beanfield.

12
Elephant Fayre and Glastonbury

There is a tone somewhere. A musical modulation. All music is inherent in that one tone – like religion. I try to follow the sound, but it fades into distance. Just the vibration is left. Maybe it's the sound of my soul, trying to break free and fulfil itself in an eternal present – not in a past that never was nor a future that will never be.

———————

Like I said, I bought my first horse down in Cornwall, that time when I seen the banshee on the clifftops – or maybe I didn't see her and she was just a figment of my imagination. Anyway, they had their own festival down that part of the country called The Elephant Fayre. It started up in 1980 when a small fest outgrew its site at Polgooth in mid-Cornwall and the organisers approached the stately home of Port Eliot, St Germans, and asked if it could be held there. It was different to Stonehenge insofar as it wasn't purely a music festival – it had different types of performance groups and experimental theatre and visual arts, as well as rock, punk, folk and reggae. The first Fayre was small, with only about fifteen hundred people over four days. But it got bigger over the years as the organisers managed to book heavier acts, like Siouxie and the Banshees, The Cure and The Fall. It was intended to raise money for Amnesty International.

You gotta remember, the tolerance of the free festival culture of the '70s was over, with the repressive Tory regime that the Sun-reading mugs elected at the end of that decade. All sorts of brutal policies would be introduced to make the rich richer and keep the people down – policies that are still having an effect today. New-age travellers and any kind of alternative lifestyle got to be a target for the Tories and their financial and media backers.

What they wanted to establish, and succeeded in establishing, was a super-rich elite – an uncaring, conservative middle-class – and a passive, brainwashed underclass of slave labour that'd allow them to get away with anything.

They didn't have a manic preoccupation with health and safety back then, so there was no restriction on what they did or how they did it, apart from ordinary common sense. They built a rickety pier in the middle of the River Tiddy with a wobbly café at the end. It didn't collapse and nobody fell into the water. The Fayre had a unique spirit about it and it was thrown together by a group of festival-organiser amateurs. They didn't have much experience, but they knew what they wanted – not just another Stonehenge or Glastonbury. They wanted to include everything – dance and poetry and music and art and circus acts like juggling and stilt-walking. That appealed to me, because my mother told me her people were original fairground people – circus performers and gaff-lads and fire-eaters and the like.

They called it The Elephant Fayre because they built a fifty-five-foot high elephant and there was a café in the middle of it, run by kids for kids – no adults were allowed in. The water supply came from a spring that was used by monks in medieval times – clear as crystal – and the toilets was a less dangerous version of the long-drop loos at the Henge. The performers included a couple of jugglers called Boris and Norris, who dressed like medieval serfs and performed with livers and hearts and live rats. There was a group of Vikings who re-enacted a bunch of bloody battles and they let kids shoot at them with real bows and arrows. No one got killed. One guy dressed like a security-guard dog-handler and went round the site ordering people to stop spliffing and clean up – the only thing was, the dog on the end of his lead was dead.

The first Elephant Fayre didn't make no money for the organisers but, as time went on, it got more and more successful. The festival gained a reputation as being well-run and a cool experience. The booking of mid-range bands meant that the crowds got bigger and younger. But, with that, logistics got harder to manage and disruptive elements started to filter in. When I say disruptive elements, I don't mean hippies I mean idiots.

There was a lot of different factions at the Fayre – we went there after the Henge, at the end of July, beginning of August. The bands were kinda punk and new wave and goth, but everyone got along in the early years of '81 and '82. Many people blame the Peace Convoy for the demise of Elephant Fayre, but the convoy was nowhere near Cornwall at that time – it was busy pissing off the authorities at Greenham Common and after that in East Anglia, where they were being demonised by the tabloid press, who were sowing the seeds of outrage that led to the persecution of all travellers.

By the '80s my horse had died and I sold my bow-top and bought an old single-decker Leyland bus and me and the Roadside Ruffians went petrol instead of horse-drawn. You gotta remember, traveller numbers increased dramatically in the early '80s and there was many convoys traversing the country at any one time. Many of the original anarchists who started the Peace Convoy dropped out in '82 and what was left was just a convoy full of less idealistic elements – or, to be blunt, infiltrating thieving junkies paid by MI5. So, the Peace Convoy as it was didn't exist after '82, but it was handy for the tabloids to call it that, and to stir the idiot Sun-readers into a vitriolic rage over anybody associated with peaceful protest against the international war machine.

By '83 the sinister elements showing themselves at the Fayre weren't hippies or anarchists from the Peace Convoy, or any other convoy, but the military in camouflage. I remember once, in '83, I was over near the ivy-covered stone wall between Port Eliot Estate and the village of St Germans. I was taking a piss against a bush when a grappling hook came flying over the wall and snagged in the ivy about eight feet above the ground. The next thing, the bush I was pissing on got up, climbed the wall and cut the rope with some kinda commando knife. Then it climbed back down, told me to fuck off and went back to being a bush. I found out later that the military had put a detachment of squaddies in the grounds to protect Lord Eliot from "subversives". The real subversives were hatching plans in Westminster to stop people travelling and protesting and attending festivals.

I don't think many people at the Fayre were aware of the army pretending to be like bushes in the grounds – they carried on peacefully. They paid fifty pence for the pleasure dome and stripped off – put their clothes in a blue plastic bag and took a shower with everyone else. There was big bass bin-speakers directed at the showers, pumping out reggae and the water came out blue and green and red and everyone had a psychedelic time.

In 1984, rasta bands like Clint Eastwood & General Saint took to the main stage. They were stopped on the way down and the bus was turned out, but found to be clean. They knew it'd happen, so they sent their stash ahead of the bus in a car with some women and it got through alright. It rained in 1985 and some of the punk bands said their music was for "burning hippies to". None of us took no notice of that, because we knew the punks were all mouth and safety-pinned trousers and were mostly pissed up on super-strength scrumpy.

There was the Round Room where you could get cream tea and a scone, if that was to your liking at a festival, and stare up at the ceiling. There was the maze, the swimming pool, the quarry, the upside-down horse-hooves, the wooden maiden and the lightning tree with the hands trying to get out. There was acid, mushrooms, speed and hash, and the Elephant Fayre was an experience not to be missed.

Bands like Urban Warriors and Mint Juleps and Happy End played and the mad circus acts continued. Hippies sold Mexican mushroom wine, which was mescaline-based and unsuspecting customers had a colourful trip after drinking it. There was a drum-beat that tried to mimic Woodstock, with people banging on dustbin lids and oil drums and filling beer cans with stones and the drumming and rattling got louder as the weekend went on. We complained about the amount of trees being hacked for firewood, but the younger people took no notice. I was thirty-seven in '85 and the Ruffians were mostly around the same – that was considered middle-aged by most of the people at the festivals then. They didn't appreciate hippie music or values and saw us as pacifists rather than anarchists – even though we weren't.

The Fayre attracted a crowd of thirty thousand in 1986 and that was its downfall. It was becoming too popular and couldn't be allowed to continue. It all ended that year. Troublemakers hired in the dark corridors of Whitehall had infiltrated the hippie convoys, with the sole aim of causing chaos and bringing travellers and demonstrators into disrepute. Their actions were then blown outa all proportion by the mainstream media and sold as truth to a gullible public. This made it easier for the repressive Tory government to pass legislation outlawing the free movement of travellers and festivalgoers. The tactics were deliberate and clandestine and the beginning of the unwarranted state control we have today. There was no single entity that was the Peace Convoy, as screamed about by the media – there was a fluid pool of travellers constantly mingling and splitting up. But it was convenient for the government to brand us as an army of medieval brigands.

Travellers were just like any other social group, you got good and bad. Trouble was, we all got tarred with the same brush when the infiltrators and agitators caused trouble. The cynical media hacks in the pay of the establishment then demonised us. OK, most of us who took up the life were from the fringes of society. We distrusted anyone in authority, with good reason. We were hippies, but not part of no convoy. It's like when we were low on petrol on the way down in '86 and we had no money left, so we picked up hitchhikers on the way. The deal was, they paid for the petrol and we'd feed them for the four days of the festival. We had a tyre blow out near Sherborne in Dorset, miles from anywhere, so we all had to sleep in the bus that night until we could get it sorted in the morning. The hitchhikers weren't hippie, but they settled in and there was no problem.

But there was all this paranoia about new-age travellers at the time. It was deliberate – planned – a right-wing revolution. Peaceful hippies were being intimidated by "security services" at places like the Fayre and goaded into retaliation. Bouncers in boiler-suits came to our bus one night and threatened to tip us over if we didn't leave. They despised us, you could tell – they hated our freedom – it couldn't be allowed, in case it rubbed off on the rest of society. If you had long hair and a colourful van, you were public enemy number one.

Then the government spooks put together this group of Nazis who called themselves the brew-crew because they were always pissed on special brew. Their job was to go about robbing and beating people. I remember once, when we were camped close to the village of Wickwar in Gloucestershire and cooking up a pot of stew, these drunken fascists came along and tried to take our grub. Normally we'd have shared with anyone, but they tried to nick it so we stood up to them.

'D'you know who we are?'

'We don't care who you are, piss off and leave us alone.'

They left and came back with their mates, all pissed outa their heads. There was other travellers camped up with us, in benders and vans, and we faced off the brew-crew with sticks and spanners. They were so drunk they couldn't fight and they buggered off when they saw we might well be hippies, but we weren't gonna lay down and let them trash what we had without a fight.

And that was the problem with the brew-crew, not many people took them on. We weren't violent, but we weren't complete pacifists either. They soon backed down when people stood up to them. It was these scumbags who'd brought heroin to the festivals, they were bullies and hunted in packs and they did their best to disband the free festival and traveller scene. They took revenge to disgusting levels, like the Nazis did, and the police rarely touched them. Why? Figure it out for yourself.

Anyway, the Elephant Fayre finished in 1986, they said it was because of the, so-called, Peace Convoy, but it was really because none of the organisers wanted to stand up to the authorities. They saw how much brutal police force had been applied to the miner's strike in '84 and the Beanfield in '85 and they didn't have the stomach for it. It wasn't the hippies they were scared of, it was the government and the people behind the government – the shadowmen pulling the strings. So they left to go work on Glastonbury, which was more of a commercial fest and not under so much threat from the dark forces of "righteousness". When the '86 Fayre ended, police roadblocks stopped hundreds of vehicles and escorted them to a huge aircraft hangar in the middle of nowhere. Plods in overalls with rubber gloves carried out strip and internal searches, mechanics took vans and cars apart and found nothing. It was a war of attrition against peaceful people – a huge and costly operation, designed to intimidate and humiliate.

The propaganda machine said after that the Peace Convoy tried to break down the gates to the Fayre and that there was violence and heroin and child prostitution. If there was, it wasn't the hippies, it was the brew-crew and other government infiltrators who were outa the control of their handlers – or maybe they weren't. They said travellers smashed up schools and set fire to trees and wrecked the village. These things never happened. But Britain was a much more repressive place in the '80s than it ever was before. Under a government that was fascist in all but name, the country was being paramilitarised and the people were being moulded into the bland, consumerist, television-brainwashed, easily managed tabloid-readers they are today.

Glastonbury originally only lasted two years – 1970 and 1971 – but it didn't make enough money for the organisers and it folded. There was a small unplanned event in 1978, when the convoy of vehicles from Stonehenge was directed by police to Worthy Farm. The festival was revived in 1980 in an event for the Year of the Child, which lost money. Michael Eavis, The Worthy Farmer, took control in '81 and it was organised in conjunction with the Campaign for Nuclear Disarmament, or CND. They constructed a new pyramid stage from telegraph poles and metal sheeting – it was a permanent structure that doubled as a hay barn and cowshed in winter. The festival made a profit under Eavis, who donated twenty-thousand pounds to CND – other donations were made in subsequent years to Greenpeace and Oxfam and WaterAid. These organisations all provided volunteers who worked for free at the festival and it was a worthy enough thing – in Worthy Farm.

I ain't got much to say about Glastonbury because it wasn't a true "free festival" like the others. It was good-intentioned and commercial and Michael Eavis did a fine job surviving through the years of persecution by the establishment during the '80s, but it was never a true hippie-fest. It was for middle-of-the-roaders who like their festivals to be controlled and safe from 'subversive' influences. Good luck to them! We didn't go to Glastonbury after the original gigs of the early '70s, but we wished them luck. Anything was better than nothing. There was a lot of bad weather there in '82. The highest rainfall for a single day in forty-five years was recorded on the Friday and that was also the year of the first laser show – Tubeway Army and Are Friends Electric. Other acts included Van Morrison, Judie Tzuke, Roy Harper, Richie Havens and Jackson Browne.

The Tory's Local Government Act, one of many pieces of repressive legislation they pushed through parliament, became law and Glastonbury had to obtain a licence for the 1983 gig, giving the authorities the power to regulate it. The council set the crowd limit at thirty thousand and imposed stringent rules about access roads and water supply and hygiene and other stuff, hoping this'd be too much for the organisers. It wasn't and the festival went ahead, with its own radio station, Radio Avalon. Acts included Marillion, Curtis Mayfield, UB40 and The Beat. In 1984, Michael Eavis successfully defended five prosecutions brought against him by Mendip District Council, instigated by the Tories, alleging contravention of the licence conditions. After all five charges were thrown out, the council announced that the 1984 licence would cost two-thousand pounds and car parking areas would be designated, with stewards hired to direct the traffic. Despite the restrictions, sixty thousand was raised for CND and other charities.

The acts were Joan Baez, Ian Drury, Elvis Costello and The Smiths.

By 1985, Worthy Farm was too small to accommodate the festival, so they bought the neighbouring Cockmill Farm to add another hundred acres to the site. Communications were stretched to the limit and people had to be towed off the site after a mud bath. Still, one hundred thousand pounds were raised for CND and the other charities. Joe Cocker performed, along with The Boomtown Rats and the Style Council and Aswad. The festival was growing every year and they improved the facilities to comply with the council's restrictions and attracted bands like The Pogues, Madness, The Cure, Simply Red and The Housemartins. But, after The Battle of the Beanfield in '85 and the closing of the Henge in '86, things were getting too uncool for an ageing hippie like me. I was thirty-eight in '86 and getting disillusioned with the erosion of personal freedom in this country. I was thinking about leaving the Roadside Ruffians and going my own way.

Solo again.

13
Battle Of The Beanfield

Violence is pointless and hatred even more pointless. Some people will never see – never shine – in their darkness. Never be any different, no matter what anyone says or does. No matter what they learn – see – hear – experience. Savagery and selfishness. Nothing will wash away the stain. And it's so hard to forgive – maybe that's what I have to learn.

———————

I need to tell you what happened on the way to Stonehenge after they banned the festival in 1985. The Tories got a high court injunction to prevent people attending the Henge that year, but it came too late for one particular group of travellers who the Roadside Ruffians were with. We camped the previous night in Savernake Forest on the Earl of Cardigan's land and there was over a hundred vehicles altogether and nearly six hundred people – new-age travellers, peace protestors, green activists and festivalgoers – men women and children. On the morning of 1 June, we set off for the Henge, not knowing that the cops had laid down an exclusion zone in a four-mile circle round the perimeter. The first we knew was when we were told that three lorry loads of gravel had been tipped across the road at Shipton Bellinger to form a blockade. We slipped down a side road hoping to avoid it, but were met with a second roadblock manned by quasi-military police.

There was a standoff and we refused to turn around because we believed we had a right to travel where we liked on the public highways. The cops didn't see it that way. Suddenly, they came at us with truncheons and riot shields, slamming their sticks into the bodywork of the leading vehicles and making as much noise as they could, shouting

'Get out! Get out!'

The drivers had no time to respond before they started smashing windscreens and hauling people out. A converted ambulance with one girl inside was smashed into and she was hauled out by the hair, over the broken glass. This caused panic and vehicles started turning off into a nearby beanfield. Now, if you read a tabloid newspaper the next day or watched the BBC, you'd have been told the field was full of heavily-armed misfits out for blood. You'd have been told the law-abiding police "officers" came under unprovoked attack by weapon-wielding anarchists and were pelted with petrol bombs. You'd have been told this by thirty-pieces-of-silver-snatching hacks who made it up as they sipped their gin and tonics in the bars around Fleet Street. If you'd actually been there, you'd have had a different version of events – a version no one was interested in.

So, less than six hundred travellers, mostly families with kids who'd chosen the road as a way of life, faced off against over thirteen hundred riot police, drawn from six different counties, in a beanfield in Wiltshire. Don't forget, the cops had the full support of the fascist Tory government and its backers the year before, when their police support unit, a paramilitary group trained in public order and riot control, beat up and arrested many miners who were trying to protect their jobs. The miners were striking peacefully, as was their right, when the cops rode into them on horseback. The courts then gave the miners brutal jail sentences instead of jailing the thugs in uniform. So, the plods knew they could do what they liked to us and get away with it. We tried to reason with them, but they wouldn't listen. Some were verbally abusing us, calling us 'scumbags' and 'pikies' and 'shiteaters'. This angered some of the younger people – maybe about a dozen or so – and they started to throw sticks and stones, to try to keep the cops back and prevent further brutality.

Next thing, the chief constable turned up in a helicopter and announced from the sky, like god, that we were all gonna be arrested. He was gonna arrest six hundred people for trying to stop themselves getting beaten up by a bunch of thugs in uniform. We were told to leave our vehicles and give ourselves up to the riot police, who were stood waiting with their truncheons drawn and sadistic smirks on their faces. People were scared – for themselves and their children. We knew if we did what they wanted, our vehicles'd be destroyed before we got back – it happened earlier at Nostell Priory, where three hundred and sixty people complied and their vehicles and all their belongings were burnt while they were in custody. These tactics were nothing less than a pogrom to force us off the roads of our own country, and we knew it. It was a Sunday afternoon in rural England, not some totalitarian hinterland or some third-world police state – but you'd never have thought so.

If you were there.

The police charged into us with shields and batons and portable fire extinguishers. Their badges were covered to conceal their identity and that meant they were no better than violent vigilantes. There was more than two heavily-armed coppers to every man, woman and child that day. They grabbed people who were sitting peaceful on the ground and dragged them away by the hair. Others who tried to get back into their vehicles for safety had their skulls split. Some of us drove round and round the field to try and avoid being arrested, but the cops threw big flint rocks and fire extinguishers through the windscreens, covering some drivers with glass. They threw shields like frisbees, not caring what damage they caused. The longer it went on, the more violent the police got. They had the taste of blood in their mouths and they wanted more.

The few people who initially resisted had already been arrested – now it was parents trying to protect their children. They were smashing up vehicles with kids inside – the kids were screaming – this seemed to excite the cops and incite them even further. One coach stopped when it was surrounded by uniforms, so's not to run them over. A woman stood up inside and held up her baby to show them there was a young child on board. Next thing, a huge flint came flying and shattered the windscreen in on top of the mother and baby, before they were dragged out. A heavily pregnant woman was wandering around, obviously traumatised – two coppers came up and clubbed her to the ground with their batons. We left our bus and took as many of our instruments with us as we could. I had my fiddle, Jake and Danny had a couple of guitars each and Kem grabbed his bongos and bodhrán. Lizzie handed me her flute, she knew we were gonna make a run for it and she wouldn't be able to come with us because of her injuries from the wall-of-death accident.

'I'm not leaving you.'

'You have to. We can't afford to replace the instruments and the cops will either destroy them or steal them.'

She was right. Still, I couldn't just leave her there on her own. The others had enough to carry, so I just sat there with Lizzie and started to play, like the guys on the Titanic that time, keeping on playing while the ship was sinking. She smiled.

In the crazy chaos, the other members of the band made a run for a small copse of trees at the top of a hill. They told me later they were outa breath by the time they got there and they couldn't run no further. Kem climbed a tree and the others handed up the instruments, then climbed up after him. It was mid-summer, so there was plenty of leaf cover and they couldn't be seen from the ground. By now, coppers had come upon me and Lizzie. We didn't offer no resistance but they still cracked me across the skull with a baton and smashed my fiddle against the side of the bus. Then we was dragged away. Lizzie couldn't walk too well, so they just carried her like a sack of potatoes. We were thrown into the back of a cop-wagon and driven off. Police were in the copse by now, but they couldn't see the Ruffians up in the tree. Others, down in the beanfield, were going round with hammers smashing up vehicles and burning them, to make sure they could never be driven again. Now, they might've been just vans and coaches to the plod, but they were people's homes and it was pure criminal vandalism what the cops were doing. The Ruffians in the tree saw all this but could do nothing about it.

Five hundred and thirty seven people were arrested that day, just for being who they were – it was the biggest mass arrest in British history. There weren't enough holding cells in the area to bang up everyone arrested, so people were transported all over the country, to the midlands and even up north. Parents were separated from their kids and anyone who tried to object was beaten up in the police stations. The coppers up and down the country joked about it – it was "beat a hippie night" and they laughed and drank whisky and congratulated themselves for being the lackeys of the über-rightwing politicians and the grotesque warmongers and the financial shadowmen and the obscenely rich.

There was a few proper journalists there, belonging to the Independent and the Observer, but they "lost" most of their negatives and video footage of the police violence. Freelance photographers at the scene were arrested and their cameras confiscated. ITN reporter Kim Sabido recorded a piece to camera and said he witnessed some of the most brutal treatment of people he'd ever seen in his entire career as a journalist – scores of people being clubbed by coppers, including women holding babies in their arms. He said an enquiry should've been held into what happened – don't make me laugh! When he went back to the ITN library to look at the rushes, most of the footage had "disappeared". An Observer reporter said,

> 'There was glass breaking, people screaming, black smoke towering out of burning caravans and everywhere there seemed to be people being bashed and flattened and pulled by the hair. Men, women and kids were led away, shivering, swearing, crying, bleeding, leaving their homes in pieces.'

But you don't have to take their word for what happened in the beanfield on 1 June 1985 – the Earl of Cardigan was also an eye-witness and made statements about the brutality of the police. Cardigan was approached by the cops the following day, who wanted permission to go into Savernake Forest and "finish off" the travellers who were still camped there. The Earl refused them permission. There was a series of trials and appeals in which the Earl of Cardigan's evidence was key in getting people off the trumped-up charges. He was branded as an anarchist sympathiser and called a class traitor by the Daily Telegraph. He sued the right-wing rag for defamation and won. In 1991 a group of travellers were awarded twenty-four thousand pounds in damages for wrongful arrest, damage to property and false imprisonment.

Police radio and video were used as evidence during the court case, but there was a recording gap in both the radio and video recordings. The recording gap in the video footage was allegedly due to the video tape breaking when the convoy was first stopped at the roadblock. There was also evidence that radio logs of conversations between cops on the day of the battle had been altered. But the cynical judge "declined" to award the travellers any legal costs and the money was all swallowed up by the lawyers.

One barrister said,

'It left a very sour taste in the mouth.'

Only one copper was ever convicted.

Lizzie and me were released the next day without charge, which was Sunday. But we were in Cheltenham nick and we had no money and no transport. They just threw us out onto the street and they said they didn't know what happened to Lizzie's crutches. I helped her limp to a local hospital and they gave her replacements and bandaged my head. We then found an open-door organisation on Grosvenor Street and they gave us some food and the bus fare to Andover. It took us a few days to locate the rest of the band and, when we did, we had no bus and I had no fiddle and a split skull – otherwise we were OK.

Roy Harper wrote a song called "Back to the Stones" and recorded it in 1989. The Levellers had a song called "Battle of the Beanfield" on their 1991 album, "Levelling the Land". The prog-rock band Solstice has a song on the 1997 album called "Circles", which comments on the beanfield. The song "Itinerant Child" on the 1998 album "Mr Love Pants" was inspired by Ian Dury's experiences on that day.

Dale Vince, who was a new-age traveller back then and owner of the green energy company Ecotricity, said this:

'It was a hideous thing, a defining point in my life. I think they always had orders to trash the convoy. They were animals. The travellers were a challenge to the established order. I slept with one eye open after that. It was hard to feel secure.'

Dale Vince left the country within a year, to escape what he called,

'A time of police and state persecution.'

I was inclined to agree with him.

You see, in the context of political dissent at the time, the Henge was small potatoes. The government knew that its suppression wouldn't cause offence to the average tabloid reader, especially as most of the establishment media were ordered not to report on it. So the government knew it could disguise its real motive – the repression of the British public's right to gather freely without prior permission, and the suppression of a grassroots movement opposed to the installation of US cruise missiles on UK soil. The best-known anti-nuclear opponents were the women of Greenham Common and it would've been a PR disaster for the plod to go truncheoning a peaceful group of women. On the other hand, the new-age travellers who set up a peace camp at RAF Molesworth in Cambridgeshire – the proposed second base for cruise missiles – were an easier target, and the Battle of the Beanfield took place just four months after fifteen hundred soldiers and police – in the largest peacetime mobilisation of its kind – were used to evict the camp.

Above all, though, the major fallout from the Battle of the Beanfield was the government's manipulation of the manufactured hysteria about travellers and protestors to introduce the 1986 Public Order Act, which allowed the police to evict two or more people for trespass, providing that "reasonable steps have been taken by or on behalf of the occupier to ask them to leave". The act also stipulated that six days' written notice had to be given to the cops before most public processions. This allowed the plod to impose unspecified "conditions" if they feared that a procession "may result in serious public disorder, serious damage to property or serious disruption to the life of the community". It was the first of many repressive pieces of legislation to be pushed through by the fascists so they could move ahead with their plans to destroy the rights of ordinary working people, so the bosses could pay them as little as they liked and the corporations could make maximum profits. That strategy can be seen everywhere today.

This is a book about hippies, so I don't want to stray too far from the subject. But it needs to be said here that the Battle of the Beanfield wasn't the end of grassroots dissent in the UK – although it gutted the travellers' movement. New "threats" emerged a few years later, when the acid house scene, with its giant warehouse raves and outdoor parties, threw the government and the tabloids into an authoritarian frenzy. Then Castlemorton Common in Herefordshire happened on the May bank holiday weekend in 1992, and was the catalyst for another assault on civil liberties. The 1994 Criminal Justice Act followed. It replaced the 1968 Caravan Sites Act and criminalised the entire way of life of gypsies and travellers by removing the obligation on local authorities to provide sites for gypsies. It also amended the Public Order Act by introducing the concept of "trespassory assembly". This allowed the police to ban groups of twenty or more people from meeting in a particular area if they feared "serious disruption to the life of the community", even if the meeting was non-obstructive and non-violent. The act also introduced "aggravated trespass", which finally transformed trespass from a civil to a criminal offence.

Both Acts had disastrous effects for all kinds of protests and alternative gatherings. They were ramped-up in the courts after the government failed to get convictions after the Battle of the Beanfield, using an ancient charge of "unlawful assembly". And, as protestors have been finding out ever since, the groundwork laid by the Public Order Act and the Criminal Justice Act provided successive governments with an excuse to suppress any peaceful protest or gathering by two or more people. When this neo-Nazi legislation was being pushed through, the people who just stood on the sidelines and let so much freedom be lost so easy, had the quaint notion that at some stage, some government would repeal the excesses of it all. Instead, we're living with its consequences today – the police right to take DNA samples from people they arrest, increased "stop and search" powers, and the taking away of the right to silence of an accused person. We have an exclusion zone round parliament where a single non-violent protestor can be arrested; all sorts of "anti-terror" legislation used to stifle dissent; we have "kettling"; and cops regularly hide their identification numbers, just like they did at the beanfield, so they can assault civilians without worrying about the consequences.

The miner's strike of '84 and the beanfield of '85 were just the start of the damage the Sun-readers' government would do. As a reward for their services the police were allowed to use whatever methods they liked, without fear of any consequences in the courts. In June 1986, they sent a paramilitary force into the New Forest, where I'd often camped, to evict a group of travelling hippies from a site at Stoney Cross. They launched a dawn raid called Operation Daybreak and used similar tactics to what they did at the beanfield. The Hampshire chief constable at the time regarded travellers as anarchists and renegades from conventional society who were not to his taste. In other words, they were people who didn't accept the work ethic of 8 till 8 – no longer 9 to 5 – for minimum wages, to buy stuff they didn't need, in order to make the rich richer and destroy the natural resources of the earth in the process. Something the chief constable obviously held close to his heart.

Throughout '86 and '87 the grotesque proprietor of News International was given full access to the government and police force in his battle with the print unions – in gratitude for his continuing support of the establishment and the brainwashing of the mugs reading his newspapers. Riot police on horses again rode into ordinary demonstrators and pickets and it was one of the most violent disputes ever seen in London. The police routinely compounded the people of Wapping and denied them access to their own streets and homes. Many other confrontations continued to happen between conscientious people and the repressive establishment and its enforcers. The rest just sat in front of their televisions and watched mind-numbing crap and read libellous shit written by paid liars posing as journalists.

Following the Battle of the Beanfield, the four-mile blockade of Stonehenge was maintained for future summer solstices. Conflict between the cops and people trying to exercise their ancient rights and reach the Henge for the solstice continued to take place every year. Even the Druids were kept out and their leader, Arthur Pendragon, was arrested on each and every summer solstice between 1985 and 1999 while trying to access the stones. In the summer of 1988 around a hundred and thirty people were arrested and in 1989 that figure rose to two hundred and sixty. In league with the government for so many years, English Heritage eventually granted "limited access" to the Druids to celebrate the solstice in 1999. That access was taken away when two hundred new-agers turned up and twenty people were arrested.

14
The Peace Camps and Taking the Stones

The act of observation changes things. Like hope. But hope isn't a touchable thing – like an electron – or a stone. The paradise lost of ignorance against the pain of developing intelligence is the widening breach between alien and animal.

———

You can't talk about hippies without mentioning peace protestors because they intermingle and become each other at times. In the autumn of 1981 a group of women chained themselves to the perimeter fence at the Greenham Common airbase in Berkshire. They were protesting about the plan to site American cruise missiles there. They called themselves Women for Life on Earth and Newbury District Council had them evicted. In December 1982 thirty thousand women joined hands and formed a human chain round the base. It was called Embrace the Base. Now, none of this suited the government or its warmongering friends in the United States and they were determined to crush the peace protestors just as they were determined to crush the trades unions and the travellers.

The rabid tabloids didn't give the Greenham women much coverage, until 1983 when seventy thousand protestors formed a fourteen-mile human chain. Then they sat up and took notice, to help out their puppets down in Westminster. But the media coverage backfired and only went to prompt more peace camps to spring up across Britain and Europe. The women circled the base again in December 1983 and sections of the fence were cut. This time the Tory police force made hundreds of arrests. The women were evicted again in April 1984, but they came back the same night and reformed the camp. It wasn't like one big camp, it was about nine small camps positioned at the various gates round the base. The first one was called yellow gate; blue gate was set up by new-agers; violet gate was religious people; and green gate was women only. This new women's movement allied itself with the CND, who harassed cruise missile convoys whenever and wherever they were carried on public roads. After a while, the missiles only travelled at night under police escort.

Just like with fire-eaters and fairground people, this book ain't about peace protestors either. It's about hippies. But the hippie philosophy was always about peace and love and not killing each other by indiscriminately dropping bombs from aeroplanes. So, many people on the road decided to support the peace women. We were with one convoy of hippies travelling to a festival and we stopped off at Greenham Common and also at the peace camp at Molesworth. This is the group that got to be known as the Peace Convoy, which I've already mentioned. After the beanfield, many travellers decided to stick together for security and there was plenty of convoys travelling the roads, not just one specific Peace Convoy. Just like us, many hippie people came to the peace camps to demonstrate their support, but weren't a permanent part of them. The main hippie aim was to "take the Stones" again and several convoys tried to approach Stonehenge in 1986. They were peaceful people and got on well with the Wiltshire locals.

The first convoy left Bath on 16 May, but police infiltrators got word to their bosses. A judge was hauled off a golf course and the site was restricted. The travellers withdrew without confrontation and settled for a while in Somerset on some uncut grassland. A tabloid newspaper of the time, called Today and owned by a "cleared" paedophile, paid to have them evicted, just to make headlines for itself. While this was going on a Stonehenge Peace March set out from London and other people picketed the estate of Lord Montagu, Chairman of English Heritage, who managed Stonehenge. In his eyes "english heritage" was reserved for the establishment and didn't belong to the common people. The evicted travellers in Somerset were made to separate at the Dorset border, but regrouped at Corfe Castle, where the plod blocked them into a narrow lane. They got outa the bottleneck and were chased by police to Stoney Cross in the New Forest, where they made camp again. This led to Operation Daybreak I mentioned in the previous chapter.

Five hundred Hampshire police, in two hundred vans, moved into the camp and evicted people from their mobile homes. The vehicles were then declared unroadworthy on the flimsiest pretexts and impounded. The hippies were told to go to a holding area, but they decided instead to set off on foot for Glastonbury. On the first day they were forced to march eighteen miles with constant police harassment. Ordinary people along the way brought out food and blankets in spite of intimidation from the cops. Another group met up at Castle Green in Bristol and walked to Bath where they spent the night in Rainbow Woods. The walkers from London came along the Roman road and camped at Figsbury Ring. Police resurrected an 1847 Act to try to stop people taking the Stones and blocked off public roads that they had no right to. The walkers and their support vehicles set up a camp on one of the forestry roads but they were harassed by cops and vigilante thugs.

Altogether, about six hundred people ended up at Groveley Wood and formed into a convoy to look for somewhere better to camp. There were walkers from Bristol and London, Stonehenge Campaign supporters from Bradford and Liverpool, a group from Scotland and another from Germany and one man from Switzerland, people on holiday or on the road for the summer. This wasn't an organised "bunch of anarchists". None of the people knew each other and everyone was making their own personal pilgrimage to the Stones, which was their right. Yet it was called the Peace Convoy again. Mutual support and solidarity was strong and organisation was spontaneous and decisions made from site gatherings. But the meetings were constantly interrupted by aggressive police and their "bailiffs" and even right-wingers with no credentials at all, apart from them being protected by the cops.

I'd got myself a new fiddle and the Roadside Ruffians were part of this group.

Police forced us to go west along the Wylye and then boxed us into a side road near Stockton for the night. Next morning, we were ordered to get moving again and it looked like the cops were driving us all towards Glastonbury. That's not where we wanted to go, so the lead vehicle turned left, over the bridge towards Boyton. A police van blocked the road and the plods jumped out, dragged the driver from his van and slammed his face into the road before arresting him. Helicopters flew over us and things looked ugly. The cops were being deliberately confrontational, hoping to provoke violence. But this wasn't a hard-core convoy and everyone kept their cool. As well as that, a BBC documentary team had joined us and the cops didn't want to be seen on television beating people like they did at the beanfield. We set up camp at Hanging Langford and were supported by the locals. Donations came from London Squatters and Robin's Greenwood Gang sent out volunteers to fetch back firewood for cooking. We then set up a stage and had a night of music – we'd become Stonehenge in Exile.

The farmer whose land we were on was forced to get an eviction order by the police and on Friday 20 June, the day before the solstice, they brought an order to the camp stating we wouldn't be allowed near the Stones as a group. We could go in, a hundred at a time, in chartered buses, which was plain stupid. Despite all the police efforts, we were seven miles from the Stones and had established good relations with the locals. We knew they'd stop our vehicles if we came within five miles of Stonehenge, but what if we camped outside this exclusion zone and walked peaceful the rest of the way? The Battle of the Beanfield would've been shown up to be a multi-million pound farce and the perpetrators would be seen as the controlling fascists they were. Hippies were trusting people and the infiltrators that'd been sent into our ranks by the cops again reported back to their masters.

Police vans were pulled across the top of the hill at Deptford, blocking the road. Transits with wire riot cages waited on the grass reservation behind them, packed with well-armed cops from eleven counties. We got blocked in front and then from behind and the cops demanded we split into groups of four vehicles, which was impossible in the confines of the kettling they'd set up. Anyway, we knew we'd be safer if we stayed together. Once we were trapped, the dogs were unleashed from their cages and they came down the line of the convoy arresting people. Anyone who resisted was clubbed. I told Lizzie to stay back and I was one of the first three hundred to be taken away, on the laughable charge of obstructing the highway. As I was being led away, I seen others trying to get outa the trap and being arrested – some managed to get into a field near Stapleford, but the cops closed the road leading to the village and they were nabbed too. I heard later that some people got as far as Yarnbury Castle, the Iron Age hill fort.

Everyone was handcuffed to an individual cop and we were taken to police headquarters in Devizes, where we was held in a garage for the rest of the day and that night. Everyone was questioned and it was like being interrogated by the Gestapo in Nazi Germany.

'Name?'

'Lee, sometimes Aaron.'

'What does that mean?'

'What I said.'

That got me a shouted threat and I had the feeling the next time it'd be a wallop of a club.

'Address?'

'My bus.'

'Where's that?'

'Where I left it.'

Wallop!

They asked me about my father and I told them I never knew him.

'What about your mother?'

'She's a wicce-witch in Reno, Nevada.'

Wallop!

There were no free cells in Wiltshire and I was taken to a police station in Gloucester at 4:00am. Next day we were handcuffed in pairs and taken to court in Salisbury. There was this guy called George of Truro and he was standing on his head in front of the cops and miming. There was a carnival atmosphere in the square outside the courthouse, with people playing guitars and singing and TV cameras and idiots arguing. I saw Lizzie among them and I knew she was alright. They let me go as long as I promised to stay outa Wiltshire. I had no problem agreeing with this – I didn't recognise their kangaroo court and anything I said in there didn't amount to the kinda promise or pledge that a man'd feel bound to keep.

Very few people got through to Stonehenge on that solstice day. Depended on which roadblock you came up against. They said about forty people from Hanging Langford made it and the Secular Druids wouldn't perform their ceremonies in protest at their brothers and sisters not being allowed to be there. The Ancient Druids performed a ritual in the road, in front of the razor wire.

Still, there was always next year.

Back at Greenham Common, police action against the women was getting more and more brutal. The mud and cold outside the perimeter fence in winter was like something outa the trenches at the Somme. Life was made even more difficult for the women by the press and the public. Local Newbury residents attacked them and the tabloids vilified them and said that Russian spies were living with them. They were threatened with rape and being gassed like animals. The disgraceful Tory government of the time was absolutely determined to get them out. They were warned by the secretary of state for defence that they'd be shot if they set foot on the base. But the women kept going, they breached the fence over and over again, despite the threats and, at one stage, a group climbed into the control tower at the centre of the base. They wrote peace messages in the manuals on nuclear and biological warfare and on the walls. They were arrested at gunpoint and, in court, the women argued that the policy of "mutually assured destruction" broke international law and they had the right to act against it. In the end, the case of criminal damage was dropped because the man didn't want to attract no more attention to what was a highly embarrassing situation for the warmongers.

But the arrests and evictions and brutal harassment by thugs called "bailiffs" went on. The women fought and fought and were joined by many people who'd been hippies.

Again and again, they were violently evicted, sometimes four times a day. They were woke by "bailiffs" pulling down the plastic sheeting and dragging them out in their sleeping bags and throwing them into a lake of mud. They cut off the water supply to the women's standpipes and the moronic Sun-readers laughed and jeered. But they still couldn't subdue the spirit of these heroic women.

The arms manufacturers were making billions – more and more nuclear weapons. More and more. The Tories in parliament rubbed their greasy hands together and took bribes and directorships from the corporations making the bombs. But the women's sacrifices were gaining international support. Then Chernobyl happened in 1986. It was a nuclear disaster with thousands of cancers and foetal deformities that're still happening today – just like what happened when they dropped the bombs on Hiroshima and Nagasaki. This prompted a treaty to reduce the manufacture of nuclear weapons.

In 1988 a Soviet inspection took place at Greenham Common and the first cruise missiles started to be removed in 1989. The women were sceptical. They kept on camping at the base. By now it had become a symbol of women's struggle throughout the world, not just for peace but for independence. Many women went to the camp to seek shelter from difficult lives at home and Lizzie helped them understand who they were. She once wrote, "I know what's turned the world into a cesspool. I know why I can't walk at night without feeling threatened by attack. I know why there's militarism and imperialism and racism and sexism. I know why the negative 'isms' exist. It's because of the media and the ignorance that hangs on the lies dripping from the bloody pages of the newspapers."

I reckoned I was falling in love with Lizzie, even though we weren't spending so much time together. She was more and more at the peace camp and I was more and more travelling and trying to be with nature. Lizzie always kept her faith in human nature, but I was losing mine when I seen the way things were going. The newspapers and television were increasingly dumbing down the morons, who were content to work longer and longer hours for less and less money. Ale-swilling idiots in pubs ran down trades union movements that were responsible for getting them the weekend and holiday pay and decent working conditions and standards of safety. The British working class seemed to have a servile nature – tugging its forelock to those who they believed to be better than them. Calling the Queen "your highness" – I mean, what does "your highness" mean? That a person's "higher" than you? "Your majesty"? Anybody who uses phrases like that must have a serious psychological disorder – a psychotic inferiority complex. The salivating hacks who wrote for the tabloids took advantage of this national natural sense of subservience. And they sold the mugs the lies we're living with today.

By 1990 the US announced that Greenham was no longer an operational base and the last of the cruise missiles was removed in 1991. By then Lizzie was involved in women's networks that were campaigning against the destruction of the Pacific Islands and the growth of militarism and food mountains and corporations supporting apartheid and the commercial exploitation of pornography. She went to Zimbabwe for a while and to support Daniel Ortega and his Sandinistas in Nicaragua. In 1997, the Greenham Common base was sold back to Newbury and, two years later, cattle were back grazing on the land. The old camp was inaugurated as a Commemorative and Historic Site in 2002, when seven standing stones encircled the Flame Sculpture representing a camp fire. It was a memorial in honour of the heroic Greenham Common Peace Women, while most of the Tories and their thugs who abused them were rotting in their putrid graves.

I left the Roadside Ruffians because I wanted to take off, like I did from Frisco. Lizzie came back from Nicaragua in 1990, after the Sandinistas was defeated due to US embargos and attacks from a brutal American-financed private army called the Contras. I was glad to see her back – globe-trotting to dangerous war-torn countries was hardly the safest thing for a woman who needed crutches to walk. She was with this person called Lauren Menéndez – half American and half Nicaraguan. I kinda felt I knew this woman from somewhere before. Maybe she was me or I was her once upon a time. Maybe in the past or maybe in the future. As with all things since I was first born, I absorbed what was being discarded – picked up the pieces – lived off the scraps. By doing that I found wisdom and strength in the most unlikely places and recognised stupidity and weakness for what they really are. I knew that only fear invites denial and everything's mysteriously and comprehensively interconnected. And the past's always about becoming – not being. We sat and drank mescal and talked and Lauren Menéndez told us her story.

It started in a flophouse on Franklin Street in Trenton, New Jersey – she said what came before that didn't matter. Lauren Menéndez packed her bags and now she headed for the door. The Elvis-impersonator would have to find his missing wife himself, or hire someone else. She just had to get outa this business, because it was getting weirder every year but what else could she do? She heard they paid good wages to people driving on the ice roads up in Alaska – but she didn't like the cold. Or maybe she could get work driving the mining trucks down in Mexico – but she didn't like the heat. It was almost midnight and she'd been stewing over what to do for several hours. If she left now, she could avoid the New York gridlock and be back in Syracuse by morning – in time to get down to the Department of Employment, see what they got to offer.

Lauren Menéndez was born in Rochelle, Illinois – small-town America. Small town, small minds. Her father was a South American meat packer and her mother was a cheerleader called Janine. She didn't know she was gay until she was about thirteen and the woman in the grocery store started giving her free apples and stuff. The woman was about forty-five and, after the free apples, she took Lauren round back and introduced her to lesbian love.

Lauren didn't mind because, although the woman was a lot older than her, she was clean and not bad-looking and she was kind and witty and good-humoured and it all seemed natural-like. Lauren had been struggling with her sexuality up until now, trying to deny she was gay and forcing herself to look at the guys in the same way as she looked at some of the girls. Now it was a relief for her to be able to come to terms with who and what she was. The grocery woman told her she must never be ashamed of that and Lauren took her at her word, not realising that being gay in small-town America was almost as bad as being muslim or black or atheist. The grocery woman got her windows busted first, then her shop set on fire and she was run outa town. Lauren and her family had to move to Rockford, where the people were a little more open-minded and her dad sent her to military school to try to knock the gayness outa her. Her father didn't realise that sending Lauren to military school was maybe the worse thing he could do on that score.

Lauren Menéndez always wanted to be a cop, like the good guys she saw on television. It was easy enough to get into the force and she got along OK with the corruption and discrimination and brutality for a while. But one night she witnessed a bunch of cops laying into this boy – he was no older than eighteen. Lauren could see he was gay and the cops were laughing as they beat the living crap outa him. The boy looked up into Lauren's eyes, just before he died. Lauren couldn't take no more after that, so she left the force, after less than a year as a rookie. She went to New York and got herself a private investigator's licence, thanks to some string-pulling by her precinct chief. Most of her clients didn't know she was gay or they wouldn't do business with her – except for maybe the gay ones.

Soon she was disillusioned with the world. It was all chasing runaway broads who had plenty reason to run away in the first place; and finding bail-jumpers for bondsmen who made a profit outa human misery; and strong-arming poor people who owed money to ruthless rich people. The whole situation was sleaze – shit and stink and sewer-sludge. She couldn't stomach it no more. Nobody had any integrity. The values she became a cop to uphold were gone – maybe they were never there in the first place? Maybe it was all just like the movies – all smoke and glass and now she saw behind the lies. She saw the dirty truth.

Everybody was on the take – on the make – and the whole life thing was reduced down to the lowest common denominator.

She had her hat on her head and her .45 in its shoulder-holster and her hand on the door handle – but she didn't turn it. She went back and sat on the bed, throwing the overnight bag in a corner. Images materialised inside her head. She believed they were inside her head, even though they seemed like they were in the room with her. Images of a young and idealistic PI with delusions of doing good – of making a difference. Images of sneering crooks and cops – images of bullets flying all over the goddamn place and confusion turning to panic and panic turning to cowardice. Fight or flight?

Flight!

It was Nicaragua where she ran off to, to get away from the crap and try to do something for people who wanted to live their own way and were being bullied by capitalism-gone-crazy America, with some senile B-list actor having his puppet-strings pulled. Pain seared through her shoulder and her butt as she ran away and her trigger-finger went flying down the street in front of her – blown away in a hundred fragments. Flying through the lead-filled air in slo-mo – like bloody fireflies in the black Nicaraguan night.

Then she saw a face in front of her. Right there across the room, by the grimy window. And she felt what she felt back then – the same attraction she felt for the older grocer in Rochelle. Not overt. Latent. Insinuating. Peripheral. Elusive. Suggestive. She introduced herself to the face in that dark bar in Buena Vista and she was bleeding from the shoulder and her pants were soaked in blood and her trigger-finger was gone.

I never really knew what went on between Lauren and Lizzie in southern Nicaragua in 1989 – and I never asked. Lauren travelled with us for a while during 1990 and into 1991, then she went back to America.

Back to the flophouse on Franklin Street? I don't know.

Lizzie heard rumours that she got involved in Native American rights and maybe she ended up in Colorado on the Pawnee National Grassland to the north of Sterling, where I spent some time with a woman called Angel back when I was eighteen. We never heard nothing more from her – until she turned up at a remote cottage where I was living.

Many years away.

15
Castlemorton Common

You hear the vana and can't tell where it comes from or where it will go. If you alter the I-ness, you create a new creature. The you that emerges will no longer be you. It will be stranger. It will be other. That's the human condition, with its silhouettes for which there's no responsibility and its senses for which there's no adequate control.

———————

After Lauren Menéndez went back to America, Lizzie and I argued a lot. I wanted to leave this country and go to India, but she wanted to stay. I told her there was nothing for us here, British society had taken the corporate shilling and was sinking deeper and deeper into the mire of apathy and ignorance. She said there was still hope – we could fight to maintain our way of life. The Ruffians had taken the bus we used to get around, so we bought an old ice-cream van and I humoured her and we kept on travelling. But it all came to a head in 1992.

At Castlemorton Common.

In 1992, Avon and Somerset police tried to end the annual Avon Free Festival, which was held in the Bristol area for a number of years. As a result, thousands of new-age travellers on the way to the festival were shunted into neighbouring counties by the plod's, so-called, Operation Nomad. About thirty thousand people gathered on Castlemorton Common in the Malvern Hills and decided to hold the festival there instead. We was on our way to Avon along the M4 and we came across a green-goddess fire engine at a service station. It was one of the vehicles taking kit to the festival, so we followed it. By the time we got close, there was miles of trucks and buses full of people. The sun was setting and we could see the site starting to pulse with light and sound as the gear was set up. There was a ribbon of headlights all the way to the horizon as more people came to the festival.

Finding Castlemorton was no problem for anyone who wanted to come. Every television station was reporting the event, showing more and more vehicles turning off the roads and onto the site. On that hot sunny weekend in May, it was a beacon calling out to all free people everywhere. An encampment grew outa nowhere. Grew. And grew. A few plods tried half-heartedly to direct people away from the site, but they were wasting their time. Vehicles pulled off the roads and into fields and were abandoned, while the occupants walked along the track into the heart of the common – drawn in by the vibe – hypnotised – moving like rhythm-robots. Spiral Tribe Collective were at the heart of the encampment, though other collectives had their own individual stages and the sounds competed with each other. Free enterprise was alive and well for the ravers who wanted to buy light sticks or whistles or tapes or whatever. It was an alternative town – a free party nirvana, vibrating to the beat of the sound systems.

There was a circle of vehicles in the centre and hard tribal techno was pumping out into the amphitheatre and a huge black and white spiral hung from one of the lorries next to the decks. People danced and waved and nodded and twisted as the tents and vans and cars continued to stretch out and fill the common from all directions. As darkness fell on the first night, fires lit up the faces of travellers and kids and dogs and it felt like this was a permanent encampment, just like in the ancient days. It was the biggest thing since the Henge and it started on 22 May.

We were there in our converted ice-cream van – me and Lizzie – and the media swarmed like flies around the mobile sound systems. Bedlam and Techno Travellers and Circus Warp. Spiral Tribe was the centre of attraction – they came together on the north London squat scene and formed a "creative forum" with music as its driving force. They bought a huge sound system for two thousand pounds and it took them a long time to pay for it. They passed the hat round at raves for donations and they made a record called "Breach of the Peace". They were an amorphous group who'd lost faith in the system and wanted people to know the score. There were big-name DJs and bands like Back to the Planet and Xenophobia and Poisoned Electrick Head. The media attention attracted more people and the crowd grew. Nobody knows exactly how many turned up in the end, some say between forty and fifty thousand. There was us hippies and travellers and weekend ravers and ordinary people on the road through unemployment and homelessness. People who had a desire to escape from crumbling urban environments, driven into the ground by years of greed, looking for something – a new way of living in a post-industrial society.

As usual, the tabloids tried to panic the public into believing the end of the world was nigh – not mentioning that nuclear weapons were far more likely to annihilate the earth than any gathering of hippies. After 1989 people started to embrace rave as the new counterculture force – a mixture of hippie radicalism, eco-activism, anti-capitalism, new-age paganism and simple music-loving freedom. The leading group in this new wave was Spiral Tribe, with their black clothes and shaven heads and alternative messages. But the Sun-and-Mail-readers didn't like a bunch of pill-popping ravers and freewheeling travellers taking over a section of "their" countryside. The West Mercia police stood back in the beginning and allowed vehicles access to the site. It was a self-regulating community that resembled a festival crossed with a shanty town – tents and generators and food stalls and sound systems that ran all day and all night for a week. The more the tabloids whinged and cried about police inaction, the more people turned up.

Let me explain the difference between travelling hippies and ravers. Weekend ravers could go back to their city jobs after the event, but full-time travellers depended on the goodwill of landowners and local communities. The loud techno riled the Castlemorton locals, and even some of us hippies. And the ravers had no experience of how to behave at festivals, to clean up after themselves and respect the natural environment. The hacks made no distinction between the two groups, writing their bile about reckless travellers spending their benefit cheques on drugs and wrecking the picturesque countryside. But we weren't scroungers, we made our living in many ways. Some of us were musicians, others were mechanics, or electricians, or carpenters. Some provided seasonal casual labour on farms and building sites. Others were skilled at crafts and made jewellery and pottery and paintings to sell at markets. Others made hash cakes, or worked on stages and sound systems at festivals. We recycled waste and scrap, but that was made more difficult by the 1990 Environmental Protection Act, which made taking stuff from skips an offence and scrapping illegal without a carrier's licence. But the media never reported this. When low-flying helicopters buzzed us like bad-tempered bees and someone took a pot-shot at one of them with a firework, a headline appeared the next day, "Hippies fire flare at helicopter" – it didn't say "Ravers fire flare at helicopter".

This new breed of techno rebels had been keeping up the outlaw tradition of the old hippie free festival circuit, getting round the Tory laws suppressing "paid parties" by not charging admission. Nobody took much notice until now. The spectacle gave the fascist Tories a new moral cause to blind the moronic voters with, and they could count on their pathological liar friends in the media to back them up. You see, the Tories and the media had nothing against the ravers, they were weekend partygoers and many were yuppies and Tory supporters and posed no threat to the establishment. But the hippies and new-agers and travellers, with their alternative lifestyle, were a serious threat to the work-for-profit ethic of that establishment.

Later in 1992 the Sun covered a Fantasia rave for over twenty-five thousand people with glowing clichés. It was just us they didn't like. The tabloids complained about "Hippie rubbish" destroying the common, while they backed the pollution of the entire planet and the destruction of the ozone layer. They called us "soap-dodgers" and "crusties", even though we were far cleaner than any of those disgusting scum-wallowing hacks. The police stayed out and didn't come in breaking heads with truncheons, that's because of the middle-class ravers. Had it been just us hippies, things would've been different.

As more and more people turned up, abandoned cars littered the roads. They came in old fire-engines and converted ambulances and army trucks and caravans and double-decker buses. They danced their way along to get spiralled – all sorts, from all over. Us hippies came prepared – campfires and food and hash and mellow music. Pushers shouted out along the way, you could get whatever you wanted – ketamine, ecstasy, acid, speed. We sold hash cakes to pay for some work on our ice-cream van.

There was a huge illuminated statue of Neptune in one tent and people danced like they were idolising it – they were lost, on another planet, another dimension. It was two completely different cultures coming together for the first time – maybe the last. It was a square mile of shanty town with no facilities. It was like wandering through a medieval fair – torch lights and campfires and relentless drumming and a life energy emanating from the land and connecting everything through the music.

The tabloids screamed and screamed, spewing venom like "villagers threaten to burn out hippies". Again, no mention of the ravers. They reported a vigilante group of hayseeds armed with shotguns and threatening to set light to the common, like they owned it or something – like it was theirs. The common was just that, common land that was there since the Middle Ages so poor people had somewhere to hold their festivals and celebrations. We were just doing the same. The rags suggested a "ring of fire" to burn us out, like we were witches or something. It was like, if they set fire to the gorse bushes, the blaze'd sweep through the camp and burn tents and vans. They didn't speculate on what'd happen to the people – but then, they didn't see us as people. The villagers had no such plan, it was the tabloids putting ideas into their heads. They'd have loved it. What headlines!

They accused "hippies" of trying to sell drugs to village kids and they graphically described lambs with their insides torn out and their faces torn off, like we were a pack of werewolves on the rampage for blood. They said "it made a policeman cry" – I doubt that very much. At one point, the cops tried to drive through the centre of the crowd. They got stopped in the middle, and a nameless hippie got passed over the crowd and started selling acid off the bonnet of the police car. After futilely attempting to get outa the car the plod ended up just laughing at the sheer balls of him. They didn't bother us after that. Later, the right-wing rags called for an enquiry and for cops to be suspended for not going in and committing carnage, like they did at the beanfield. And their hysterical screeching could be heard all the way to hell.

Despite the poisonous diatribe of the media, Castlemorton Common was a unique event. Free, like in the old days, with thousands of peaceful people enjoying themselves in a beautiful place – bright days and starry nights, travellers, the earth beneath our feet, music, dancing, the sweet air and human harmony. It was well organised and safe and nobody tried to annihilate society like we know it. Castlemorton was massive in its size and bravado. It marked the peak of the free party scene in Britain and also its death – though we didn't know it at the time.

We need to recap here, to understand what was going on. The term new-age traveller was born outa the hippie ideology during the 1970s as the travelling scene grew from the Free Festival movement. People bought vehicles to transport themselves and their possessions from one event to another. By 1980 a network of Free Festivals had become established throughout the country. Stonehenge got to be the site for the biggest festival and the spiritual centre for people who identified with ancient pre-christian religion. There was an emphasis on communal gatherings and observance of the seasons. In an attempt to stamp out this phenomenon, the Tory government of the 1980s spent many millions of pounds on police operations, court cases and legislation.

You gotta understand, there was conflict between landowners and commoners since before the Diggers revolted in 1649, it was an old struggle that took on a new form. Hippies and travellers wanted remote pieces of land to live on and hold their festivals on. This couldn't be allowed, because it might catch on and the corporations wouldn't have a ready workforce to produce bombs and useless consumables in order to make more and more profit. So, the fascists drafted ever more draconian laws, leading to the introduction of the Criminal Justice Bill which gave the police power to break up and arrest the organisers of any protest or party. But the police already had too much power to act in, so-called, cases of trespass and the argument for more legislation was capitalist bullshit. The 1986 Public Order Act was designed to smash public gatherings, and contained specific "anti-hippy" clauses where people could be imprisoned for six months or fined a thousand pounds.

The corporate puppet masters who controlled the politicians viewed us travellers as "rural terrorists" and used surveillance in tracking our whereabouts. I've already mentioned Operation Solstice in Wiltshire, and Operation Nomad in Avon and Somerset, and there was a Central Intelligence Unit based in Thames Valley solely to "keep an eye" on hippies and other "subversives". Most of the time, the major offenders in breaching the peace were the cops themselves. They spent vast sums of public money on undercover operations and surveillance and manning roadblocks – wasting time in false arrests and filling up cells with people just trying to follow their chosen lifestyle. Policing by consent was replaced by coercion and I was getting fed up with the harassment and violence meted out to people by cops and them being called "defenders of the peace and public order" by the media. Any real journalist or photographer who tried to tell the truth and show what was really happening got silenced with the threat of prosecution and having their equipment confiscated and even losing their jobs.

When the party finally wound down, West Mercia police swooped on Spiral Tribe, impounding their equipment and arresting thirteen members. By avoiding another Battle of the Beanfield, they comfortably won the public relations war, licensing the authorities to take further action. Every attempt to mount a free party that summer was stopped by a slick police operation, and at the Tory party conference in October the prime minister taunted: "New-age travellers? Not in this age. Not in any age!" Spiral Tribe was charged with public order offences and their trial became one of the longest running and most expensive cases in British legal history, lasting four months and costing the UK four million pounds – a monumental waste of public money. The sound systems and equipment confiscated by police were all returned, like there was no legal reason for it. They were acquitted of all charges relating to Castlemorton in March 1993 – shortly after, the group moved to Europe.

So, after failing to convict Spiral Tribe, the Tories introduced the Criminal Justice and Public Order Act 1994. I already mentioned this piece of legal vandalism in Chapter 13, but it's relevant here, as it was one of the reasons I decided I'd had enough of the harassment and coercion of the fascist government and the libellous media in this country. And I wasn't the only one, many hippies were choosing to leave Britain for other countries where alternative lifestyles were still tolerated. I was forty-six in 1994 and getting too old to put up with the way people like me were being treated. The sheep kept crowding onto their trains and roads in the rush-hour mornings and back again in the evenings for diminishing wages, and anyone who didn't want that kinda life was being crushed under a mountain of legislation. To me, this Act was the most serious threat to civil liberty in a series of threats to civil liberties, where all kinds of unofficial demonstrations could be stamped out. It was also used against other groups, like ramblers and hunt saboteurs and environmental protestors at places like Twyford Down and Newbury. It did away with the right to silence of an accused person and gave the cops powers to forcibly take body samples and keep them on file forever. It increased the use of "stop and search" and did away with councils' obligations to provide sites for traditional gypsies, in an attempt to assimilate those people into "settled" society.

It's important for people to know what was passed into law by the MPs who sat on their arses in Westminster and pretended to be representing the people of Britain and not the vested interests of corporations and warmongers. This is just some of the stuff included in part five of that piece of shit legislation, the Criminal Justice and Public Order Act 1994 (CJA):

∞ Raves were banned – defined as "amplified music characterised by the emission of a succession of repetitive beats".

∞ Vehicles and sound equipment could be "confiscated".

∞ The right to assemble was banned.

∞ Squatting was banned.

∞ "Unauthorised" camping was banned.

∞ No more gypsy sites.

∞ Peaceful protestors could be "kettled".

∞ Journalists and peace campaigners could be classified as "terrorists".

∞ No more right to silence when questioned by police.

∞ Increased stop-and-search powers.

∞ Compulsory taking of "intimate and non-intimate samples" – such as hair, saliva, skin, blood, urine and semen.

∞ Privately-run prisons, unaccountable to public scrutiny and run on a profit-making basis, along with prison ships and "secure training centres" for children aged twelve to fourteen. These young inmates can be strip-searched forcibly by a single member of staff; all their mail can be read and censored; all family visits can be stopped on the order of the Centre's Director.

So you can see that the whole of part five of the Act covered "collective trespass" and legislated against festivals and other traditional gatherings – laws that affected squatters and campers and protestors and the criminalisation of a whole section of society.

A group made up of sound systems and civil liberty organisations coordinated a campaign of resistance to the Act while it was still under debate. Two demonstrations were organised in London and ended up as a party in Hyde Park. Another group, called the Zippies, protested online – it was called the intervasion and used electronic disruption techniques that harassed MPs and shut down the prime minister's email server. The band Dreadzone released a single called "Fight the Power" – the song had samples from Noam Chomsky that talked about "taking control of your lives", meaning political resistance to the Act. The cover artwork had a picture of a young woman with a baby stroller and a poster attached to it saying "Kill the Bill".

Electronica band Autechre released a three-track Anti EP on Warp Records, stating:

> *Warning. "Lost" and "Djarum" contain repetitive beats. We advise you not to play these tracks if the Criminal Justice Bill becomes law. "Flutter" has been programmed in such a way that no bars contain identical beats and can therefore*

be played under the proposed new law. However, we advise DJs to have a lawyer and a musicologist present at all times to confirm the non repetitive nature of the music in the event of police harassment.

The fifth mix on the internal version of Orbital's "Are We Here?" EP was titled "Criminal Justice Bill?". It consisted of four minutes of silence. "Their Law", a song by electronic dance band The Prodigy with Pop Will Eat Itself, was written as a direct response to the Act. A quotation in the booklet of the Prodigy's 1994 album "Music for the Jilted Generation" read "How can the government stop young people having a good time? Fight this bollocks."

The Six6 Records music compilation album NRB:58 No Repetitive Beats was released in opposition to the proposed Act. The album's liner notes said:

For every copy of "No Repetitive Beats" sold Network will pay a royalty to D.I.Y./All Systems No! The money will be used by D.I.Y./All Systems No! towards the cost of a sound system which will be on hand to replace any sound equipment seized by the police using draconian powers granted to them by the Criminal Justice Bill to stop music "wholly or predominantly characterised by the emission of a succession of repetitive beats". The Bill is unjust and tramples across common sense and civil rights. If you want to help throw the CJB out contact the human rights organisation Liberty. Fight for your right to party.

The B-side to Zion Train's "Dance of Life" single included a track entitled "Resist the Criminal Justice Act". UK garage act The Streets also criticised the legislation in the track "Weak Become Heroes" from their debut album "Original Pirate Material" – one lyric goes: "and to the government I stick my middle finger up with regards to the Criminal Justice Bill".

But the campaign against the bill was mostly toothless and the Act became law. The anti-corporate culture was absorbed into the steel and brick clubs – the muddy fields and wobbly tents were blown away. Dress how you like became smart trainers and designer jeans and the original festivalgoers couldn't make it past the doormen. The underground was gone, the mainstream was here. With new clubs springing up across the country every month, most ravers had little incentive to campaign for freedom, leaving us hippies and travellers and activists to fight a losing battle.

The Act of 1994 was a draconian piece of legislation, explicitly aimed at suppressing the activities of alternative counter-cultures. It was about politicians judging people's lifestyles and making laws to protect the capitalist establishment. The main targets were us hippies and travellers, squatters, direct action protestors, and festivalgoers. It was drafted in an atmosphere of "moral panic" engineered by the tabloids and their morally deformed proprietors.

The free-festival dream was already dead by the time the government introduced the Criminal Justice and Public Order Act. Castlemorton was both the pinnacle and the swansong of a '90s version of festival counter-culture. It was unsustainable because of its following – pseudo-renegades, imitation anarchists. The radical idealism of Spiral Tribe couldn't convert the ravers, so they took off.

I was soon to follow them, but not to Europe. To India on the Hippie Trail.

16
Encountering Alice

Bad isn't good no matter how you phrase it. Maybe not. But to become good, I have to admit that I'm bad. It's just a matter of control – and understanding. Come out of the darkness of conscience – of scruple.

———

Between Castlemorton and the introduction of the Criminal Justice and Public Order Act, Lizzie and I kept moving, but things weren't the same. I was determined to leave and she wanted to stay. In the end, I said I was going – with or without her. Our relationship was a loose one – no strings attached. She'd gone for short stints to Zimbabwe and Nicaragua and I didn't mind. I missed her while she was away, but I knew I could live without her. Still, I knew she'd be sad if I left, and I'd be sad to leave her. Where would I go? I didn't know.

Long as it was outa here – make a new start somewhere. Away from all the crap. I always wanted to visit India and plenty of hippies had been along the trail there before me. It was a place where a man could travel in peace, be left alone and not kicked about like a mongrel dog just because he didn't want to take the corporate shilling.

I was a bit nervy about it – I don't know why. I'd travelled across America on my own when I was nineteen, and up and down the length and breadth of Britain since then. India would be a piece of cake – so would getting there. There was two routes, through Istanbul to Tehran and Herat and Kandahar, then Peshawar and Lahore and on to India. Or, after Istanbul, I could go through Turkey and via Syria into Jordan and Iraq, then Pakistan and India. In the end Lizzie said she didn't think she could make it, hitchhiking on crutches all that way. But she'd fly out to join me when I got to wherever it was I wanted to go – just let her know when I was there and she'd come. We gave away the converted ice-cream van and she went to live with a friend of hers from the fairground days and take a break from travelling. She was forty-two – four years younger than me.

I started out from Hemel Hempstead after saying goodbye to Lizzie. I hitched a ride in a transit van that was full of a football team on their way to play a Sunday league game. They dropped me near London and I took the underground all the way down from Harrow-on-the-Hill to Greenwich, south of the river. From there I hitched through Dartford and Chatham and Canterbury in a lorry that was crossing from Dover to Calais on the ferry. At the other side of the Channel, the lorry took me as far as St-Quentin in Picardie and I bunked down there for the night. It brought back memories to me – hitchhiking, from when I crossed America. I was a lot younger then and optimistic about the world, searching for something I never found – at least not in Britain. Maybe I'd find it in India.

Next day was Monday and I left the cheap hotel in St-Quentin and hitched another ride through France and into southern Germany with a British guy driving a Leyland six-tonner and he took me as far as München in Bavaria. I didn't want to hang around in Europe too long, so I kept going through Slovenia and into Croatia, which was a dangerous place because of the war of independence. OK, fighting was intermittent after the ceasefire of '92, but the JNA was still active and likely to shoot tourists who they suspected of being UN spies. I spent an uneasy night in a hostel in Zagreb, before hightailing it outa there on a series of local buses to Požega and then Bǎcka Palanka on the Yugoslav border. Even there, things were dodgy and unsettled and people were suspicious of strangers, so I thought it best to get over into Romania. Hitchhiking was too dangerous, so I caught another bus to the border and then the night train from Timisoara down to Bucharest. It was a ten-hour journey on the train – we left at 10:00pm and arrived in Bucharest at 8:00am the next morning. I didn't have a berth or anything and I only managed to sleep intermittently, as the train kept stopping at stations in between.

Bucharest in September was a nice place to be and I decided to hang around for a bit, catch my breath after the sprint through the Balkans. I didn't have much money to be spending on buses and trains and the aim of this trip was to hitchhike like I did in America. I checked into a cheap hostel and they told me there was a free concert at the Sala Polivalenta in Tinererului Park – it was a band called Cargo and I decided to go along. The park was huge and green, with playgrounds and bike-riders and a funfair and a lake. The concert venue was right in the middle and there was a couple of hundred people there when I arrived. The band was heavy metal, which didn't turn me on much, but I decided to stay because I needed to chill and I had nowhere else to go. A makeshift bar served some kinda plum alcohol called *tuică*, but I couldn't see no hashish, which I thought was strange, being this close to Turkey.

I only stayed about half an hour because it wasn't really my scene. I took a walk along the Bulevardul and into Strada Vişana. It was still early and I was hungry, so I looked for somewhere to eat. I realised I hadn't had no food since Zagreb and I was never a big eater, never needed much to sustain me. Sometimes I thought about stopping eating altogether. See how long I could last – become so light I might float away on the warm breeze coming up from the Mediterranean. Light as a bird's wing, a feather. But maybe not. That just wouldn't be practical and I'd only get ill. Maybe die. Everyone has to eat. Everything must devour something else to stay alive. One of the laws of nature. Something must die for something else to live, and so on and so on, even if it's only an ear of corn. And I couldn't be the odd one out. I decide to look for somewhere cheap.

There's a little place on the corner of Vişana and Intrarea Trestiana, serving Thai food, so I think I'll give it a try. There's only a few people in the place and plenty of vacant tables. The menu's in Thai and I don't speak the lingo. I'm struggling to understand what everything is because I don't want to order something I can't eat – they might think I was being an idiot. There's this woman sitting at a corner table. She sees me twisting the menu and comes across.

'Having trouble?'

She's got an Australian accent and looks about thirty, with red-red hair and black eyebrows and she introduces herself as Alice. She sits at my table and calls the waiter and tells me she's a financial analyst with Morgan Stephens & Thaksin and used to getting her own way. She orders *khao tom* followed by *kai phatmet mamuang himmaphan* without asking me, and two bottles of Miller Light. She smiles and puts a finger to her lips as if to say don't talk. With your mouth full.

She only speaks again after the meal and as an aside from ordering more drinks. I tell her my name's Aaron and I'm on the Hippie Trail. She says she'd love to do something like that, just drop out and walk away from it all. I say why don't you and she answers that she's bust her balls getting to where she is and she ain't gonna throw it all in now. Alice smokes a long thin cigar called a panatella and blows the smoke my way.

'How long you staying in Bucharest?'

'Till tomorrow.'

'Why don't I show you the city?'

'Thanks, but I'm on a tight budget.'

'Don't worry about money, I got plenty.'

We leave the restaurant and make our way back to the park. It's twilight but there's still joggers and kids playing and old people strolling and chess players in a kinda pavilion. She sits by the lake and I sit with her and we watch the evening go by. She seems lost in her thoughts and I don't want to intrude – until she offers me a cigar. She smells of Chanel and she's wearing Gucci sunglasses and a light two-piece suit by Belle De Jour and a diamond ring by Tavernier of Bond Street, which she says was given to her by a perfect man and she's never had the heart to throw it away – even though she threw him away.

She looks me up and down and blows smoke into my face. Her eyes are sad – a deep sadness I ain't seen before.

'I must say, you look a bit old to be a hippie.'

'We're all old now.'

'Who?'

'Hippies.'

'Let's walk.'

She gets up and strides away along the edge of the lake towards the city to the north. This takes me a bit by surprise and I gotta hurry to catch up with her. I don't have to catch up with her, but I want to – because I need some company and this Alice is as good as company's likely to get in a strange place. She stops walking and throws away the butt end of the panatella.

'Let's get a drink.'

She takes my arm and we leave the park and flag a cab on Bulevardul Tineretuliu and make our way through crowded streets under a darkening sky to a club called Interbelic, in the Old Town. She says it's a place she goes sometimes when she wants to be alone and I say she's not alone now. She says that's different and it's just she's not in the mood for the usual superficial company of her social set tonight. It's dark and discreet in the club, with an easy saxophone blowing soft blues in a corner and we take a table away from the rest of the sparse clientele. She orders a half bottle of Barao de Vilar port with two large Rémy Martins. She mixes the port and brandy and I see the low club-lights reflected in the dark, sensuous colour of the liquid.

'I saw him again, Aaron.'

She says this like she knows me well and like I should be aware of who it is she saw again. I play along, wondering if this woman's mistaken me for someone else – maybe someone she knew once – or was once – in a different life.

'Who?'

'The man.'

'The man?'

'The perfect man.'

She lights up a cigar. She's edgy. Unpredictable. Better not to push things. I mean, I'm edgy myself. Nervous. Not really a good combination. I know without her telling me that she's damaged.

Psychologically. She was hurt by her perfect man. Perfect in form and face and hair and eyes and laugh and libido – in an imperfect way. Perfect. The imperfection making him perfect. And she loved him – told everyone he was perfect. And it's fine until they start to live together and she sees him really. As he really is. Then the imperfection becomes caricature. Grating. Irritating. And now she hates him. Would like to kill him – for the imperfection that made him perfect. They parted, as they were bound to eventually – and now she don't trust perfect men. That's why she's here. With me.

We make some small talk and it's difficult to know if she's interested or not. It seems like we've always been close – not like we just met about an hour or so ago. Like we were in love or something at some time that neither of us can remember. Like we shared confidences when there was no-one else to listen and we don't know when we first met – maybe way back. We don't know where and we don't know how and it don't really matter. Alice and I are a fact of more than one life – or so it seems. That's all that matters.

I ask if the man was following her – the perfect man. And she says we're all being followed, in one way or another. We're all being spied on – manipulated and activated and deactivated and castrated and masturbated – by fashion designers and television producers and art critics and gigolos and gurus and marketing executives and pharmaceutical researchers and the general public and thirty-third degree masons and magazine editors and detergent manufacturers and liars and deceivers. It's the way of the modern world. It's inevitable and there's nothing we can do about it.

I disagree and tell her I believe it's all connected. Everything. A huge global public relations conspiracy, managed by degenerate media moguls. She shrugs her shoulders. I tell her I believe there's greater forces at work behind the scenes in the world – behind the ideal, behind the cynosure, behind the political and the correct, behind the face, behind the word, behind the gesture, behind the essence and the quintessence. And she says I'd know that more than most, wouldn't I? I think maybe she's just humouring me – being cynical – listening to my hippie philosophy – my narrow parochial view, as she calls it. And now she's bored with it. I can tell. Today she don't feel like humouring anybody. Today she's the one who needs to be humoured.

'I don't want to be here, Aaron.'

'I know. Let's go.'

'We can go to my place.'

'Can we?'

We leave club Interbelic. It's dark and the downtown's alive with sinister types at this time of night. All looking for something. What? The same thing as me? Safety? The same thing as Alice? *Felo de se*? Our taxi takes us through the crowded streets of happy hunters and we're both relieved when the door of her apartment closes behind us and we're away from it all. Separated from it all. Only ourselves in this little oasis of *bienséance*. Just the two of little us. She opens a bottle of Chianti and lights up a couple of panatellas.

'It's haunted me forever, Aaron ...'

'Your perfect man?'

'No, of course not. Not him. Seeing him made me realise I can't be content with any man. And that made me so melancholic.'

'Why? Why do you need to be with a man?'

'I'm thirty-two, Aaron. I want a child. After twenty-seven, a woman's child-bearing powers start to decline.'

Her voice breaks and she stops speaking. I want to put my arm round her shoulder and comfort her – shield her from whatever it is that's hurting her. But I don't.

'You can have a child, Alice.'

'I want a perfect child, Aaron ... and I can't find a perfect man.'

This is crazy. A perfect child – the second coming. She wants a clone of herself – a child that'll carry her genes and no-one else's.

'A clone?'

'Are you insane?'

She laughs. Sarcastic. If only. Drinks her wine and stubs out her panatella.

'The technology's out there.'

'No it isn't! I'll be too old by the time it is.'

I'm trying to understand the situation and the thing that keeps coming to mind is Alice herself. What makes her what she is – a disappointment to herself? Not physical or mental or in achievement or nothing like that – but maybe something in her childhood. Some disappointment that left a huge gaping need. An empty place that can't be filled by herself – only by herself. And I see my mother with her railroad man and I see myself and my own childhood and the father I never had. I see him in my dreams sometimes – even now. But we don't come together. Don't come close to each other. I can tell his heart's desolate. I can feel his despair – but I can't do nothing. I feel helpless – useless – heavy. So heavy. Everything's futile and life itself is an inadequate thing.

Alice laughs again. Sarcastic. Biting into my thoughts. She opens her mouth to speak but no words come. It's like she's in suspended animation and stays like that for some time. Then her lips come together without saying anything at all. She empties her glass and fills it again. It seems to me that, even with everything, she believes she has nothing.

'Even with everything, Aaron ... I have nothing.'

She wants what women with nothing have.

'There are women in the world with nothing ... and they have more than I have.'

'Not so.'

'Yes so, Aaron. Women in the rubble of Gaza, women in the slums of India, women in the jungles of Burma, women in the poverty of rural China ...'

I let her talk. Was her childhood like mine? Is that where the source of her problem lies?

'My childhood was an idyllic thing, Aaron … in Australia. My mother was a warm, loving woman and my father was one of those good guys, you know, you see them sometimes in the movies. They always do the right thing.'

'Then, what's the problem?'

'I want it back. I want to relive the past, Aaron. Don't you?'

I say no! No? But maybe I do – not the same way. Different. With everything changed. So it wouldn't be the past, would it? It'd be the future. Alice stands in front of me. Looking. I look back at her. She's about to laugh again – but she don't. Instead, she gets up and leaves the room. I don't follow. I don't know where she's gone – maybe the bedroom, maybe the bathroom. She's gone a long time and I wait for her to come back. We're kinda alike, this Alice and me, even though we're completely different. Both affected deeply by something – the past. Our pasts. Childhoods neither of us can understand, except that Alice wants to relive hers and I want to forget mine. The force that surrounded me as a boy is still here. I know that. I've seen it, even if I only imagined it. It's everywhere. Omnipresent. So also is the force that surrounded Alice as a girl. I wanted to escape from the one into the other. And I wanted to take Lizzie with me – but she wouldn't come.

Now I sit here waiting for Alice.

I go to the kitchen and find her there. She walks across to where I'm standing, by the door. Her face comes right up close to mine and she blows gently across my eyes and nose and her hand takes the glass from mine. She keeps blowing on my face while guiding my hand up under her dress. The insides of her thighs are warm and moist and she's wearing nothing underneath but stockings. I kiss her and she pulls her mouth away from mine – keeping her lips real close and running her tongue across them. She collects a glassful of ice cubes from the freezer before pulling me after her into the bedroom. She helps me strip and slips her own dress off over her head and we fall naked onto the bed – except for Alice's stockings. I try to kiss her body, but she pulls away again and pushes me down onto my back.

176

Then she removes the stockings – slowly. Alice is at the foot of the bed and she begins to crawl forward – like a snake. Coiling herself over my body until her eyes are directly above mine and full of something I don't recognise – something I ain't seen before. Or maybe I have and I don't remember.

She wraps one of the stockings round my wrist and ties it to the bedstead. Then the other one to the other wrist. I'm about to say something, but she clamps a hand across my mouth. A dribble of spit emerges from between her lips and I see it fall in slow motion. She removes her hand in time to let it strike my mouth – like an exploding bomb. Alice climbs across me and manipulates me up inside her. Then she begins to move. Slow at first – slow – slow – slow. She's light – so light. Almost weightless. I can hardly feel her on top of me. Her head's thrown back and her fingers are deep inside my mouth, searching for my throat and almost choking me. Before long I can feel myself coming. Alice feels it too. She reaches for an ice cube from the glass and the cold shock of it has the effect of halting the climax. Alice keeps on gyrating until all the ice is melted and she's reached orgasm herself – how many times I don't know. She rolls off me before I can explode inside her and finishes it with her hand. Then she unties the stockings and pulls the dress back over her head and leaves the bedroom without a word.

I lie in a pool of sweat and melted ice – wondering what it is that's just happened.

When I come outa the room I find Alice smoking a cigar and drinking the last of the wine.

Her voice is husky when she speaks.

'Feeling better?'

'Sure. Are you?'

I stayed the night and, when I woke in the morning she was gone. No note, no message of any kind. Like she was a mirage. An apparition. A visual fallacy – that was never really there and only gave the impression of presence.

17
The Hippie Trail

All longings for physical immortality are nothing more than
the aspirations of fools. We should be looking elsewhere for
that elixir of life – not at the body and blood.

———————

After the night with Alice, I collected my gear from the hostel and had a cheap breakfast. Then I headed out on the road to Istanbul. I was walking for about an hour without no luck, when I was picked up by a farmer driving a cattle truck. He didn't speak no English, but he took me over the border into Bulgaria. I was another day trekking and getting sporadic lifts before I made it through Bulgaria and into Turkey, and I walked the final few miles into Istanbul. I carried on through the commercial centre and into Asia to the sound of the muezzin calling the faithful to prayer and the ships' sirens and the shouts from the bazaars.

The days of the Magic Bus were long gone and there weren't so many hippies on the trail in 1994. But there were backpackers, trudging their way through the miles to gain some kinda knowledge of life before they went back to whatever was mapped out for them in the mundane world. So I was surprised to come across a battered old coach pulled over onto the side of the road on the eastern side of the Fatih Sultan Mehmet Bridge. It was covered with peace slogans and had the words "Bombay or Bust" scrawled across the front. There was about a dozen people around the engine, none of them knowing what they were doing.

Having been on the road for so many years in all kinds of clapped-out vehicles, I knew the basics of mechanics, so I took a look.

'It's the sparkplug.'

'Can you fix it?'

'Sure.'

So I did – and earned myself a lift. Most of the people in the coach were young, not more than twenty-five, and full of enthusiasm. They were trying to recreate the days of the old Hippie Trail back in the '60s and '70s, even though the landscape had changed a lot from that heady time. They were surprised and delighted to find out I was an original hippie and they welcomed me with open arms. Cool!

On the way outa Istanbul we came across a street party, with the locals dancing and playing zurnas and davul drums. I joined in with my fiddle and we all got invited to dance in a circle, until the jandarma came and broke it up.

The journey to Ankara was uneventful and I slept a lot of the way. We arrived at a campsite at 8:00pm and cooked up some food. A couple of the bus people played guitars and I joined them on the fiddle for a bit of a jamming session that lasted into the night and we were joined by other campers who sang along and drank Atatürk Forest Farm ale and I finally found someone with an ounce of resin.

We made a late start the following morning for the six hundred and fifty-mile trip to Erzincan. The terrain was starting to get steep, with dusty hills covered with sparse dry grass. Because of our late start, we didn't make Erzincan by nightfall and we had to camp by the side of the road because nobody wanted to drive in the dark. We took turns in standing watch, to guard against local bandits and feral dogs, under a sky that was so clear the stars were like a glittering blanket of diamonds.

Next day, we drove the rest of the way to Erzincan and the hills started to become mountains. I wondered if the old bus'd make it the rest of the way to India. Doubtful. We stopped in a lorry park the following night, but I was woke up several times by loud explosions. Next morning, I asked a couple of English lorry drivers, but nobody seemed to know what made the noise during the night. We drove on to Erzerum but the coach broke down before we got there. This time I couldn't fix it and we had to be towed into town to a garage. The guys at the garage took half a day to fix the bus and I wandered round town while I was waiting. Erzerum was also known as The Rock and it was six thousand feet above sea level. By the time I got there, there wasn't much of the old medieval city left to see, so I just bought some watermelon from a roadside vendor and went back to the garage to escape the flies.

We passed Mount Ararat, where Noah's Ark landed after the great flood, and started through passport control at Bāzargān. The Iranian border guards were hostile and it took us a long time to get through. They searched everyone and all the backpacks and nearly took the bus to pieces, in case we were smuggling drugs. Just as well we'd smoked the ounce of resin and had nothing else, otherwise we could've ended up spending a long time in some shithole prison. One of the bus people was American and they gave him a particularly hard time. When we finally got through, we put our watches forward an hour and a half and moved on. Iran was an edgy place, just like the Balkans, and we wanted to get through it as quick as possible. There was armed guards everywhere and we were stopped continuously as we moved through the country, from village to village. Most of the women wore burqas and I couldn't help thinking about the crazy sailor back in Frisco.

It was almost October and the heat of summer was starting to ease, but it was still hot inside the coach as we drove on down to Tabrīz. We found a proper campsite there with showers and a grassy park and we cleaned up and cooked some rice and green stew and drank some Persian love-tea. Like I said, we didn't want to hang around in Iran, so we set off again down to Takestān. On the way, we passed these villages made completely of mud and I would've liked to have stopped and explored, but the bus people were a bit paranoid and we kept moving. We camped for the night in a windy field on the outskirts of Takestān, before moving on the next day to Tehran. We found a campsite with a pool and I got stomach cramps from the green stew and possible dehydration from drinking local water. I slept outside, under the stars and felt better the next morning. It took us nearly three hours to drive through Tehran and we came out into the Reshteh-ye Alborz to the north.

The bus people wanted to see the Caspian, so we drove through spectacular mountain scenery with steep gorges of grainy rock that gave way to forested hills. We reached the Caspian near Khezerābād and went for a late-night swim in the warm waters of the inland sea.

We decided to take a break from travelling the next day and I just spent the time resting and recovering from the dehydration. Then we moved on across the desert to Mashad and down to the Afghan border at Islam Qala. Again, they was heavy on drugs here and everyone on the bus got nervy. We drove into the compound and the searches started again. In late 1994 the Taliban had a series of military victories in Afghanistan and the country was virtually at war with itself and no place for western tourists, even if they were only passing through. It was a lawless place, with large areas controlled by warlords. The worst fighting was in the east, around Kabul, so we decided to head south, sticking close to the Iranian border, until we could reach Pakistan.

We keep going, down through the foothills of Chalap Dalan and the sparsely populated Pusht-i-Rud and the Dasht-i-Margo desert. We stop only to use the primitive toilets in remote villages that remind me of the loos at the free festivals – raised platforms with a hole cut into them and pigs foraging below. We cook on the bus, porridge and fried eggs with flatbread and chai and we're followed by hordes of local kids looking for baksheesh. At one stop, I buy a light linen shalwar kameez, a kufti and some sandals which are more comfortable than the shirt, boots and jeans I've been wearing up to now. I tell the others to do the same and we'll look like natives – but they don't listen. We see a mirage in the desert – a kind of oasis in the distance with water and trees and people that's not really there. When we get to it, it's gone. In the old days, the hippies would've travelled via Herat to Kabul and then Peshawar. But we can't do that because of the war, so we gotta keep to the remote Registan region, populated only by camels and Baluchi and Pashtun nomads who give us suspicious looks when we drive past in a cloud of sandy dust. And we're all praying the bus won't break down again – or we're done for!

There's nothing out here and I can't help wondering how these people survive. But we come across lone tribesmen walking in the desert – women too, and children. Where are they walking to? Where have they come from? There's nothing here. Then, without warning, we see a couple of vehicles heading towards us – fast. It's pointless to try to outrun them, as we gotta be careful where we're driving and not go into the deep sand. We hope they're not the Taliban. When the armoured jeeps come close, soldiers jump out and order us off the bus. We're searched at gunpoint and pushed around a bit, but we keep our mouths shut and don't give them no hassle. Their officer in charge speaks in Afghani to me, as he thinks I'm a native guide. I try to explain that I'm English, which makes him think I'm some kinda spy.

The others are then sent on their way, with a military escort, and me and my gear are thrown into the back of one of the jeeps and driven off in the opposite direction.

I'm taken to a remote military barracks and thrown into a cell, while they go through my gear – papers and passport and visas and stuff. After a couple of hours, I'm taken to a room and sat on a chair and a couple of armed soldiers stand behind me. This officer comes in and he speaks perfect English, in an upper-class British accent. He turns out to be a major in the Pakistani army and he's here like an "advisor" – to who, he don't say. He says they've confirmed that I'm English and he asks if we knew we were driving through a restricted zone.

'No, we didn't.'

'Why are you here? Don't you know there's a civil war going on?'

'We just want to get to India.'

'Why don't you fly there?'

'We're hippies.'

A smile breaks across his face and he says he remembers all the hippies from back in the '70s coming through his hometown in Pakistan. He was only young then, but it was real enlightening to meet these people from the west and talk to them. It was they who inspired him to go to England for his education and he attended Eton and Oxford, before gaining his commission in the army. He had his men bring me some food and coffee and asks if I'd like to take a shower. I say sure.

It was late by the time I showered, so I stayed the night at the outpost and, next morning, I was driven to the border at Chaman in a military jeep and the Pakistani officer came with me – I think he was glad of the diversion. The border crossing was chaos, with dozens of brightly-painted lorries jockeying for position and horns honking and people with loud voices everywhere. The officer, whose name was Major Khushk, made sure I was processed quickly, as a kind of apology for me being taken away from my travelling companions and detained. But the bus people were gone – I was on my own again. I thanked the major for his help, knowing I'd probably be dead if he hadn't been there "advising". He commandeered a lift for me in a truck which took me through the hills and down onto the plain, as far as the Indus River at Dera Ghazi Khan.

Although it was early October and the end of the monsoon season, the temperature was still in the mid-thirties Celsius on the plains of Pakistan and the humidity was intense. I crossed the road bridge over the Indus and started hitchhiking the two hundred and eighty miles to Lahore. It took me three days and I camped in fields along the way, finally making it into the capital of the Punjab late on Friday evening. I spent some of my remaining money on a hostel room in Lahore, because I was exhausted and needed to sleep for at least forty hours. The place was cramped and sweaty, but I slept well into the next day. Breakfast was *bhatura chole* from a roadside stall because I didn't trust the stuff in the hostel.

While I'm eating, I get talking to this guy who knows London and has family in Southall and he invites me to dinner at his house later that day. He gives me his address and I'm not sure whether I want to go or not. But I'm here to experience things, so I take a tuk-tuk over there at 7:00pm. We eat spicy *bhuna gosht* with rice and some green stuff I don't recognise. We drink tea with the food and then some Pakistani moonshine because Muslims are prohibited from buying alcohol. I'm worried about the 'shine, as I've heard it's made with methyl alcohol and can make you blind, but it would've been offensive not to drink it. The guy's name's Wahid and he introduces me to his family and we talk into the night, mainly about England and specifically about London, even though I don't know the city well, apart from the Family Squatters and the Street Commune back in 1970.

The Indian border was only seventeen miles from Lahore, but getting through it wasn't easy. The Indians meticulously searched my pack and asked me lots of questions about drugs, trying to trick me into admitting I used the herb. They used the old "good cop, bad cop" routine and said that everyone must have, at some time or other, smoked hash. I said I never touched the stuff, I was a strict Christian and didn't even drink alcohol, even though my head was woozy from the Pakistani 'shine the night before. In the end, they got tired of trying to crack me and let me through. I made my way to Amritsar, which wasn't far from the border. I wanted to go there to perform *seva*, which was part of my goal for taking on this trip in the first place – to find what I'd failed to find in America and Britain – the meaning – what it's all about. Like I said, I already knew the answer to "what" – I was looking for the answer to "why". People I met on the road in Britain told me anyone could do seva – work that's offered to god in selfless service.

The Golden Temple was impressive, standing in the middle of its reflecting pool, but it seemed to me that the many tourists were intruding on something sacred – wandering round, gawking and taking photographs while people were worshipping. Sikhism advocates unity and equality of all humankind, engaging in selfless service and striving for social justice for the benefit and prosperity of all. That seemed like a worthwhile place to be and I thought I'd give it a try. Seva was supposed to cleanse the soul and, after Alice, I reckoned my soul needed cleansing. My first night in the free dormitory was comfortable enough. I went to bed early and fell asleep almost immediately. I woke at 4:00am and sat cross-legged on my bunk, closed my eyes and tried to meditate. I prayed to Goddess Lakshmi, reciting the three-part prayer ninety-nine times in my mind. Then I went back to sleep. Just before dawn, I dreamt I was walking towards the main gate of the Golden Temple, along with hundreds of other pilgrims. Someone tapped me on the shoulder. I stopped and I looked back. It was Lizzie. She smiled at me, came close and whispered in my right ear.

'Be brave. Be brave.'

I woke again at 7:00am, when the alarm clock of the man in the bunk on my left went off. It was an old-fashioned, wind-up, spring-driven thing with two bells. The noise was loud enough to wake the whole dormitory – but not him. It took him at least three minutes to hear it and switch it off. Then I was able to think straight again. I sat on the bunk and remembered my dawn dream and thought about it. It wasn't the first time Lizzie came into my mind since I left England.

Later that morning I went down to the local bazaar and bought shoe-cleaning stuff – black polish, brown polish, neutral polish, four pieces of cloth, three wooden handled brushes, three dusters, a sponge and a bag to carry it all in. My mentor in the temple was a guy called Dilip Singh and he was waiting for me when I got back. After saying a short prayer, we both went down to the northern gateway where Dilip arranged for me to be given a space to sit and do my seva. Very soon, the pilgrims were queuing up to leave their shoes with me to be polished. My seva had started!

I cleaned and dried the shoes with a cloth and then applied the polish, using a brush to spread it evenly, then rubbed the polish in. I buffed the shoes with spit and a dry cloth to get up a good shine. The results were spectacular as far as I was concerned. I'd never done this before, but I soon got to be an expert shoeshine boy and my speed increased with practice. I catered for all kinds of footwear: black shoes and brown shoes and white shoes; men's shoes and women's shoes and children's shoes; new shoes and old shoes; worn shoes and even some torn shoes. Dilip Singh said, for seva to be really effective, I needed to do it for forty days – so I started to count. For the first two, I only did the shoe-cleaning seva. But on the third day I started doing other stuff as well. Dilip organised for me to walk around holding a sign with a top-loading poster frame and a square piece of white cardboard, on which was written an announcement in English, Punjabi and Hindi: "You May Leave Your Shoes Here To Be Cleaned and Polished."

This gave me some exercise from the sitting and was a break away from the monotony of the northern gateway.

On the sixth day, I moved outa the free dormitory to a small bedsit-type room, which I rented from an aunt of Dilip Singh's. When she heard I was doing full-time seva at the Golden Temple, she wouldn't accept no rent from me.

'Giving free accommodation to a sevadar like you will be counted as my seva in the Kingdom of God.'

But I insisted she take some money, because I didn't want anything to interfere with the selflessness of the seva or have anything or anyone else contribute – except myself. I was hoping this'd get me where I'd always wanted to go and I wasn't taking no chances. Her name was Geena Kaur and I gave her a month's rent upfront, which more or less cleaned me outa cash, but she said she'd throw in food as well as lodgings for the money and that was me taken care of.

I liked my room. It was spacious, with two large windows that allowed plenty of sunshine in. Not that it mattered much, as I was away from early morning to late evening.

The room had some basic furniture – a bed and a table and two chairs and a small wardrobe. It was on top of a grocery store in the middle of a bazaar, not far from the Golden Temple. There was no rats in the room, but I did see a lizard on the wall on the first night. It disappeared the next day – I don't know where to. Geena Kaur owned two other similar properties in Amritsar, but they were very far from the Golden Temple. This one was ideal for me. A small staircase led to an open air rooftop where I went to sleep on the occasional night in Amritsar when it was hot.

The days rolled by and I took the seva real seriously, working from 9:00am to 5:00pm, seven days a week. My other sevadar colleagues were kinda impressed with me, especially when they realised I was a non-Sikh and from England too. In India, backpackers from England were often regarded like crazy drug-addicts. But not me. I started to grow a beard and stopped having my hair cut. My beard grew real fast and my hair was already long and was now over my shoulders.

'Hello Aaron, you look like a hippie.'

'I am a hippie, Dilip.'

When I wasn't doing seva, I sometimes sat cross-legged on the floor of the temple to meditate. I had no problem with meditating in a Sikh Temple, even though I didn't really believe in a monotheistic god and, as a sceptical agnostic who knew the "what" but not the "why", I was probably closer to Buddhism than anything else. I believed in the "oneness" of all things and this universal "being" was at the core of who I was and who I'd become. But the simplicity of the seva cleared my mind – it helped me to shed the clutter of materialism and concentrated my thoughts on what was important.

The Buddhists advocated removal from the material world and a solitary, singular existence. Here, I was surrounded by a sea of humanity and I started to see it as it really was – for the first time. I saw myself in every man's eyes, in every woman's smile, in every child's wonderment. I was Mohammed and Jesus and Siddharthu Guatama, I was Blake with his visions and Juliana with divine love, Swedenborg with his journal of dreams and Browning with spiritual insight and Alighieri with his hell and Elohim with his heaven and Nostradamus and Donne and Rasputin and Bayazid of Bistun and a hundred million others.

Three weeks into my seva, I called Lizzie.

'What're you up to?'

'Polishing shoes.'

18
Weightless In Nepal

The light grows brighter. Shining with the unbearable attraction of disembodiment – the new reality. Then blurring as my brain performs its evolutionary function and creates the illusion of waking consciousness. Of filtering reality – of selecting from the wider spectrum of awareness – of preventing overload.

––––––––––

It's the middle of November 1994 by the time I finish my forty days seva. I feel refreshed when it's over, ready to find my old life again. The disillusionment's left me and I believe life can be worth living, despite the greed and manipulation. I say goodbye and thanks to Dilip Singh and Geena Kaur and set off for Delhi. I still have a bit of cash, but I know I'll have to get a paying job to survive and provide my fare back to England. I find a cheap hostel in Delhi – a small shared room and the window's a hole in the wall where a brick's been removed. I gotta go to the Nepalese Embassy to get a visa to visit Kathmandu, which ain't no trouble and, after, I take a walking tour round Delhi and have something to eat at a cheap roadside stall. By the time I get back to the hostel, the doors are locked and I have to sleep outside on the street. I have my Afghan clothes on, so nobody takes me for a tourist and I'm left alone.

Next day, I found an agency where they spoke English and they got me a job as a peon at one of the big houses. The wages weren't much and the work was as a general servant, but I needed the cash for train fares and I stayed there until the end of November. When I was ready to move out, I went to Delhi Station to book a seat on the night train to Jaipur. It's the biggest train station in India and it was a nightmare trying to get a ticket. It was my first experience of an Indian sleeper and it was chaos trying to find the right carriage and establishing my entitlement to the booked seat. The rows of open compartments meant I had to sleep with one eye open to make sure my gear didn't go walking during the night. I got to Jaipur at 5:00am and couldn't find anywhere to stay, so I set up camp in Jai Niwas Garden, near the Pink City, only to be moved along by stick-wielding cops. I wandered round the Pink City after that and had some *dal batti churma* to eat with a bottle of water at the Amber Fort. The old fort was huge, overlooking an artificial lake, with long walls all around it, broken by watchtowers that stretched into the distance over the hilltops. Down below, the green valley spread away out towards the distant misty plains.

I catch the bus to Agra at 4:00pm and manage to get some sleep on the way. From there I catch another sleeper to Varnasi. I've decided to take the trains and buses rather than hitchhike because India's huge and I'm running outa time. I got my three-month tourist visa in England and I've already been here over two months and don't want it to expire and get involved in a lot of diplomatic hassle and maybe have to spend some time in an Indian jail. I meet this rickshaw driver who speaks good English and he offers to take me to see where the dead bodies are burned beside the Ganges. The journey's through narrow streets that get narrower and narrower, ending up in a maze of dark passageways. We finally arrive at the river bank where the bodies are burned in large pans. Once they've been burned, they're tipped out into the river where people are cleansing themselves just a few yards away. I expect this to be a spiritual place, but it ain't – at least not to me. It's like a crematorium in England, with one funeral following another in conveyor belt fashion.

I called Lizzie before I crossed into Nepal from India at Raxaul and she said she'd fly out to meet me in Kathmandu. I didn't have much hassle because my visa was in order and they didn't have the same obsession with drugs like they had elsewhere. So I bought some chai from a guy selling it out of a big kettle and pouring it into little clay pots. Once the water'd been boiled, it was OK – or so I hoped. People just threw the pots away when they'd finished and there was loads of them smashed all over the place. It was nothing to do with hygiene, but because of the caste system – so people wouldn't have to drink from a pot that'd previously been used by someone of a lower caste.

The Himalayas were in sight now and they were an awe-inspiring spectacle and the air was cold and rare. The people here were different from India, they seemed preoccupied, almost nonchalant, which was something fresh. It was too cold for my native clothes, so I was back into my boots, jeans and jacket – some guy wanted to buy my jeans, but I wouldn't sell them.

It's only eighty-five miles from Raxaul to Kathmandu, so I decide to hitchhike again. I've hardly any money left and I want to experience the road after so much travel on trains and buses across India. There's few cars on the roads but the second truck I signal stops. The driver seems to be used to picking up hitchhikers and is real friendly, even though he speaks little English. I have a phrasebook and manage to make myself understood. After a truck rest stop and some cool food that the driver insists on paying for, he drops me at a toll booth. The people there also seem used to hitchhikers and have no problem with me asking drivers for a lift from there. Another truck picks me up at the toll booth and takes me the rest of the way into Kathmandu.

The City of Temples was the end of my journey and I arrived after a night trip in the truck to see the sun rise over the Himalayas. My first job was to find a cheap guest house with a squat toilet and a cold shower. Once I stowed my gear, I got my head down and slept for the rest of the day, then went and got a traditional meal of *daal*, *bhaat* and *tarkaari*, along with a local beer called *jaan*. That night I went to a temple with a fifteen-foot high Buddha that was intricately carved and beautifully painted. There was a smell of incense and a chanting coming from somewhere that wasn't obvious. After a while, I looked round to see that I was the only one there – the smell of incense stayed, even after the chanting had drifted off to somewhere distant. It was an atmosphere of pure serenity – and I didn't want to leave. This was it, the culmination of where I wanted to go, and now I sat cross-legged on the floor and allowed myself to feel the lightness of being.

Gradually, the temple became kinda insubstantial. I hadn't taken anything and I knew I wasn't tripping. It got like smoke or mist, undulating and drifting and the walls closed in and then retreated from me. Back and forth. Back and forth. I saw myself when I was real young – with my mother. The wicce-witch. I was moving slowly away from her – in slow motion. She was silently calling to me, but I kept moving away, towards a clump of trees in a translucent landscape. My mother was calling for me to come back. Calling. Calling. But I couldn't hear her voice, just the loud chirping of the birds in the trees as I came closer and closer to them.

The birds are high up in the branches and they're calling to me to fly up and join them, but I don't know how. The branches of the trees are alive, waving to me. Everything's alive – glowing with life – even the stones and the rocks under my feet. And I'm part of it. Everything. I want to be absorbed into it, the oneness – it's me and I'm it. My mother doesn't and she's calling to me – calling. I'm getting further and further away from her, approaching the glowing trees. I don't have no friends like kids of my age and my mother doesn't send me to school because we're on the road all the time. We're always moving and she teaches me herself – her wicce-witch knowledge.

I rarely speak to people, except when they ask me a direct question and people think it ain't normal, but my mother thinks it is. When I do speak, my answers come slowly and are accompanied by little sharp sounds from deep inside my throat. Now, with the translucent landscape and the glowing trees and the calling birds, everything's so alive and animated and exciting and I run towards it, away from reality. If it's reality I'm running from. I get to the clump of trees and look up into the labyrinth of leaves and waving branches and chirping calls. I want to fly up there, but I don't know how. The birds are calling, telling me to come. The branches are waving, inviting me into their arms. The trees are glowing, smiling at me, saying I'm part of them and I can do anything. But I can't fly. I want to fly – but I can't. I can see my mother coming closer, bringing her reality with her. I know she'll soon be beside me and I'll have to go back.

A small bird flutters down, maybe a thrush my mother thinks from her distant viewpoint. It lands on my outstretched arm and stays there. My face is alight now and my mouth moves and seems to be saying something. The bird's beak's trembling, like in some response.

My mother tries to move faster but it's like in a dream and her legs are lead.

Another bird almost tumbles down from the tree, like it's been pushed by some bully-bird up in the branches. This one's bigger than the first, maybe a blackbird. The landscape's growing more opaque and my mother's scared she'll lose sight of me altogether – that I'll be absorbed into the essence of everything – became part of the oneness. Other birds follow the first two – varying sizes and colours, all trying to perch on my shoulders with talons slipping and wings flapping and the noise of chirping growing so loud that my mother's almost deafened. So loud that it's scary. There's a noise from somewhere – like a gong or something. I look round. A monk's come into the temple. The birds fly away.

That night I'm restless in sleep. Dreaming, I think. My father comes into my dream, even though I never knew my father – I know it's him in my dream. He comes to my mother and says he's worried about the way she's bringing me up. My mother's a strong woman and tells him it's none of his business. He says it is. She says he left her – they were never married so he has no rights. He was a lout, spending most of his life on the fringes of the law. She made a mistake with him and now she wants him to go away and leave us both alone. He wants to try again but she says it'd be a waste of time – he never understood her and, if he didn't understand her, he'll never understand me.

As it happens, my mother's also worried about me. Not because I got no friends my own age or because I don't go to school, but because of the birds. They want to take me and she don't want to let them. I paint pictures of the birds on the walls of our caravan and she wipes them away, but they keep coming back. Images of birds – small birds and large birds and indigenous birds and exotic birds and wild birds and tame birds – and whenever I go outside I just want to be with the birds. Most peculiar of all is the fact that the wild birds respond to me. They don't seem to be scared of me like they are of people in general. They perch on my head and shoulders and, when she comes near them, the birds straight away get hostile and try to attack her, swooping at her and screeching, like they're protecting their young from a cat. She don't tell my father this, of course, because he'd only use that against her and try to take me away.

When I wake in the morning, I find feathers on my bunk in the small guest house. At least, I think they're feathers. I tie a band of cloth round my head and stick the feathers into it. Now I look like the guys in that field in Reno who I seen, or didn't see, when I was very young.

On my second day in Kathmandu, I decided to go outside the city for a good look at the mountains. I hiked west into the mid-hills. The environment was remote and solitary, with dense forest and barely accessible paths. It was fresh and vibrant and the trees around me were alive, like in my earlier trance. After an hour and a half of climbing fairly steep terrain, I came to a level place with an incredible view of the valley and the mountains. It seemed like the centre of the universe – you know, when you've reached that spot that's the essence of everything. Axis Mundi. A place you only get to once in your life and you feel like god. I sat down to rest and get my breath back and the lightness came again, just as it did in the temple the day before. The trees came alive and I could see the sap running through their veins. The view got hazy and the sound of birds singing got loud. Down on the slopes, I could hear someone calling to me – calling for me. Shouting for me to come down, that I wasn't ready. But I thought I was. Ready. The voices got louder, searching, but so did the birdsong. I lay on the ground, arms outstretched, and felt myself lifting up – defying gravity. Higher. Higher. Until I was level with the tops of the trees. The bird sounds were reaching crescendo and I closed my eyes so I could drift into the dharma. When I opened them again, I was back on the ground.

I had two more days in Kathmandu – it was Thursday and Lizzie was arriving on Friday with airline tickets and we were flying back to Britain together on Saturday. That night, I dreamed again. My mother was talking to the railroad man and telling him how, when I was born, the hospital was overrun with starlings – an "epidemic" of them some smart-arsed newspaper hack quipped at the time. She thought nothing of it then, but in the months and years that followed, she was always pestered by birds, swooping on me and scolding her, like she'd stolen something from them. I took little notice until I was about three, then my fascination with birds developed. The railroad man thought this was weird and kept his distance from me when we ran away with him to America. By then I was five and had forgot about the birds, but now it was coming back to me – in my dreams. That's if it was true at all and not just dream imagining. I went missing once when I was that young age and when they found me and after all the questions and admonitions, I just sat and said softly, with little chirping sounds sometimes between the words, that I was only talking – to the birds. Ha ha ha.

I was told there was caves in the remote region to the north of Kathmandu, so I trekked up there on the day before Lizzie arrived. It was a religious and wildlife conservation region and for the most part untouched. The morning was hazy and I came to a dirt road lined with elder and oak trees that led to cement steps and I could hear the sound of drums and cymbals and horns and chanting voices in the distance. I followed the steps and the sounds to a kinda hermitage for women and I wasn't sure if I should be there or not. But it was OK, nobody said nothing and I found out the place was called Nagi Gompa and more than a hundred nuns lived there, from young girls to old women. The nuns were there to learn the esoteric vajrayana known as *chöd*, which means severing. I find out that, through practise, they're able to sever their personal demons – neurotic self-cherishing and painful negative emotions. Chöd works in three ways: to transform harmful mental states such as fear and hatred into courage and selfless love; to understand the perfection of wisdom taught by the Buddha in the sutras; and to realise their own true nature.

I was keeping outa the way in a small clearing and just observing what was happening from a respectful distance, when I was approached by a woman in billowing saffron robes.

'There are a hundred and seventy species of birds in the trees above your head.'

'You don't say?'

'Yes, I do.'

Her voice seems to drift from her rather than being spoken. I hear what she says not like sentences. Not like strings of words. I don't hear them – I know them, like complete things! Complete images. The complete meaning comes in the same instant. Not in the clumsy focus of separate sound-symbols – but complete pictures. Concepts. Understanding of what's meant to be conveyed. I hear my mother's voice again, and the sound of waves. The morning mist encircles me, along with the crying and wheeling of seagulls. And I can see them – just a few at first, but more and more flocking with every wing flap and wild cry.

They're aggressive birds and won't let my mother get near me. Then men come with guns and the shooting starts, with blood and feathers flying. I go berserk at the killing and try to attack the men with the guns, kicking them and screeching at them in a high-pitched voice – until my frenzy's spent. I lie on the ground and my mother holds me.

All this I see from the outside, like I'm me but I ain't – a different me – a me who existed once but no more. And it's this place that brings it back – the forgotten memories, if they are memories. This spiritual place of lightness. The past's strange – difficult – perplexing. I don't know what the birds mean, but I know they mean something. A weightlessness maybe? A metaphor? My father comes again and I look pale and drawn to him and he's angry again with my mother. I don't speak to him, my mother tells me not to. My father ain't a man who can express himself real well. His life has, for the most part, been a difficult one – never having much time for thought. Consequently, my mother's too strong for him and he can't cope with her wisdom – her wicce-wisdom. She makes him feel less than what he is and this absent strata of experience, this lack of full character development, prevents him from relating fully to the woman and her strange little son. Sometimes he wants to say more to her, to do more for the boy, but he don't know how. He's scared of things that are alien to him. He can't compete in her arena, so the relationship remains unfulfilled, and even though little rays of hope and loneliness are reaching out from him – they can't quite connect.

When the mist cleared, the nuns were all gone into the little huts that were spread round the hermitage and I left the place to hike back down to the city. I was trying to understand how this place could evoke memories that I never knew I had – recollections I was too young to be able to remember. Maybe they were just figments of my imagination – wishful thinking.

That night I dreamed again, that I had to be rescued from the high branches of a tree and my mother lost her temper in a vain attempt to communicate with me, because I told her real coolly that I was just learning to fly. She shouted and raised her arms above her head and said that I was breaking her heart and I had to stop or I'd be taken away to an orphanage. I shrank back from her and rolled into a ball and she realised she'd lost her objectivity – her sense of justice. She apologised and said she didn't mean it, but I was sobbing now and wouldn't be consoled.

People speak to my mother about psychiatrists and special care and help from people who know more about these things, but she won't have none of it. She says the boy's her son and she'll sort things out and she don't need no shrink's help to do that and who do they think they are anyway? My mother's always been different to the rest and she keeps herself to herself and we're always on the road, so it's nobody's business but hers – and mine – the bird thing. If there is a bird thing. People resent her for being so independent and headstrong and they keep their distance from her – except when they want their fortunes told.

And she don't care – it's the way she is. Then I see her sobbing – in my dream. She looks tired and troubled and I'm not there. I'm gone. She went to my room in the trailer out near Hidden Valley and I'm not there. She's worried because I come home one day with a passenger pigeon feather and she knows that bird's been extinct for a long time. Now maybe I'm gone back there – or gone forward, to somewhere else. And all her wicce-witch skills are useless. Useless.

Somebody said they saw a photograph in some wildlife publication. A small black and white print, buried in the bird section – of a strange, unidentifiable object, almost human in shape, flying south and barely distinguishable among a flock of wild geese.

But it wasn't me, I was in Florica's vardo, heading down to Frisco.

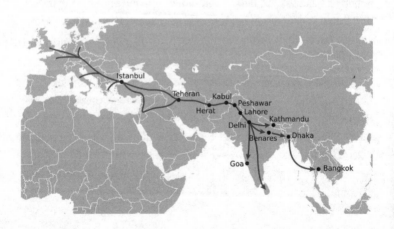

19
The Incident

Sorrow is a goatsong. Sorrow? Samsara. The brute. The coarse. And I don't know if sorrow is the right word for the sentiment – maybe compassion? Except there's no compassion. To move on is to move away – become less human? Subhuman? Or superhuman? It's inevitable. It's reconciliation – of the brute with the beauty.

———

Lizzie flew into Kathmandu on Friday 25 November 1994. We spent the night together in the small guest house then made our way to Tribhuvan Airport on Saturday. I was glad to see Lizzie after almost three months. My money'd run out and I didn't fancy hitchhiking all the way back to Britain. I'd come to Nepal on the Hippie Trail to find what had eluded me all my life, and that night with Lizzie I finally found it. It'd been with me all along – since I first met her in 1970, twenty-four years ago. We lay together in the small bunk and it was good to be beside the woman again – feel her body close to me.

I know it's good for her too because she responds to my touch. Breath comes fast from her mouth when I move my hand across her back. Her eyes are open and staring into mine. Her voice is like velvet when she speaks – words of love and longing. Her face is sensuous and serene. Her hair glows with moonlight and her skin's almost luminous in the semi-darkness. Our naked bodies perspire in the night's coolness, in an embrace that's been waiting all the long weeks. And I feel an overwhelming of emotion for this woman who I've known for so long but have only just recognised – whose body now moves gently in rhythm with my own. All my searching flows away on a river of passion that pulls me down until I'm drowning and the sound of my desire is like some distant animal and her words float like kisses up into the star-filled sky.

Our flights leave at 2:00pm and we get talking to some people on the plane who're travelling back to Europe – two couples, I can't remember their nationality now. We're in the air for a few hours when the plane's diverted for an unscheduled stop at some airport – I can't remember which one. My memory of that evening's hazy – sporadic – incomplete. I know the pilot announces that there's a minor problem with cockpit controls and we'll be airborne again in a few hours. I remember that. The people we're with say let's go get something to eat while we're waiting, but Lizzie don't want to leave the airport in case we miss the flight when it takes off again. I tell her it'll be OK – the pilot said it'd be a few hours. It's growing dark by now and we find a place in a street close to the terminal – a small brasserie on two levels. We go downstairs –

Our friends and us.

It's early evening and quite warm outside – maybe not warm. No, it was November. Not warm, but not cold either. No – I'm sure it's cold, with rain falling. Or is it snow? I know it's early evening, a real busy time. The ambience is cheerful inside, even if outside the evening's dull. Young faces – some happy, some sad. All chattering and chirping and explaining and arguing and ordering this and that. Young shop and office workers from the surrounding vicinity. Young. Now and then a chorus of laughter rises above the background music – I think it's Creedence's "Tombstone", from the "Green River" album – or is it Van Morrison – or Eric Clapton? No, I'm sure it's Fleetwood Mac. It might be any restaurant in any city in any part of the world. But, of course, it ain't – it's this restaurant, in this city, in this part of the world. We study the menu –

Our friends and us.

It reads "loin of veal in marsala sauce" and "bagún agus cabáiste" and maybe "roast beef and yorkshire pud" then again, it could be "khao tom with kaffir lime and ped dang", definitely "parathas and sabz chai" and also some "kasha varnishkas and pumpernickel with hah-lah". We decide on the regional cuisine, which don't appear real appetising when it's eventually served, but it tastes alright. We wash down the food with a carafe of Chardonnay Moulin d'Aurore – or maybe it's Guinness at room temperature in half-pint tulip glasses, or it could even be Punjab brandies or a couple of bottles of Kahlua liqueurs. We raise our glasses in a toast and there's a kind of optimism in the air – a sense of relief about something or other.

The voices around us are happy – they speak in many languages, some we can understand and some we can't. Maybe English or Arabic or Irish or Russian or Hebrew or Thai or maybe all of them –

And others.

I can remember why we've come in here. It's early evening and we're hungry. The airport cafés are crowded with people – even though it's cold, with rain blowing from the west. At least, I think that's the day in question. Maybe it's another – when it's hot and we've come in here to get some shade and shelter from the setting sun – maybe to rest our feet. Or in autumn when everything's soft – trees and grass and birds and words and we're going on a journey, but we come in here first for refreshment or to wait for something. No – it's November, and we're going home. We decide on passion fruit bavarois for dessert – or a basket of mixed sorbet – or borekas de nuez – or murabba el balah.

It's a small brasserie, intimate and cosy. Our new friends sit with me and Lizzie down on the lower level – in a secluded corner. It's nice in here. We whisper confidential things to each other and smile in a knowing way and remember the day before and wish for other days like that. The meal's good after initial reserves and the liquor relaxes us to the point where we feel warm and contented inside. At peace with the whole world. It's so lovely to sit here, away from the rush and bustle of the airport. We talk about the friends we've met and the journeys we've made and will be making, and dreams and hopes and aspirations, and to-morrow and yesterday, and music and love and there's nothing to frighten us –

For us to fear.

Nobody can guess anything's wrong – how can they? How can we? It's such a lovely evening. Early. We've come in here for no specific reason – just a whim – a shot in the dark – the flip of a coin.

Nothing more.

It was either here or there – one or the other. We chose here. It might have been there, if we'd chosen otherwise. But we chose here. It was unanimous – just to spend a short while together before –

What're we gonna to do after? I can't remember. I think we're gonna say goodbye – go our separate ways. Maybe we plan to go to a bar first, have a few beers – or listen to some music somewhere? Or do we want to get some travelling gear or some maps of the vicinity? We want to do something out of the ordinary – something extra-ordinary. Or maybe we're just drifting – going with the flow of the early evening. Golden. It's golden down here – so golden, on the lower level of the brasserie. A golden glow. Maybe it's the decor, or maybe the mise en scéne. I can remember something golden for some reason.

What is it?

Or maybe that's outside – after. I can remember the young waiters and waitresses are real busy, rushing here and there with trays held over their heads as the early evening crowds spill out from the shops and offices and into the cafés and bars around this area. I also remember shivering suddenly and laughing as I tell Lizzie that someone just walked over her grave. It's strange that I can only remember her face like I last saw it – not laughing or talking or joking or eating. Not like it is now, but later –

Outside.

The last time I saw her.

The restaurant's full to capacity – mainly with young people, excited about one thing or another like young people usually are. Talking about tonight, or last night – living like only young people can live. Lizzie and I ain't that young, but our friends are and we once were and we understand the young people around us. We fit in with them and are the way they are. People come and go – probably getting on home or keeping a rendezvous with a lover or just with somewhere else to be at that particular time. Those who go before, or come after –

Such a random thing.

Such a random, indiscriminate thing. An instant in time. A casual, orderless moment. Such a thing.

When we've finished our meal, we try to decide what we should do now, before we gotta say goodbye. No, that's wrong – we gotta get back to the airport. We don't want to miss the flight. I remember one of the young people coming to our table and asking for a light. We don't understand the language, or one of us does – or maybe we know from the body movements. I'm sure one of our friends smokes. No, I'm the one who smokes – one of us gives the young person a light and they say '*shalom*' or '*salaam*' or 'thank you' or '*alwidaah*'. I can't remember where we are – which city. Yes I can – it was Jerusalem, or maybe London or Srinagar or Baghdad or Belfast. No, I'm wrong – it was none of them. I can remember sometimes, but not right now. Maybe I should write it down – when I can remember – to jog my memory –

When I can't –

We decide we should go, as there's people waiting for our table. I remember them standing at the top of the stairs, waiting for a table. They look so hopeful. So eager.

It seems, as we stand up to go, that everything's happening in slow motion. It seems to me, at least, that there's no past and no future – only an eternal present. A golden present, without anticipation or reflection. An essential moment of being, in the golden brasserie. We climb the steps, me and Lizzie and our friends, to the upper level. We move slowly, gradually, step by step, one foot after the other – Lizzie's slower than the rest of us – it's difficult for her, with her crutches. Some of the people who were standing at the top pass us on the stairs, heading for our table, which has been immediately cleared away and wiped down. I remember the floor of the upper level coming into view as we climb the steps. I remember the feet of the diners under their tables. I remember the street lights outside shining through the window. I remember faces all around us – talking and laughing and eating. I can't remember Lizzie's face like it is now, coming up the steps.

Only like it was outside.

It's evening and the tables are full of animated people and busy waiters and waitresses carry trays of food to and fro above their heads. We're a little disorientated at first. We look round for the cashier and see a young girl seated behind a counter near the door.

She's busy on her cash register – many customers are paying their bills. Our friends argue with us over who should pay for the meal. I say I'll do it and they say they will. We eventually agree that it'll be our turn today and they'll pay next time – if there is a next time, because I think I remember this is a farewell meal. Maybe an *au revoir* meal or a fair-weather meal. I'm sure we've planned to meet again. We would've planned to meet again. We wait in the queue until it's our turn at the cash register – me and Lizzie. I can't remember how long we stand in line.

Maybe if it'd been a minute or two less – or if there'd been a customer or two less?

Maybe if the young cashier had been quicker? Maybe if we hadn't argued over who'd pay the bill?

Maybe if there'd been no eternal present – only a past and future?

I move towards the door and wait for Lizzie because she has the money and I have none. I can remember the tremendous noise – the ear-shattering blast and the blinding flash of fire. I can remember being thrown through the glass of the brasserie door and across the street – ending up against the wall on the opposite pavement. I can remember debris raining down on top of me. I can remember the fearful screaming of the injured and the sound of sirens in the distance.

I believe I try to stand up. Inch by inch along the wall. I think I look across the street to where the brasserie used to be and see some of the young people struggling out through fire and smoke. They look traumatised and scared and unsure of what to do or where to go. Many are horribly injured and being helped by friends.

Everybody's screaming and crying and shouting.

Except the dead – who make no sound at all.

I know I search for Lizzie and I find her just where the cashier's counter used to be. I look down at her face – so beautiful inside the brasserie only a moment ago. So golden. It's difficult to distinguish her features now – just blood and bone and a kinda –

Kinda –

I reach down to touch her and realise I got no right arm. The arm on my right side's gone. Just gone. There's no pain, just a lot of blood. Emergency services arrive on the scene and police keep back the crowds who're congregating from nearby streets.

I remember a sensation of falling and I try to fight against it. There's no pain – just a feeling of euphoria. A strange thing, as I remember it.

The scene of carnage seems to grow brighter and brighter until I can't see anything at all, just a brilliant white light. All sounds of screaming and shouting and sirens die away and get replaced by a serene silence.

And I surrender to the light and float away on the calm gentleness.

20
Valediction For Lizzie

*She was out there – half out there – gradually coming back
into a body that was independent of, yet linked to, herself.
And she struggled to find herself, what was left of herself,
when she was half in and half out.*

I spent some time in hospital after the explosion. I don't know how
long – I was sedated for most of it. Then they flew me back to Britain.
I managed to sleep some on the flight, despite the churning in my
stomach – despite the dread. Lizzie was all over the cabin – the sight
of her, the smell of her, the silent sound of her smile. I kinda wished
the door would open and I could jump out into the blueness of the sky
and disappear into the whiteness of the clouds below. I felt truly alone,
abandoned in the endless sky and aimlessly falling to oblivion.

Apart from the shallow sleep, I spent most of the time staring out
the window at my thoughts and wishing I could go back to before I
went on the Hippie Trail and start over again from there. I had nothing
to go back to – no home and no money and no lover and no right arm.

Nothing.

And the moment of truth was fast approaching, as the plane circled
Heathrow for a landing slot. I was forty-six years old and I might as
well be newborn. I had nowhere to run to, no sanctuary, stuck inside
the metal fuselage that was taking me towards my fate. Now and then
the sick feeling in my stomach would go away – for a second or two –
and I'd think maybe I'll be alright, maybe it never happened and it was
all a dream and Lizzie will be waiting when I land. Then I seen dark
and dismal London looming up outa the greyness and my heart fell
down into my boots again.

We came into land and I started the slow walk to the arrivals
terminal, along escalators and moving walkways. Everyone was
watching me, everyone knew I'd left more than my arm in that

brasserie. I could see myself on the CCTV screens – I looked old and beaten and dishevelled. Terminal three arrivals was packed with people. It was a busy time of day and passengers were milling round and looking happy to be home from their travels. I wished I was invisible, able to disappear, to evaporate into the ambience around me – into the milieu of movement and become a ghost. I was getting dizzy and needed to piss. I finally found my bag after forgetting what it looked like and I lifted it off the carousel with my left hand. I seen the green channel looming ahead and two customs officers looking straight at me. Maybe they'd arrest me for being so careless. For losing the thing I'd been trying to find all my life.

'Where are you travelling from?'

'I don't know.'

'You don't know?'

'I can't remember.'

The customs men whispered to each other and I think it was made known that I was a victim of the bombing in November and I was coming home for physiotherapy and a prosthetic limb. The one who questioned me smiled, apologetic, and let me through.

The walk to the exit seemed surreal – like a dream – like I wasn't in control of anything anymore – like my life was drifting away from me, being pulled away from me by uncontrollable circumstances. I carried my bag through to the arrivals lounge – the bright lights and tannoy announcements and babel of voices. Home.

'Lee ... ?'

Someone was coming towards me. A woman.

'Lee?'

'That's me.'

'I'm Angela.'

'Do I know you?'

'I'm Lizzie's sister.'

I didn't know she had a sister, but she had. Angela was thirty-eight and lived in Hertfordshire. She was married and had a husband and two kids. She told me I could come stay with them while I was having my physio at St Albans. We made our way through the crowds to the lifts and then across the footbridge to the car park.

The drive up to Hertfordshire took three quarters of an hour. Angela didn't say much and I didn't encourage her. We pulled into the driveway of a detached bungalow near Berkhamsted and went inside. Angela's husband was Mike and her kids were Danny and Linda, who were aged fourteen and twelve. They showed me to my room and I said I wanted to rest because I was fagged out after the flight. Someone knocked the door lightly later that night, maybe to see if I was hungry, but I pretended to be asleep and they went away.

When I got up next morning, Mike was gone to work and the kids were gone to school. Angela was in the kitchen.

'We were waiting for you.'

'I was tired.'

'No ... I mean ... to bury Lizzie. The funeral's tomorrow.'

They'd flown her body back – what was left of her – a couple of weeks ago and Angela'd kept it at the undertaker's. I didn't know how I felt about that. I didn't know how Lizzie would've felt about that.

'There's compensation.'

'Compensation?'

'Yes, for the ... accident.'

It was no accident. It was deliberate. But the criminal injuries compensation people forked out a hundred thousand for Lizzie and twenty thousand for my arm. Angela said she didn't want the money, so I could have it all.

'I don't want it either.'

'You need it, Lee. You have no home.'

She was right, but I didn't want to think of that just then.

'Where's Lizzie now?'

'At the church.'

'Can I go there?'

'I'll take you later.'

It was cold! January. I didn't realise more than two months had passed and I remembered the winters on the road with Lizzie. After Mike and the kids came home that evening and Angela fed them, she offered to drive me down to the church. I preferred to walk. It wasn't far and the sleety rain'd stopped by then. Spectres played hide and seek all along the lanes. Ghostly hands touching me with cold fingers. Ghostly sounds and smells and flickering shadows that disappeared when I turned my head. I didn't know this part of the country. I didn't know this life – this family. Angela told me she and Lizzie shared that life down the long years ago. Lizzie was a restless soul and had to go, when she was old enough. She stayed – Angela. The first time Lizzie came back was when I dropped her in Hemel Hempstead to set off on the Hippie Trail. She didn't want to – wasn't going to, but Angela came across her in the street one day and pleaded. Now, walking along the lanes with the poltergeists, I wished they'd just left me alone. I wished they'd kept them away from me – the buried memories of long ago. I'd come to terms with my own childhood in Nepal, and I wanted to remember Lizzie like she was on our last night together – in the guest house in Kathmandu. That was my Lizzie.

This here was Angela's Lizzie.

Lizzie's body – what was left of it, had been taken to a church near the village.

That's what Angela said. It was the second time she told me, in case I didn't hear her the first time. But I did. We was going there now, me and her, to pay our respects before the funeral tomorrow. I shivered as we walked along. The ghosts screamed at me from the trees, they ran round me and away across the fields to some place I didn't know. To wherever they lived. I shouted at them to go away and leave me alone, but they kept coming back.

And back.

If only.

If only I hadn't gone to Nepal – if only I'd come back the way I went – if only I'd kept some money – if only we hadn't met those people on the plane – if only we hadn't been diverted – if only the airport cafés hadn't been so busy – if only we'd been a bit earlier – or a bit later.

But it was too late for all that now. I'd said the same things to myself a million times already. I knew Lizzie lived on, all around me – but that didn't make it no easier. And now I was going to the church with Angela, who I'd only just met but it seemed like I'd known her forever. I didn't want to go there, but I was being pulled by some bond or promise from long ago – some absurd umbilical cord that'd have to be severed. It was dark in the January evening and no moon or stars was visible in the sky. A wild wind played among the branches of the trees and whispered words of love in my ear. Words I didn't want to hear, words that reminded me of the times –

The times!

The lights were dim inside the old church and I could see candles flickering up near the altar. They cast an eerie light over the coffin and bier – motionless in the gloom. It reminded me of that other church, many years ago in Cornwall, when I hallucinated and saw the ghost of someone from another life. That memory made me feel anxious – maybe even scared. It was ridiculous to be scared, I was a man of the world – seen many things – experienced many things. Knew the "what" – and Lizzie was the "why". And the why was gone – for me. I didn't have to be scared, but the anxiety stayed. It wouldn't leave me.

I moved slowly forward, taking each step like I expected to have to turn and run at any second. I sat in the front row, looking at the coffin, which was covered with wreaths and cards. I lit a cigarette. Angela looked at me like I was crazy.

'You're not allowed to smoke in here.'

'Why not?'

'It's against the law.'

'So's a lot of things.'

Angela sat beside me in the pew and took the cigarette from my hand. She put it in her own mouth and took a long pull, then she replaced it between my fingers.

'I suppose you're right.'

She stood up and moved towards the coffin – placed her hands on the brass handles, gripping them so tight her knuckles turned white. She seemed to be reading the cards and the messages on the wreaths. The smoke from my cigarette spiralled up into the gloom of the church. We didn't speak for what seemed like hours – but was really only seconds. The cigarette burned out and I dropped it onto the floor. Angela turned to me from the coffin.

'Do you want to see her?'

'No!'

'Why not?'

'I'm trying to remember her on the last night we spent together.'

'Did you love her?'

'Sure.'

Suddenly, Angela brushed all the cards and wreaths off the coffin, scattering them across the nave. Flowers cascaded everywhere. I was surprised, but said nothing. She opened the coffin lid and looked inside, beckoning to me to come. I hesitated for a second or two, then got to my feet. Apprehension almost choked me, but something made me move forward. There was nothing to be scared of – was there? Lizzie didn't look like I thought she would.

They'd done a good job on her and her lips had a half smile on them, like there was a joke only she was getting. She looked like she was still alive, except for a black mark down the left side of her head and face that they couldn't cover up. Still a beautiful corpse!

I put my hand inside the coffin and touched her, to reassure myself that she was really dead. I told myself this was only the shell, the mechanical bit. There was no soul, no emotion, no pain, no love, no hate, no recriminations.

No life.

I wanted to ask Angela why she did what she just did, but she was sobbing and I kinda knew anyway. OK, Lizzie never told me why she tried to commit suicide on the wall-of-death that night back in 1970, but I had a feeling it was something to do with her father. Now I knew for sure.

I spoke softly to Angela.

'Maybe we better go.'

'Not yet.'

We sat back down in the pew.

'Were you there ... when it happened?'

'Sure.'

'Of course you were ... your arm got blown off. I forgot.'

'That's OK.'

There was a kinda resentment in her voice, like because I was there when it happened and she wasn't.

We was two strangers, sitting there, but in a way we weren't. We was linked by the woman we both loved – even if Angela didn't know that. We was relying on each other now, for strength and comfort and hope and forgiveness.

Lizzie left home when she was fourteen and nobody really knew her after that, except me. Angela was eleven when Lizzie left and nobody else knew her before that. We was the only two people who really knew her – before and after.

Lizzie hated herself for leaving, but she had no alternative. She couldn't stay – if she had, there would've been a lot of trouble. The father was glad to see her go – relieved to be rid of her. She would've caused trouble, sooner or later. She hated leaving her sister and there was resentment in Angela's eyes the day she left – the same resentment that was in her voice now. Like she'd been betrayed. But Lizzie had to go – there was no choice! They'd never written or kept in touch because Lizzie was always on the move – always moving and nobody knew where to find her.

'I'm sorry ... '

'For what?'

'That she left you.'

There was no reply. She just accepted the apology – or maybe she didn't accept it. I closed the coffin lid and started to pick up the cards and flowers. She didn't help me. I arranged them as best I could on the coffin and then went to sit beside her in the pew.

'Can I have one of your cigarettes?'

Before I could open the packet, a priest came out from the sacristy behind the altar. I was startled by his sudden appearance because I'd kinda forgot about the other world – the world of reality, the real world. It was like everything else had faded away, except for Angela and Lizzie and the coffin and the night.

The priest looked at the cards and flowers still strewn in the aisle.

'What happened?'

'I'm sorry father, we had a slight accident. We'll make it all right.'

'Very well, but I'm closing up the church now. You can leave by that door near the chancel. I'll leave it open, just pull it to behind you when you go.'

The priest closed up the main entrance and disappeared back into the sacristy. A door slammed and a heavy bolt was pushed into place. We heard his car starting up outside. He drove away and silence came back.

I took out my cigarettes and we both lit up. We sat there for a while, not speaking. We were alone again, even though Lizzie's dead body lay before us. It started to get cold.

'Think we better go now.'

'Not yet. Let me have another cigarette.'

'Ain't you got any of your own?'

'I don't smoke – as a rule.'

I gave her another cigarette and, suddenly, the lights went out and the church was filled with grotesque shadows from the candle flames. I got to my feet.

'Come on.'

'I can't see too well ... wait for me!'

Angela took hold of my hand and I led her towards the chancel door. I turned the metal handle but the door didn't open. I tried again. Angela helped me pull, but the door was locked. The priest was obviously mistaken. Someone'd locked the door earlier and he never realised it.

I was scared again – was this déjà vu? Like back in Cornwall when the ghost nearly raped me. I took a candle from the altar and went down to the main door. That was locked too. Angela stumbled after me, not wanting to be left alone. I walked back up the aisle and past the altar to the sacristy. The door inside was locked. There was no way out!

Angela began to light more candles, placing them in a ring so we were encircled by the flickering light. It seemed to her that she'd be safe within the circle. Outside was darkness, but she was safe inside the ring of light.

Time meant nothing to me and seemed to stand still. I can't remember how long we sat there. Every time a candle started to burn down, Angela made me replace it with a fresh one. I'd go to the altar each time and get another – she was scared to step outside the circle and relied on the light to keep her safe. After a while, she started to sob. I watched her, but didn't try to comfort her. It was like I couldn't move, like I'd been petrified by some sorcerer's spell and was condemned to stay motionless forever.

'Why don't you do something?'

'What you want me to do?'

'Get us out of here!'

'I can't. You know that.'

'You must! You must!'

'Have another cigarette.'

I wanted to help her, but there was really nothing I could do. We stayed inside the circle of light as Lizzie came through the door. She took Angela away and locked her in a safe place. She smiled reassuringly and put her finger up to her lips. Be quiet.

Their father wanted love – their mother never gave him what he wanted. So he demanded love from his girls. It was his right, after all he'd done for them. It wasn't much to ask – was it? Afterwards he was violent, like it was their fault, like they made him do it, like they enticed him, made him drunk and lured him into this world of desire and abuse and violence and turmoil. He'd do something for the church to make amends. They'd be punished – the kids. The mother never interfered. She closed her eyes and her ears. She was scared of him, scared of finding out, scared of knowing, scared of her own frailty, scared of confronting the thing that lived in her own house. Then she died.

It was getting colder. Angela was shivering. The church lights and heating were obviously on some kinda timer switch. Her voice shook when she spoke.

'I have to get out of here.'

'Won't Mike come for you?'

'He's probably gone to bed, and the kids. I said we'd be a while.'

I took off my coat and put it round her shoulders.

'I got ill when Lizzie left.'

'I'm sorry ... '

'I wanted to write to her, to call her, but I didn't know where she was. It was like she'd died, like she'd been swallowed up by the earth.'

'Maybe you should've left too?'

'How could I?'

'I don't know.'

'She should have took me with her.'

'How could she?'

'I don't know.'

She was quiet for a while – reflective. I finished my cigarette and flicked the butt down the aisle. Sparks flew. The circle of light flickered violently as a breeze came from somewhere and blew at the candle flames. We sat close to each other. She wiped her tears away with a red handkerchief and rocked to and fro and hummed a tune that she remembered from long ago.

All the darkness outside the circle was filled with ghosts. They moved round the ring of light and asked to be let in. Angela told them to go away but they wouldn't. She shouted at them and they disappeared for a time, but came back again and again. I kept the candles lit and she rocked and hummed. She could smell the heavy whisky breath. She could hear the crying and the pleading – Lizzie first, until she went away. Then her. She could feel the fear and revulsion and pain. There was no more candles on the altar to keep the circle intact. The ghosts were getting in!

'No!'

Angela sank to her knees. She started to rock to and fro, to and fro. Then she collapsed onto the floor and started to convulse, like she was having some kinda fit. I tried to help her. I rolled up my jacket and put it under her head, but she kept on shaking. Foam began to ooze from the corners of her mouth and her eyes rolled in their sockets. More candles were going out and more ghosts were getting in. I had to do something.

I stepped outside the circle and went to the coffin – swiped all the cards and wreaths off again and opened the lid. Then I gently lifted Lizzie's broken body out and carried it back and laid it beside Angela. She stopped shaking and the convulsion left her. Then she slept.

The candles flickered out one by one, but an inner peace glowed through the darkness of the old church and the two sisters lay together like in their confused and frightened childhood – until the first streaks of morning light came through the stained glass of the windows.

I lifted Lizzie up and put her back in the coffin and replaced the lid. Ravens circled outside the church, looking for an early breakfast. Their harsh cawing woke Angela and she looked up at me, trying to remember where she was. I was smoking a cigarette and she sat up slowly, rubbing sleep from her eyes.

'What happened?'

'You fell asleep.'

'The candles?'

'They went out.'

I passed the cigarette to her and we both sat in silence for a while. Rainbow light shone down from the stained glass windows and struck the bier. The coffin seemed to be surrounded by a sort of bluish luminescence – just for a few seconds, then it passed on. We heard a heavy bolt being drawn back and a key being turned in a lock. Then the priest emerged from the sacristy. He stared at us in disbelief for a moment, his mouth opening but no words coming.

'We got locked in.'

The priest rushed across to the door by the chancel and tried it.

'I'm so sorry. It must have been dreadful for you. I don't know how this could have happened.'

'We're OK.'

'Are you sure?'

'Yes, we're fine.'

We didn't leave immediately, but watched as the priest fussed around, clearing away the candles and picking up the cigarette butts and the cards and the wreaths. Then I stood up slowly and pulled on my jacket.

Outside, I turned my collar up against the early morning chill. Angela walked on ahead as I stopped to light another cigarette. I thought I heard a sound behind me and looked round quickly.

But it was nothing – just my imagination.

21
The Commune

There's not all that much difference between the living and the dead – except that the dead are dead and the living are still alive – in the human context at least – in the body and blood context. Such a small thing. Such an insignificance.

I stayed with Angela until the summer of 1995. By then I'd had my physiotherapy and they gave me a prosthetic right arm. It didn't do anything, just hung there lifeless, but it looked better than the sleeve of my jacket pinned up. My fiddle playing days were over – I knew that. But by the time I left Hertfordshire the criminal injuries compensation money had come through and I bought myself fifty acres of land with a big, crumbling old farmhouse and a few barns on it. It was on the edge of the Lake District, close to Ambleside, but remote from it at the same time. I just wanted to get away and be on my own, kinda leave the world behind for a while. But it didn't work out like that. People from the old days got to hear about the place and many of them came to stay and park their vehicles on the land. It was a transitory place, people coming and going all the time, and the local press started to call it a "commune".

As time went on, there was all sorts of rumours and reports about orgies and other kinds of deviancies going on and that didn't surprise the locals because they always knew the place was the root of all evil. There was an incident in January 1996 when a woman was assaulted near one of the barns and the police found an empty cider flagon – but nobody was able to identify the culprit. Probably a passer-through who was long gone the next day. But it led to more rumours, and stories have a tendency to grow as they travel and the place got itself a dangerous name. Some said there was a ghost haunting the area, but others believed it was some kinda crazy person and there's never no smoke without fire and strange stuff was going on. I was interviewed by the cops.

'What's going on, sir?'

'Many things, officer. Most of which we're totally unaware of.'

'I can see that!'

'What do you know about black hole singularities?'

'Very little.'

'That's what I mean.'

The cop didn't have a sense of humour. Not many of them do, in my experience. Maybe he just wasn't happy in his work and would rather have been somewhere else.

'The woman, did you know her?'

'There was no woman, officer. It was a hallucination.'

I waved to the cops as they drove away. I knew they'd probably be back.

It turned out she was a vagrant, taking shelter in the barn. After making the complaint to the cops, she disappeared and nobody ever seen her again. Then I got sick – not physical sick, but more in my head. I think it was the after-effects of Lizzie's death. Post-traumatic stress disorder they call it these days. I'd never grieved properly for her and it was all inside me, trying to get out. They sent for a doctor, the people around me. I told him some things he couldn't understand and he gave me a sedative before making his report.

'There's really nothing wrong with him.'

'There has to be something wrong with him.'

'Physically, he's in good shape.'

'And mentally?'

'Lucid, in control. Not paranoid nor schizoid nor depressed nor obsessed.'

They couldn't understand. There had to be some logical explanation for my behaviour.

'He's simply telling the truth. All the time.'

'Dear Jesus!

How positively and totally dreadful – to tell the truth all the time. Such a selfish thing –

The doctor said I'd reverted to a kinda childlike state, even though I certainly wasn't suffering from dementia or Alzheimer's. A childlike state insofar as the truth's concerned. I'd regained the child's candour and, while this was charming in a kid, it could be extremely embarrassing and dangerous in an adult. They tried to absorb what the doctor was saying, but situations without circumstantial explanations were alien to them.

'What should we do?'

'You must keep him isolated for the time being. I've given him a strong sedative.'

The doctor gave them a container of capsules and a knowing look. They came to where I was lying motionless and bent over and looked into my open eyes, which didn't register their presence. They were worried for a moment, but I seemed peaceful enough, with my new childishness. My new child candidness. Child truth. Child lies. Child eyes.

I was in some sort of trance, like I was dreaming – half-smiling in my equilibrium.

Still.

The stillness that allows the mind to know what is, that eliminates the need for work and struggle and conflict and drama and introduces an independence from life's battles. Still and safe, so the mind's relieved of the need to monitor the environment around it for opportunity and danger. The time of vision. Altered states. Knowing. The imaginal field still evolving and separate consciousness sampling separate elements and no unanimity as to the final form of reality. And even though I'd changed, I was still all I once was. What a difference a day makes. If it was just a day. Or several days. Several worlds. Several universes.

Lost in the symphony of the universe. Beyond the universe. Beyond the beyond the beyond.

I got up late one summer night – when they were all in bed. I checked they were asleep and then left the place I was in and headed for the closest barn. There was no light and no noise – except for the constant hiss of insects. The barn door opened with a squeaking sound and I went in. I realised after a moment or two I was holding a flagon of cider. I took a slug from the flagon, then lit a cigarette and moved slowly through the old building.

Searching. I knew no one was there, but I kept looking – went everywhere and looked back out the door at the black primitive night. I felt no guilt. No fear. I understood it all. The insects devoured each other outside the window – one life for another. Death giving life. From one to the other. The two inexorably entwined. Two sides of the same coin. Each unable to exist without the other.

I lay on the straw and knew we'd have to meet again to end it. She'd have to end it. It wasn't over.

There'd be another time – to make up for what happened. If there could be any making up – now. Maybe lay the ghost in her like it was laid to rest in me. She'd know it too – wherever she was. And she'd come back to finish it forever. Because she'd know, just as well as I did, that the love thing we were looking for was that moment when two souls who

– in words and actions

– thought they were separate

– saw

– in knowing

– they were one.

Rumours were running wild all over the commune. The people there couldn't handle my self-obsession – calling me a lunatic and a crazy schizophrenic nutcase and how it was lucky they found out now and not later. It got into the media and was a godsend for all the holier-than-thous who wanted the commune closed down and burned to the god-forsaken ground. And although people expressed their revulsion with the menagerie, they loved nothing better than someone else in the dock. They called me a criminal and, even though there was no logic to their assumptions, they reckoned I was a crook and a confidence trickster and a lying manipulator.

That was outside.

Inside, the person I was had been taken away in the night by the faeries and this thing had been left behind in my place. This bad thing. This honest thing. They didn't love me anymore. They hated me. Because I didn't reflect anymore what they believed themselves to be.

I reflected what they actually were.

I didn't know them anymore. I didn't understand them – what they wanted from me. Nobody liked being told the truth. And they forgot I was human – I was less than human. I had the insect in me and they didn't like that because it was still in themselves – even though they'd never admit it. Instead, they decided to hold with the convenient maxim that a lie can always get to be, with constant repetition and a good haircut, the truth. I wasn't Lee or Aaron anymore and never would be again, because they believed I'd broken the great taboos of compromise and diplomacy.

I got increasingly restless and the tranquillisers had less and less effect on me. I insisted on telling the people what they didn't want to hear. They told me not to but I wouldn't listen.

I wasn't aware of time passing. Or maybe I was aware but just didn't care. It was unimportant. Inconsequential. Irrelevant. I started to be preoccupied. Meditative. Staying in a restricted space for most of the time.

In the outside world, other stories were hitting the headlines and they gradually forgot about me. I took to writing. Prodigiously. Obsessively. Reams and reams of stuff. Pages of words that made no sense to anybody but myself and mathematical formulae that would've stymied a rocket scientist. I said it was my thesis. My gospel. A bible.

It'd explain everything to everybody. There was no need for anybody to feel afraid. Or ashamed. Or guilty. Ever again.

But the hippies gradually drifted away – the kindred spirits. They washed their hands of me and the commune broke up and I found myself alone. Which was OK, because I knew it was inevitable, the same way I knew everything else. And, in any case, all things had to separate in order to come together again. So it was cool.

All I needed to do was explain, but it was difficult. It wasn't that I was scared of anything out there – of the police or the public or the pedants or the press. I wasn't. I just thought the job was too big for one man alone. Even Jesus had twelve apostles. So I gathered a group of misfits round me.

Hallucinogenic visionaries and disillusioned environmentalists and political pariahs and sexual nonconformists and medical limners and religious dissidents and equalitarians and globophobes and transgenics and travellers and down-and-outs and freeloaders.

The commune on the edge of the Lake District got to be an open house for philosophers and prophets and gurus and sages and seers and witch doctors and drifters of all declensions – they came and went and the barns was always full of people at any time of year.

They listened to my words and accepted them because they all wanted something – were looking for something. The truth. Or the pseudo-truth. Or the quasi-truth. Or the nouveau-truth. Or the neuro-truth. Or maybe just a meal-ticket.

They came from all over the world once word got out. A new messiah. Offering to share with anyone who was willing to listen. The commune soon attracted even more notoriety than before and was raided at regular intervals by cops and drug squads and vice squads and special branch – looking for conspiracies and narcotics and bail-jumpers and easy books and backhand bribes. I was in and out of court all the while. The judges didn't appreciate my quantum logic in defence and I was fined many times and served a couple of short stretches in prison for a variety of misdemeanours.

I got to be notorious, like the commune, with subliminal stories in the media about orgies and black magic and child sacrifice going on inside the grounds – all the time.

My previous acquaintances doing backgrounders and calling me a Charles Manson and a Timothy Leary and a Karl Marx and a Ted Bundy and a lot of other undesirables all rolled into one. A dangerous man. A threat to stable society. They all said somebody oughta do something about me. The media screamed "CLOSE DOWN THE COMMUNE FROM HELL!". Burn it down! Scatter the degenerates to the wind! After first crucifying Lee or Aaron – or whatever I called myself – in the marketplace. Because the whole evil thing was a blight on the azaleas and dogwoods of Lake Windermere.

I got the word out all right. But it wasn't the word I wanted the world to hear.

Me and my guests weren't greatly concerned with immediate issues of politics or society or finance or conservation. We concentrated on the bigger issues. I dispensed the knowledge and put my writings into book form, which I distributed to my disciples. It was difficult for me to know for sure if these people were really interested in what I had to say – or if they were just interested in a free place to stay for a while. But I believed that, if even some of it sank in, then I was doing good.

I tried to get my book distributed to a wider readership but nobody'd take it on – even for its curiosity value. A couple of dozen copies were handed out on the streets of Bradford and Blackpool by a few of my more dedicated followers. But the people just threw them away. Or tore them up. Or set fire to them. Or spat on them.

Nobody really wanted to listen to what I had to say – even the chatterers and the camp followers. They listened for a while, but eventually drifted away to more mundane things. And I couldn't blame them. Didn't blame them. The word was going nowhere outside the commune. And there was stagnation inside – on the inside. They were only human – didn't know what I knew – hadn't seen what I'd seen. So how could they know? How could I realistically expect anyone to understand? Yet. It was too early in the evolutionary process.

They still thought in terms of the images that obsessed them – in terms of who they were – or who they thought they were. Identity. Whatever that meant? They still clung to it, even though it meant nothing no more. Identity was still part of what made them human, so they could never understand, no matter how many words I spoke or how I explained it. The universe was an overwhelmingly hostile entity to them and its nature was obscure – writing its secrets in mathematical code that was only understood by the very few. They didn't care that all objects had influence over each other – even though those influences weren't apparent. That Time and Self were different sides of the same coin. Or that real happiness was always insignificant and never grand nor dramatic. Or that togetherness told the truth and separation spoke confusion. Or that the end was always implicit in the beginning.

I got more and more disillusioned as time went by. I wondered if I'd done the right thing in coming here. Maybe things couldn't be changed? Many tried before me – many. All failed. Maybe things just had to follow their own route and nobody could change that – no matter how much they knew?

Then a strange feeling started to obsess me, of being watched by somebody. Something. Just a feeling. A sense of eyes on me. Unnerving. There was always lots of people coming and going and I was rarely alone, yet this was singular. Not part of the whole. Separate. I couldn't think what it might be – maybe vigilantes setting up surveillance. Or the police. Or the press. They all watched me from time to time – until they got fed up and went away, only to come back again when they had nothing better to do.

Paranoia? No such thing. Guilt? Didn't know it.

The feeling of being watched grew stronger and stronger. I knew something was there – in the commune – but I couldn't see it. Couldn't catch it – whatever it was. Sometimes I'd sense it behind me, but when I turned there was nothing. Nobody. Or across a room full of people. Staring. But I couldn't visualise it. It was invisible. Stalking me. Prowling. Waiting for the right time to strike.

Gradually, the population of the commune thinned out. Natural selection – of an unnatural collection. Other things were contributing too, people ultimately couldn't understand what I was trying to say – so the cabbalists and transcendentals took off to the next new phenomenon. The freeloaders weren't getting loads for free anymore. And there was very little publicity these days for the camera cravers. A few psychedelics and schizophrenics hung around for a while longer, not really knowing where they were – or why they were there. And the fewer people occupying the commune, the stronger the feeling of being observed grew.

I started to take notice of those still around – which was a lot easier now than before. One or two were long-termers who'd been there from the beginning. Others came recently and probably wouldn't stay for long. And a few I wasn't sure about – could've been there a long time or maybe just turned up that day. Anonymous people, who you'd see every day and still not recognise – not know anything about. Or want to.

All sexes and all ages.

Sexes and ages blending into one another until everybody seemed androgynous and perpetual. Except for one. A woman. Maybe forty or a little older – it was difficult to tell. Difficult to know precisely. I noticed her more than the others. She stood out among them because she walked with crutches. I caught her watching me. Her eyes. Watching me. Eyes I recognised from somewhere before, even if I didn't recognise the woman who owned them. She seemed like a wraith. An illusion. A hallucination. A mirage. A vision. Anamorphic.

There when I observed her – disappearing into the fabric of the commune when my concentration was distracted. Fading away when my mind focus shifted. Concentration on the individual bringing her into being – lapse of attention allowing her to return to the commune. But the eyes remaining. Watching. Observing. Waiting. All around. Looking inside my soul. I could feel them burning – dissecting and destructuring. Knowing everything. Being everything. Being the act. Being the guilt.

The guilt was back! Like an old friend. Like a missing but essential part of the whole. I knew this and felt a contentment in the knowledge.

'Lizzie?'

'You've recognised me, at last.'

'It is you?'

'It's me.'

Now that I said the name, it was like I always knew it was her. The admission sealed the fact.

'What're you doing here?'

'You knew I'd come back.'

'Why?'

'Because you wanted me to.'

'Did I?'

I couldn't remember. I didn't remember wanting her to. Maybe I did – but I couldn't remember it. Maybe I asked her because I knew I could – knew she would.

She moved closer to me. Closer. She was right, I did want her to – I knew she'd come back, because it could never be over until she did. Then I felt the overwhelming guilt and I backed away, looking for someplace to hide inside myself. But there was nowhere. My hiding places were all gone. I was naked. And maybe that's what it was – what I wanted.

Elimination. To give up the ghost. Become part of the – part of the – absorbed into – into – falling. Falling. Into the flames.

'Can you kill me?'

'No.'

'Please ... '

'No. It wasn't your fault.'

Then she was gone, back into the commune. I didn't know where. Maybe waiting in the barn for me to come, so she could kill me. I didn't know whether she was real or a figment of my imagination. Coming and going. Appearing and disappearing. Haunting me.

Bringing back old feelings. Old emotions. Old instincts. Desires I didn't want. Dragging me back to when I was a human being. Guilt. Anger. Elation. Despair. Desire. And all the others. Coming at me like old ghosts.

I talked to the other people in the commune for reassurance. The ones who were left. But they were no help.

'Get out!'

'What's the matter, teacher?'

'Get the hell out. All of you!'

'But ... '

I went berserk. Shouting and ranting and raving like a lunatic.

'I don't want you here anymore.'

'What about your message?'

'Fuck my message!'

'We gotta tell the world.'

'I don't care about the world. Fuck the world too!'

Because the world didn't want to listen to the truth. Because it was all too confused. Traumatised. Neuroticised. Desensitised – to the pathology of it.

The guests grew surly. Snarling. Like the other dogs on the outside.

'You're a bastard, just like the rest of them.'

'Sure I am. Now fuck off!'

I got violent – always a way to overcome frustration. Anger masking guilt. Hostility holding back humiliation. I threw furniture round and tossed things through windows and ripped down curtains.

The hangers-on gathered up their stuff and headed for their various vehicles. Beaten up old psychedelic vans and pick-ups and a few customised Harley Davidsons. Others left on foot, carrying backpacks. I drove them all out, like Christ with the temple moneylenders.

I followed them down to the gates to make sure they left. Shouting all the way. And they went. Because there was nothing worse than a bitchy benefactor – a conscientialist who'd lost his cool.

Now I was alone again – not quite alone. But it felt like it was how it was meant to be. Always. And I'd only just realised it. There was nobody left around now but myself. And the ghost.

'Lizzie!'

I searched the commune for her – everywhere – but I couldn't find her. She was always one step ahead of me. Or one step behind me. I knew she was there, somewhere. I could feel her eyes. Watching. Waiting. Sometimes I could hear her voice. Whispering. I wanted her to leave like the others. I wanted to get rid of her, to throw her out – so I could get my mind right again – focus my thoughts on what was real and important. I was starting to forget it, some of it, all of it. Starting to go back. Regress. Because I was obsessed with Lizzie.

Preoccupied by a ghost. If she was a ghost. Sometimes I didn't know for sure. She seemed like a ghost – the way she could melt into the essence of the commune.

But she wouldn't go, no matter how much I shouted or threatened or pleaded or ordered or asked.

The commune's still and empty, except for eyes watching. No life. No feeling. No humanity. No warmth. Even though there's no cold. No right nor wrong. No words. No conflicts. Just concepts. Of what is. What was. What will be. Between one thing and another. Neither one thing nor the other.

Aaron's tired. He drinks some cider straight from the flask. Fatigued. Exhausted. He moves outside, where he can't tell if it's night or day. But he can hear the insects. He carries the flask in his hand and feels the grass alive under his bare feet. The sky's mauve and there's no wind. He can't see the million stars he knows are overhead. More than a million. Billions. Beyond the mauve sky. He moves, instinctive, towards the nearest barn. Only a hundred yards away. Fear fills him. Gives an extra edge to his senses.

Tiredness leaves his body. Evaporates into stagnant air. He's alive. Human again. Adrenaline rushes through his veins and the short hairs stand up on the back of his neck. He knows again who he is, what he is, as he moves closer to the barn. Every step becomes its own little lifetime. Death. Life. Birth. Again. Again.

The barn's quiet. He listens. Quiet. The door's open and he steps inside. He moves silently. No sound. He pauses and takes another slug from the cider flask. Sees the ghost sitting on the straw – looking at him. The danger's palpable, like a heartbeat. A separate entity between them. His brain's full of white noise. Her features are obscure – except for the eyes.

Was she waiting for him? Did she know he'd find her? Did she want him to find her? Now. After all the haunting. He moves closer to the eyes that reflect his own. There's no guilt in them. Everything's acceptable within the context of the eyes. He touches her and she doesn't react. She lifts her face to him and he kisses her gently. His hands move across her body, to make sure she's real. She is. A light reflects in the corner of his eye. Glinting from the blade. He ignores it. Knows it's there but wants it to come. To end it. End everything. She lifts the blade. High over her head. Behind his back. He knows it's there. He sees the glint of steel in the corner of his eye and he waits for the pain – to end it. End everything. He looks deep into the eyes.

I jerked back violently away from the woman. Cider spilled across the straw from the flask that dropped from my hand – stained the ground a golden colour. My face was full of horror as I backed away to the wall.

'I'm sorry!'

She didn't reply. I could see the anger in her eyes.

'I'm sorry!'

She turned her face away from me and stared to move towards the door.

'I'm sorry!'

I crept away, back out into the insect night, across the wild grass. Head hurting and heart on fire. The black sky was infinite with a million stars overhead. I quickened my pace until I was running.

Running.

Running.

Away from the commune. Away from the primeval darkness.

22
Millennium

I've seen the fall from Eden. I know the real trauma of that forgotten moment, when man stepped out of the quantum and into time. I recognise the brain for what it really is – a tool of survival – evolved for the purpose of maximising self-life in a risky contaminated environment. A filter, whose prime function is to contract consciousness, not expand it.

I had this recurring dream while I was in hospital – that I was someone from the future called Limbo Jones, then I'd wake in a cold sweat.

Limbo Jones woke in a sweat. Cold perspiration covered his entire body. He tried to remember the vision, the dream that was so real it caused him to wake up in this state, but so obscure he couldn't make no sense of it. He climbed outa the sweat-soaked bed and headed for the shower. It was 5.00am and he knew he'd never be able to get back to sleep now. He had to leave for work at 6.30am, so he might as well get ready at a leisurely pace.

Under the piercing shower-rain, he experienced that feeling of extreme loneliness again. It was fleeting, momentary, like some sense of nostalgia that sometimes came and pierced his heart. He didn't know where it came from and it hadn't always been with him. He only knew it for the first time about a month ago and it came upon him unexpected, intermittent, since then.

After showering, he made some decaf and spread a thin layer of cottage cheese on a couple of crispbreads. Limbo Jones ate a healthy diet and exercised regularly. His job as a geneticist with the Universal Life-Science Institute was demanding, as was living in a big city. Both required that he be fit and healthy and he tried his best to accommodate them.

The big city was located in a well-developed country on a medium-sized planet at the edge of a fairly unspectacular galactic star-system.

In fact, unspectacular was a word that could be used to describe Limbo Jones and his life – up till now.

It wasn't the first time he'd woke up in this state from the same dream. It had happened a few times before and started to manifest itself on his psyche about the same time as the nostalgic feeling of loneliness arrived. It was like someone, or something, was trying to communicate with him in this way – through the dream and the emotional sense of loss.

However, the message was opaque, distorted, ambiguous and he couldn't be sure if it was a message at all, or just his subconscious playing tricks on him.

Limbo Jones dressed and took the subway to the city centre. He was early, because of the dream, and there weren't many people about. It was a bright day and, when he emerged from the subway, he looked up at the powdered blueness of the early sky and thought to himself that life was really such a strange thing – so important and self-centred at ground level, yet so minute and fragile on the universal scale. This was no great profundity, it was a normal, everyday thought and, thinking it, he almost walked into someone as he continued to look up at the brightening sky-blue, with sunlight rising from behind the tall buildings to the east.

Deciding he better concentrate on the rest of his journey to work, Limbo Jones walked the final few blocks to the Institute. This was his first job since graduating with a Master's degree and he'd been with the research department for almost two years now. At twenty-five, he considered it to be a good career and, if he worked hard, he could expect to be promoted to assistant departmental supervisor by the time he was thirty. The salary and job perks were competitive and the working environment was one of the best in the city. The only drawback was the long hours – full commitment to the job was expected and this left little time for a meaningful social life.

After signing in at reception, Limbo Jones took the elevator to the sixth floor. He put on a white coat and entered the empty research department. Then, as he walked to his workstation, he had a flashback. It was like something from a movie. It only lasted a second or two, but it momentarily disorientated him. It was a face – a face from his dream. Not a human face, or at least not a human face like he knew a human face to be. Rather, a morphing visage, half image and half numeric code, appearing and dissolving somewhere on the mesolimbic pathway of his brain, dancing between the synapses and neurotransmitters and receptors and tracts.

Limbo Jones was a scientist and, as such, he didn't believe much in things he couldn't explain. Every working day, he dealt with genes and enzymes and strands and nucleotides and carbons and bases – stuff that could be seen or, if not actually seen, indisputably proven with mathematical formulae and test results. Alright, his intuition told him that science couldn't explain everything, that there was much to be discovered. But he believed that, eventually, everything would be explainable in scientific terms. However, for now, he was seeing this thing – this vision – this dream, and he couldn't explain it. Even if he could, he wasn't sure he'd want to. It unnerved him.

There were more than twenty buildings on the Institute's campus – labs and offices and recreational facilities of various sizes and functions. The lab where Limbo Jones worked was spacious, in research institute terms, with stations for a dozen technicians and scientists to work at the same time. The supervisor was Stephanie Tallis, a tall, genial enough woman in her late forties – or early fifties, it was difficult for him to tell exactly. Stephanie ran the lab with a relaxed, laid-back approach – and this suited Limbo Jones – except when it came to working the hours and meeting deadlines and milestones, then everyone was expected to put their shoulder to the wheel, without excuse or exception.

The assistant supervisor was called Camilla, a mid-thirties woman of ambiguous origin with a serious and somewhat secretive approach to her work. She stayed mostly apart from the others in the lab, except when it came to supporting and standing in for Stephanie. She'd be leaving in a few years, to follow an alternative career in medicine, and Limbo Jones would inherit her position. He knew this because Stephanie told him one evening when they were working late and she was anxious to reassure him that he was a valued member of staff and his hard work and dedication would be rewarded. He just had to wait until Camilla left and not go looking elsewhere for career advancement.

Limbo Jones made his way unsteadily to his work station and sat heavily on the grey upholstered swivel-chair. The window close to him faced out into the hall, so he never knew what the weather was doing, except when arriving in the morning and leaving late in the evening. Most days he ate a light lunch in the staff self-service cafeteria and some days he skipped lunch altogether, just snacking with a tuna-and-cress black-olive ciabatta, that he bought from the vendor who came round with his basket mid-morning and again mid-afternoon.

He wanted to just get started on his work but, before doing so, Limbo Jones paused and took a couple of deep breaths. The vision, or whatever it was, had disconcerted him, taken him by surprise. He wasn't expecting it this early and so soon after the trauma of the night-time dream – it'd ambushed him when he wasn't prepared.

He took a sip of water from the plastic bottle he took from his fridge before he left for work, then turned towards his microscope. Other people were beginning to arrive in the lab and it was best not to give anyone cause for concern, in case they assumed he'd been contaminated by something and had to be placed into quarantine.

Limbo Jones was working on a project called Aglibol, which was a government commission and kind of covert. A total of three scientists and five technicians were working on the project and none of them were really allowed to know what the others were doing. Limbo Jones was told it was a cosmological development for space exploration, to design a statin-based drug that would improve human ability to see in total darkness. That's all he needed to know.

The drug would allow human eyes to draw in the most remote, minute point of light and magnify it, very much like a cat did. His own particular role in the process was to design and develop the hybrid esther bonds that'd attach themselves to a sequence of amino acids along the chromosome of the base material.

But he was an inquisitive person and Limbo Jones did a little extra-curricular research and discovered that Aglibôl was an ancient lunar deity in the old city of Palmyra. Could it be coincidence that this name had been given to the project he was working on, just when it was discovered that his planet's moon had begun to drift away into space?

'Good morning Limbo.'

He turned and smiled at Stephanie Tallis, who patted his shoulder as she passed his workstation on the way to her own. Stephanie was always cheerful in the morning, like she was happy just to see the new day once more. But lately, as the day wore on, she'd become more and more morose, scowling inwardly and frowning at anyone who approached her. This was uncharacteristic, a new dimension of the woman that hadn't been apparent before, and Limbo Jones wondered if she had some heavy weight pressing on her soul that she was reluctant to share with her colleagues.

Or maybe it was something to do with the moon, as the world leaders were saying.

The drift started unnoticed, registering first on magnetic recording instruments and gravitational charts in remote tracking installations across the planet. Then on the shift of radio signals from orbiting satellites. A distortion was observed in the mascons, the large positive gravitational anomalies associated with the moon's impact basins, caused by the dense basaltic lava flows that filled the basins. Once they started to investigate, scientists soon discovered that the moon's axial tilt had increased and this could only mean one thing – drift!

There'd been no major impact on the planet yet, apart from some tidal effect, but this would change as the drift increased and nobody could predict the long-term problems it'd cause. There was another dimension to the crisis – this manifested itself in the symptoms that Stephanie Tallis was exhibiting. Moroseness, or a gradual descent into negativity, which was becoming noticeable in an increasing section of the population.

At least, the symptom was being attributed to the moon's drift by governing bodies throughout the world. They said it was a temporary thing, this increased introversion, this cynicism, this negativity. They said it was a phase that would pass once people acclimatised themselves to the drift.

The negativity manifested itself on a more global scale as greed, with the richest in society wanting to be even richer, at the expense of the poorest in society. These people were not the everyday shabby, gutter rich, but the obscene super-rich, who were out of touch with every reality except their own. Out of touch with what they really were and where they came from. So out of touch they believed themselves to be the nouveau gods. They were brainwashing the population with television and trivia and personalised religions, so that everyone was forgetting they were part of a oneness that was whole, not fragmented, nor splintered into millions of little egos, all competing with each other for shallow, worthless prizes.

The negativity was manifesting itself everywhere. In the media nobody addressed the real issues of the day, but increasingly obsessed over celebrity and the shiny little trinkets of illusory reality, the fool's gold of stardom and wanting to be special at the expense of everyone else. It manifested itself in selfishness and suspicion and cynicism and a hardening of hearts. It was spreading across the planet and was affecting all aspects of human life.

It manifested itself on a personal level inside Limbo Jones, almost subconsciously at first, but with an increasing sense of frustration and disappointment. It was like negativity was growing inside him, spreading like a virus through his nervous system and his genes and his brain functions. He was feeling levels of negative emotion that were alien to him – fear and doubt and a kind of baseless paranoia. It was like some natural equilibrium inside his soul had been disturbed.

He began his work for the day, testing the samples of nucleic acids and reforming chromatin proteins and histones and subdividing genetic codes and chromosomes. Soon he was lost in the complexity of his research and the world around him became hazy. Other voices in the lab got garbled and incoherent and the people around him passed by like shadows with blurred outlines. Colours blended into a chromatic soup and time travelled at a pace that was unique to his concentrating mind. Gradually, the space that was the interior of the lab grew brighter, the voices disappeared altogether and the shapes and colours faded into nothingness.

Limbo Jones saw the face in front of him again, the half-image, half-code face from before. Only this time the features were more distinct, and this time the emotional sense of loss wasn't so acute – like it was dissolving in the allness of the moment. It was a beautiful face and intrinsically female in nature. Not beautiful in a humanistic way, but in an eternal, wave-like way – coming and going, appearing and disappearing, like an apparition coming out of a mist, then fading back into the opacity, before becoming visible again. It was smiling – not smiling in a way that'd be recognisable like a smile, but in a way that was all-encompassing, like the whole face was a smile. Like it wasn't made up of the component parts of eyes and nose and mouth and chin and ears, but was just a face, the component parts inseparable and indistinguishable from the whole.

The smile reassured Limbo Jones and he lost his apprehension. There was something eternally glorious about the vision, something familiar and welcoming, like a glimpse of a long-lost friend in a crowd, or a piece of nostalgic music heard in the distance and rekindling emotions of overwhelming déjà vu. The eyes were starlight, and the mouth was the moon, and the skin was the sun, and the hair was strands of shining double-helix. The face spoke to him, not in a sentence, not in a string of words. And he didn't hear it, he knew it. Like a complete thing. A complete concept. The complete meaning came in the same instant, not in the clumsy focus of separate sound-symbols, but like a complete picture. A complete understanding of what was meant to be conveyed.

'Limbo Jones is me and I am Limbo Jones.'

A hand appeared in the vision. It reached out to Limbo Jones in the lightroom that once was the laboratory where he worked. There was nothing else in the lightroom, except himself and the vision and the words that weren't really words, but an entire concept. No walls, no floor, no ceiling. Just light, and face, and voice, and Limbo Jones. Floating in dimensionless suspended animation.

'I've come to be with you.'

Again, the sound wasn't a sentence, the complete meaning of the words was conveyed instantaneously – warm and friendly, like a blanket enveloping a cold body.

'With me?'

Limbo Jones heard his own words in the same way as he heard the words from the vision. A question with complete meaning and not ambiguous in any way.

'With you.'

Something shattered on the floor – a glass dispenser. It brought Limbo Jones back from wherever it was he'd gone to. The people were back in the laboratory and the voices spoke and laughed and the colours were white and opaque and transparent like they were before. And Limbo Jones remembered the feeling of unbearable loneliness that came back and pierced him through the heart.

After the commune I was in the psychiatric unit at Carlisle Hospital for eighteen months, until September 1999. The new millennium was approaching and the doctors said they'd cured me of my illusions and delusions and it was time for me to face the world again. My feelings fluctuated, back and forth – pulling me this way and that – one way and the other. My time there was hazy. I was in the middle of a half-enlightened, almost-aware, nearly-known agony. Being broken down and put back together again. Humpty Dumpty. Being reduced to my most basic level and then built up again. What comes back ain't what went in – bits missing or added or changed about. Same ingredients, but a different person. The theory of beta decay.

What's seen can't be separated from the act of seeing itself.

Nobody visited me while I was there, except for Angela, and I went back to stay with her in Hertfordshire when they let me out. By now, I was fifty-one and not getting no younger.

Most of the people I'd been on the road with in my earlier days had gone to settled living, but there was a hard-core of new-agers still travelling. Some of them had reached their third and even fourth generation on the road by now. They helped each other, looking after kids and maintaining vehicles and "skipping" – salvaging food from supermarket skips that was perfectly edible and wholly immoral to be thrown away. One guy I met told me he hadn't bought no food for six months, even though retrieving thrown-away grub from supermarket skips was still illegal.

The old hippie philosophies were mainly environmental now, not so much political. Though it was sometimes difficult to separate the two. They were involved with initiatives like back to the land, co-operative enterprises, alternative energy, organic farming and other issues like that. The new way was to be positive and progressive, not confrontational and negative.

The fascist Tories of the '80s were gone and replaced by a new breed of neo-conservatives, posing as liberals, who failed to repeal the vicious legislation imposed on us by their predecessors.

Despite everything, there were still pockets of alternativism alive and well on the roads of Britain – and I wanted to join them. There was a new face to the original hippies who dropped out so many years ago and I was probably the last of that ambivalent line that stretched back for nearly fifty years. More and more new-age kids were opting back into the mainstream of society and it was a struggle for parents to balance the life and stick to principles, and still give their kids what they wanted.

The commune went derelict while I was away, but land prices in that part of the world went up and I was able to sell it for twice what I paid for it. I was richer than I'd ever been in my life – money-wise at least. But it wouldn't be easy, an aging hippie travelling the roads with one arm and a big hole in my heart.

But it was the millennium – a new millennium.

I stayed with Angela over Christmas and into the New Year and then I had to go. I wanted to be at Stonehenge for the summer solstice in millennium year.

23
The Mystic and the Recluse

The more you understand, the less you can predict. Voluntary actions are prompted by circumstances that aren't voluntary at all. The way to consciousness is through subconsciousness – and the way to subconsciousness is through the chemistry of the animal. We're made of those chemicals – we are those chemicals.

————————

I got down to Stonehenge for the summer solstice in 2000. There was limited access, but it was the first year people were allowed back up to the Stones. It was all real sanitised and it wasn't the same like the old days and it never would be, but at least things were improving. Over the years that followed, festivals started to happen again – the Sunrise Celebration and Bearded Theory and Pagan Pride Acorn Fayre and the Eden Festival and Beautiful Days and Cornbury and Holifair and the Shrewsbury Festival and the Sonic Rock Solstice and Alchemy and the Acoustic Festival of Britain. Many small events were springing up around the country, like new shoots after a hard winter. They were all well-managed and health-and-safety conscious and conformed to the authorities – but they were better than nothing.

The new millennium rolled on and I was sixty in 2008. I bought myself a reconditioned vardo and a young horse to pull it and I went back to the way I first travelled the roads when I came home from America. New horse-drawn routes were being established in rural areas, where you could travel a few miles and then find an inn that'd cater for you and your animal. It was a leisurely life for a wanderer like me – on my own and not in convoy no more. Just laying back and staying cool.

Then I met this woman who was into mysticism and alternative medicine and she reminded me of my mother, even though she was younger than me – probably mid-forties, older than my mother was the last time I seen her.

We was staying at the same inn one night and she sat beside me in the garden while I was smoking a joint.

'Can I take a draw?'

'Sure.'

She said her name was Holly and she was a vegan and knew about hundreds of mystical and supernatural health treatments. It was all about forms of energy that were alien to physics – believing in alternative realities, in forces that are outside the universe. This interested me. It was kinda like a melting pot of paganism and folklore and parapsychology and guesswork. It was a sprawling enchanted forest of alternativism where wishful thinking was an industry and faith was a ticket and death was a transition. What's wrong with that? She told me about pranic healing, which was something to do with colours, and the twelve steps that said a power greater than ourselves could restore us to sanity – which might've been a good thing for me if I'd known about it earlier. There was flower therapy and holistic systems and biosonic repatterning and blood crystallisation and chiki energy-flow and acupuncture and esoteric toning and shaman stuff that I'd heard about on the Great Plains and lots of others. I listened and showed interest, but then she asked me if I wanted her to tell my fortune.

Now, all my life I believed I knew more than the average person, that my mother had put something into me when I was young that allowed me to see beyond the brain. So I thought if the future was there to be seen, I'd have seen it by now and I wouldn't have got on that plane with Lizzie. But what the hell – it was late summer and we were in a nice garden and I was smoking the weed. She looked at both my palms first, then placed her hands on my head. It was weird, because I could feel a kinda energy passing through her and into me – like a very mild current of electricity.

'I have to tell you about your past before I can tell you about your future.'

'I know all about my past.'

244

'Do you?'

She said she wasn't talking about my recent past, so I shut up and let her get on with it. She said nothing for a while, then told me I was once called Malik and I lived at the beginning of time. I said time has no beginning and she sighed and said she meant the beginning of human time. So I shut up again.

She said my circle of life got fragmented and influenced by a negative energy that'd existed in the universe when only energy existed. That energy was made of both good and bad stuff and the good side created the material universe and the bad side wanted to destroy it and go back to being pure energy. Back at the beginning of human time, we were more aware – we were somewhere between angels and raze-humans and we knew about the circle of life and other stuff that we forgot now. She said I had to get back to that and I kinda knew what she was talking about – I knew getting back there involved connecting. Thing is, only a few thousand humans existed back when I was Malik, so it was easier to be connected. Being a twenty-first-century human ain't so easy – too many distractions – too much artificial light blocking out the stars. She said it was a combination of animal instinct and human sentiment.

The thing about it is, all this materialism makes us vulnerable to the negative energy stuff – that's what she said and I guess she was right. In a way. The other thing is, we got this humanity, this thing that makes us human – and I didn't think I could truly understand everything, like I thought I did when I was younger – until I stopped being human. Now, a lot of mystics have a solution for that – like meditation and yoga and the astral plain and all kinds of other stuff, just like this Holly had. But I tried all that over the years and I was still human – still had all the flaws. It all goes back to connection, I guess – singly, you're just a human on your own, but connected, you're part of everything. The billionaire controllers of this planet are outa touch with their true nature because of greed and lies and self-obsession and the misuse of power. They believe themselves to be god-like and immortal. But that negativity will destroy them, along with everyone else.

This negative energy's spreading like a virus, Holly told me. You can see it everywhere – escalations in violence and disease, infant mortality, school shootings, earthquakes and tsunamis and the return of torture as a legitimate governmental resource. Positivity's taking a beating, everyone's cynical, apathetic, suspicious, hostile – there's no peace and love. There's no more hippie code. People who try to stay positive have a tough time of it. If you ain't connected, then you can't know about the circle of life – you can't see the truth. The negative energy will blind you. Every negative thought and action makes it harder to get back to being positive.

Holly came for a ride in my horse and vardo. She was supposed to get off at the next staging point, but she didn't. We travelled round the lanes and back roads of Wiltshire through the summer of 2008 and she talked to me about lots of things – some I knew and some I didn't. I listened and took what I needed from what she said and discarded the rest. She said people were becoming paranoid, scared of every shadow and distrustful of every contact and association. Most of them don't understand what's going on. What she said was like that recurring dream I had when I was in the hospital – Limbo Jones and the moon drifting away and all that stuff.

Holly's mind was full of strange landscapes. The eyes that looked back at her when she stood in front of a mirror weren't her own. They vanished quickly, before she could identify them. Her head was filled with alien sounds and smells and sometimes she thought she was going crazy.

I knew the population of the planet was being increasingly brainwashed by television and trivia and celebrity culture and personalised religions and political charlatans – it'd been like that for a long time. Everyone was just out for themselves and not for existence as a whole. Most of the old hippies were either dead or assimilated into the establishment and people like me were pissing against the wind. So I just drove my horse and vardo and thought my own thoughts and tried not to interfere with anybody.

And I told Holly to do the same.

The thing is, there was signs all over the place for people who wanted to know the real truth – about the past and the future. There's fragments of the circle of life everywhere, but they're just fragments – incomplete. It's hard to understand the signs, unless you're like Holly. Or me. People don't want to go back to the beginning, where they belong, to see things clear and get the order right. It's like Holly's a mystic, but there's others – watchers and knowers and healers and visionaries and transformers. You gotta find out what you are man, and the only way to do that's to go back to the beginning. Once you know, then you got a handle on energy streams and the circle of life. It's like there's millions of circles of life, all trying to connect at the same time. If one's successful, it's like a domino effect and all the rest will happen after that. Holly said people can identify their own circle of life by colour – but I ain't convinced about that. Once you find your circle of life, then you can see the bigger picture, how all the small circles of life combine to form a circle of total life, where the oneness of all things becomes apparent.

Here's how Holly sees it. The growing total life circle gets more and more powerful as it expands and negativity gets weaker and weaker. Equilibrium's restored and the forces that started the spiral into negativity get defeated. This reflects itself at all levels of life on the planet and it spreads out through the universe. Human beings gotta realise that they can create positive energy through thoughts and words and deeds, to keep the negative energy in check. Otherwise, it's a descent further down into war and greed and fear – until there's nothing left. Holly reckons people need to rediscover love and truth to stop the drift downwards. Only then will human nature flourish and self-obsession fade away. The universe is fundamentally positive. It's filled with promise, waiting to be known and understood. No more fear and doubt about life after death, because death don't exist no longer – only life in the form of positive energy. It's then we can travel through time and dimensions and accept that we're part of one energy force. In the end, everything fades in the face of pure love.

Holly left in October, when the weather started to turn. She went her own way. I was sorry to see her go, but I was sure I'd meet her again. I decided to make camp somewhere for the winter. Not literally make camp, like pitching a tent and sitting out the hard weather – I was too old for that. I had a lot of money now, so I didn't need to. I put the horse into stables and the vardo into storage and I rented a small cottage in the Vale of Evesham. I lived alone there through the winter of 2008 and into 2009, hardly ever coming into contact with another human being. I read a lot of books and did a lot of thinking and I stopped eating meat and became a vegan, like Holly was. There's different kinds of vegan, like dietary vegan and ethical vegan and environmental vegan – I became all three. That don't mean I was gonna pull the vardo come spring and let the horse sit on the driver's seat, it just meant I'd value the animal and take care of it properly and wouldn't ill-treat it.

Christmas came and went and 2009 came in with a lot of snow and below-zero temperatures. I had enough food and fuel so I didn't need to go out nowhere and I was happy looking through the window at it. I think it was a Friday, early on in January, but I can't be sure now. I heard a knock on the door, faint at first, and I thought it was just the wind. Then it came again, a bit louder. It was late, after midnight, and I wondered who'd be calling at that hour. I went to the door, but I couldn't see no one out there in the darkness. It was snowing a blizzard, so I shut the door again to keep in the heat. After a few minutes the knock came again. I thought maybe it's someone pulling a prank – some kids who wanted to test the hermit – so I ignored it. Then it came again, real loud. When I opened the door a second time, a woman I vaguely recognised was standing there in a long coat and boots. I tried to remember her name, but couldn't.

'Aaron? Or Lee, which?'

'Whichever you prefer.'

'I'm Lauren Menéndez. Do you remember me?'

She was an older woman than I remembered – maybe mid-fifties. She'd come back over from America on business and wanted to find Lizzie. She found Angela instead, because Lizzie told her she had a sister, even though she never told me. I was keeping in touch with Angela, that's how Lauren Menéndez found me.

'It's real late.'

'I know.'

'And snowing.'

'I know.'

I took her coat and offered her a chair by the open fire.

'You could've waited till morning.'

'I could have, but I didn't want to.'

'It's pretty remote out here.'

'I know.'

She came by taxi as far as she could, then trudged the rest of the way on foot. After knocking a couple of times, she went round the back – that's why I couldn't see her when I opened the door. She came back around after I'd closed it. She saw the light and knew someone was home, but she thought I might be asleep, so she knocked louder.

'You took a chance.'

'I've taken many chances, Aaron. Nicaragua, Zimbabwe ... remember? And a lot of other places too.'

I made some coffee and she warmed her hands on the cup. I had a bottle of the local 'shine and I offered her some. She nodded her head and I poured a good measure into the coffee.

'Can I stay here tonight?'

'There's a spare room.'

The 'shine had a narcotic effect on Lauren Menéndez. She sank back into the chair and let the tensions of getting out here flow away. I could see she was drifting on the mixture of malted barley and treacle and the scent of witch hazel, and it took her a few minutes to realise she was listening to music. When her mind came back to her body, she saw I was playing an acoustic guitar. She didn't recognise the piece of music, but it sounded Celtic, with a haunting, far-away melody.

'What is that?'

'It's called "Greysteil" ... Greysteil was an invincible medieval knight, who was eventually defeated with a sword made by a woman.'

We drank more 'shine and burned more wood and I wondered when she was gonna ask what she came here to ask.

'What happened to Lizzie?'

Next morning, I woke early and fried up some bread and mushrooms and tomatoes and made fresh coffee. Lauren Menéndez climbed outa the little cot-bed in the spare room and found me in the kitchen.

'Good morning.'

'Breakfast?'

She looked at the food and her nose twitched.

'No bacon?'

'I'm vegan.'

We ate in silence. There seemed to be an understanding between us. Nothing needed to be said. Words would've been somehow superfluous – would've got in the way.

Of our nexus.

Our mutual loss.

It was still snowing heavily and Lauren Menéndez didn't fancy the trek down to where a taxi'd be able to pick her up. I said she could stay at the cottage if she liked, until the weather cleared – or longer if she wanted to. As long as she liked.

'When will the weather clear?'

'Who knows?'

She considered my offer. She was in no rush to get back to wherever it was she came out here from. There was no television, just books. I read and she looked out the window at the falling snow. At lunchtime she found some potatoes and root vegetables and some other stuff and cooked up a kinda vegetarian stew with thick slices of soda bread.

'You didn't have to do that.'

'I like to earn my keep.'

We sat at the table and I told her I didn't eat much and she said no wonder I was so skinny. She served up the food and poured the coffee and, when we finished, I tuned the radio into the BBC weather station and the forecast was for the snow to let up the following day.

'I'll take you down to where the taxis come.'

That night, we sat by the fire together and drank more 'shine – this time mixed with hot water, brown sugar and cloves. I didn't play the guitar, because Lauren Menéndez wanted to listen to Beethoven's "Sixth Symphony" on the radio. I didn't know it was Beethoven, or that it was his sixth symphony, until she told me. I'd heard classical music before, but only small snatches in passing, never for a sustained period of time. It took me a while to get used to the melodic effect, to the unusual synchronicity. But when I did, it reminded me of summer – of the countryside – of my childhood, travelling on the remote back roads and lanes with my wicce-witch mother – and later in the vardo with Holly.

The "Sixth Symphony" was followed by a quieter piece, "Clair de Lune", which meant moonlight, by Claude Debussy, Lauren Menéndez told me. She slipped down from her chair onto the mat in front of the fire. She was quiet, meditative, listening to the soft piano music, letting the 'shine take hold of her. She seemed to feel at peace in this place and she smiled with her eyes. I wanted to put an arm round her, but I didn't. It felt like we were kinda kindred spirits – more than that, we'd shared the same soul. The clock hands turned and time slipped by, surreptitious – in harmony with the 'shine and the fire and the music.

I got up early again the next morning and started breakfast. I waited for Lauren Menéndez to get outa the little cot-bed and come into the kitchen, but she didn't. The snow'd stopped falling, just like the weather forecast said it would, and the low clouds were dispersing, leaving a sky the colour of cornflowers. I waited. The breakfast went cold. At eleven o'clock, I looked into the room.

Lauren Menéndez was gone. Outside, footprints led away from the cottage, down in the direction of the taxis.

When winter was over, I left the cottage and collected the horse from the stables and the vardo from storage and set out on the road again. I travelled north, up into Gloucestershire and through the Forest of Dean, where the Roadside Ruffians heard a musical note in the moonlight and came across the psychedelic glade after eating mushrooms all those many years ago. I remembered the clearing and the ramshackle cabin surrounded by wild flowers – and the old shaman with long white hair and dark skin. I tried to find it again, but it wasn't there. So I moved on up towards Tewkesbury.

And that's where I found Croft Farm.

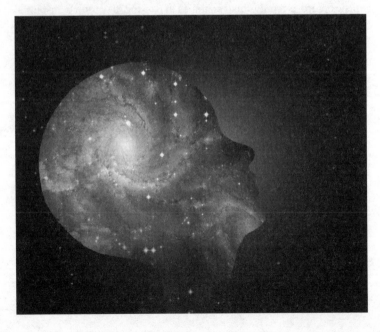

24
Lakefest – A New Dawn

The mystery of life shouldn't be a problem to be solved – just a
reality to be experienced. If there is such a thing as experience.
The shedding of old feelings – emotions – longings – wants.
And the knowing that there will be no more disturbances.

I've always been a hippie – and still am. There's many names for it nowadays – new-ager, alternative, itinerant, backpacker, whatever. To me it's hippie, because that combines the two essentials – travelling and music. To know what it feels like to travel the roads in a horse-drawn vardo and understand the relevance of music and certain types of plant life. To understand that there's a different way to live, away from the madding crowd. I guess we're all hippies in our own way, ain't we? Or, at least, we'd like to be. Those of us who're lucky enough to be able to break away from the corporate shilling can do it – and I don't denigrate those who can't. If you have kids then you gotta support them – I never had no kids, so I could do as I liked. I never had no strong relationships – except with Lizzie for a short while – and that's what it takes for a life on the road. Some people do it with families, but it's hard – especially now when the kids want the stuff the other kids have. When they're subjected to non-stop consumerist marketing.

Anyway, I'm coming to the end of my story.

I travelled up towards Tewkesbury and came across Croft Farm, in the hamlet of Bredon's Hardwick and unmarked on any map. It was a potato farm for most of the twentieth century and got turned into a sand and gravel quarry in the '70s. It was located in the River Avon Valley and had its own lake. In the '80s, landowner Alan Newell built a water park there, with a caravan and camping site. There was hiking and fishing and water activities, but no music. So, I got involved with a few enthusiasts and we talked about a festival at Croft Farm like in the old days.

'Course, it never could be like the old days because of health-and-safety and other rules and regulations, but we'd try to make it as laid-back and easy-going as possible. On 9 April 2011, Croft Farm Waterpark hosted its inaugural music and cider festival. It was just a one-day event – a giant booze-up with thirty-two different ciders and real ales. The music was provided by The Wurzels and Avert Francis and The Roving Crows. Nine thousand pints of cider got sold to the festgoers, who seemed to enjoy themselves in the sunshine.

In 2012 we expanded things and Lakefest was born. We decided in the beginning to stick to the old hippie philosophy of peace and love and the fest'd be a friendly, westcountry affair. The scenery was more than magical and music'd be a mixture of folk and rock and country – a coming together of mainstream and alternative. We couldn't offer a "free" festival, like Windsor and the Henge, but we vowed we'd keep ticket prices as low as possible, just to cover our costs. We was more interested in legacy and memories than profit and we published our personal telephone numbers in case anyone wanted to talk to us – something that was unheard of with the other fests around the country, but in keeping with our ethical approach.

The new festival started out like a two-day event on 18 and 19 May 2012. The Friday line-up included EMF, Erica, Kickback, Rainy and the Dust, 3 Daft Monkeys, Toploader and Reef. On the Saturday we had Tim Parkes, Avert Francis, Missing Andy, Smoke Feathers, Miles and Erica, Chesney Hawkes and The Roving Crows. The Levellers were booked, but couldn't turn up and got replaced by Athlete. We advertised a traditional family-friendly fest, keeping true to its hippie roots, with bars and food and funfair acts. The music started at 4:00pm on Friday and 12:00 noon on Saturday, which would be a fancy-dress day. As Croft Farm was located in a small hamlet, to be fair to the locals and not antagonise anyone, we said the site'd be quiet by 2:00am on each night. Dogs was allowed on leads and if people wanted to bring their own booze they could, as long as they kept it on the camping fields and didn't bring it into the main festival area.

Despite our break-even policy, we found out the hard way that music festival promotion was a high-risk business – we lost fifty thousand pounds in 2012. But we weren't put off, because everyone who came said they had a truly cool experience – that was our real payoff. So, we expanded the fest to three days for 2013, from Friday 9 to Sunday 11 August. New headliners included Ocean Colour Scene, The Beat, Duke Special, The Crazy World of Arthur Brown, Jim Lockey & The Solemn Sun, Willie & The Bandits, Ruffanti, Gaz Brookfield, Frazer Kennedy & Friends and Funmilayo. Other new acts included The Levellers, who turned up this year, Chas & Dave, Cosmo Jarvis, Baka Beyond, The Chip Shop Boys and Erica. We sold out early and 2013 was a big success – financially, we broke even.

We kept to the three-day timetable for 2014 and the line-up included Spunge, Young Kato, Bad Cardigan, Sons of Navarone, Jar Family, Sarah Warren Band, Sons of Earnest, Phoney & The Freaks, Radio Riddler, Gaz Brookfield, Coco & The Butterfields, The Leylines, Edd Keene, No-Good Nancys, Megan Lara Mae, Victorian Dad, Foreign Affairs, Pheasants and Their Enemies, The Quakers, Moon Brothers, Tess of the Circle, John Adams, Edd Donovan & The Wandering Moles, Blue Horyzon, Future Set and Whipjacks. A very big bill! Others who turned up included The Bad Shepherds, The Neville Staple Band, Fun Lovin' Criminals, Snap!, Buzzcocks, Shed Seven, Lightning Seeds, Doctor & The Medics, Lee Scratch Perry and others. We sold out early again and 2014 was an even bigger success than 2013. We were really moving.

More and more people kept turning up over the few years we was running and the word spread that there was a true event, as close to the old hippie fests as you could get. It was a meteoric rise, but we kept to the original peace and love ethic and built a fest that was friendlier and more fun than any other. We managed to start making a small profit, which we ploughed back into making the fest better, while still keeping ticket prices as low as possible.

In 2015, we started to get too big for the venue. Thousands of people were turning up and having a good time and we never expected the fest to grow that quick. It was held from Friday 7 till Sunday 9 August that year and the acts was getting bigger too. We had Billy Bragg and Embrace and The Magic Numbers and The Cheeky Girls and D:Ream, along with Dreadzone, Ferocious Dog, Hayseed Dixie, Lloyd Yates, Nizlopi, The Selector, BabaJack, Notorious Brothers, Haunted Soul, Simon Murphy, Jasper in the Company of Others, The Lounge Crusade, Lisbee Stainton, The Cracked, The Outcast Band, The Robin Pierce Band, Woo Town Hillbillies, The Hawthornes, Skewwhiff, Crow Puppets, Mark Harrison, Claire Boswell, along with many bands from the previous years. Another huge bill!

The critics said we created something special – there was a sense of community, of bonding, of common purpose and shared enjoyment. We had something the other festivals didn't have. What was that? It was a vibe – an atmosphere that everyone worked hard to make happen. An opportunity for people to be part of something larger than themselves. To be part of a "collective" and forget all the hassles of the universe for a few days. As well as that, we was family-friendly and provided lots of stuff to entertain the kids – all free. And our festgoers were a diverse bunch of all ages and types and everyone gelled. It all worked. The music arena was compact and well-designed and a vibrant location, with people in transit to and fro. We was lucky with the weather too, over the years, not that that matters much to true festgoers, but the sun raises the spirits, as Wally Hope would've told you – if he was still around.

The facilities were as good as any, with free showers and food stalls and good choices and prices in the bars – Old Rosie and Country Perry and Henry Westons and Hardywood and Five Mile Mountain and Rusty Beaver and many more – along with a late-night cocktail bar. We had three tented stages and a Secret Disco scene with great beats and a chilled atmosphere. The quality across the stages was as good as it gets and so were the sound systems. Punk-folk band Ferocious Dog kicked off on the Friday, with "Fruitbat" Carter on guitar, and got a great reaction from the crowd. The performance was as good as any headline act. The place bounced with reeling folk-rock and had the "Dog Pit" full of moshing youngsters. Goldie Lookin' Chain were funny and visual and hyperactive and produced some fine beats and driving rap. They were fast and full-on. Ash were a class act and one of the sets of the weekend. The years were physically and musically kind to these guys, they had variety and vitality and freshness, with classic hits seeded throughout the performance. They closed the main stage with a singalong of "Girl From Mars" – a fitting end to the first day.

The Roving Crows provided some great country blues on Saturday, with Caitlin Barrett's addictive fiddle playing. I wanted to jump up onstage with her, nearly forgetting I only had one arm. It was a heady mixture of hoedown and Celtic reels and they finished up with a foot-stomping "Devil Went Down to Georgia". Dreadzone were one of the headline acts of 2015 – they're a band that always delivers – from "Ironshirt" through to "House of Dread", the place was rocking off its feet. Frontman McSpee fed off the Lakefest vibe and then sent it back into the crowd. It was what festivals should be about. Billy Bragg brought some humorous political action to the scene. "New England" got the people singing along and brought back a feeling of the anarchic old days. The Outcast Band were and are as good as any in the music business. They blew the intimacy of the Floating Globe tent apart with a sweaty set of power and intensity. Their sound was a combination of rootsy melody and driving folk-rock with an undercurrent of blues. The interplay between vocals and fiddle was something to hear. The Roadside Ruffians were never as good as this.

N-Trance filled the Garden Tent on Sunday. Lynsey-Jane Barrow and MC B were in the groove with a polished interplay of dance and rap. Hayseed Dixie hit the mark in the late afternoon with their tongue-in-cheek rock, and Magic Numbers closed things off with a hard-edged rock set from the talented four-piece – and class bass playing from Michele Stodart. For some people I spoke to, the Silent Disco was one of the highlights of the weekend. Everyone got into it and the Garden Tent was packed as the magical vibe kept building. It was surreal, and that was the beauty of it – everyone dancing to their own tune. Then someone piped in "Hey Jude" and a crowd came onstage – the organisers and stewards and volunteers and kids and anyone who wanted. One-by-one, people started to take off their headphones and began to sing. Technology was forgotten. Humanity was remembered. One community. One family.

That's what Lakefest was about.

But crowd sizes were getting on for ten thousand now and we had to start thinking about a bigger venue. After the 2015 event, we decided to move Lakefest to Eastnor Castle at Ledbury, the former site of The Big Chill Festival. The plan wasn't to compete with Reading or Glastonbury, we could never do that, but to build a festival that was laid-back and easy-going, like I said. Lakefest was for people who wanted to bring their families and have a laugh and a drink and a dance and a party atmosphere. We tried hard to keep the commercial edge away and we'll keep doing that.

In 2016, over fifteen thousand people will turn up to party in the Deer Park, with the Castle and the Malvern Hills for a backdrop. Our promise to them is the coolest weekend of world-class music, fairground acts, beer and cider, drinking and dancing and a few other surprises along the way – whatever the weather. We've extended again, to four days now, from Thursday 11 to Sunday 14 August. We have Primal Scream booked, along with We Are Scientists and Starsailor, The Coral, Newton Faulkner and Afro Celt Sound System.

There'll be more. Much more!

So, that's my story. Not just my story, but the story of the people I met along the way. I only found what I was looking for once – it only lasted a short time and then I lost it again. But it was worth it, for whatever little time I had it.

There's a thing I once read, I think it comes from Wuthering Heights:

I've dreamt in my life dreams
that have stayed with me ever after,
and changed my ideas:
they've gone through and through me,
like wine through water,
and altered the colour of my mind.

D'you know what I mean?

259

Illustrations

We have attempted to locate the originators of the illustrations in this book but given the nature of the internet this has not always been possible. These are the sources:

Cover © BenG.Photography

p. 11 © www.jerrystoll.photography

p. 23 © binkski / 123RF Stock Photo

p. 34 © tonobalaguer / 123RF Stock Photo

p. 46 © objowl / 123RF Stock Photo

p. 59 © BenG.Photography

p. 70 © lesyanovo / 123RF Stock Photo

p. 81 www.examiner.com/article/feel-like-i-m-fixing-to-die-country-joe-and-the-fish

p. 91 © soloway / 123RF Stock Photo

p. 104 © Novic / 123RF Stock Photo

p. 115 © NejroN / 123RF Stock Photo

p. 124 www.ukrockfestivals.com/henge-history-84.html © Herb

p. 133 www.ukrockfestivals.com/e-fayre-83-photo-gallery.html

p. 143 https://libcom.org

p. 155 https://s-media-cache-ak0.pinimg.com/736x/39/88/e6/3988e6fb3798b0047de3ee1f37c4c61c.jpg

p. 167 © Spiral Tribe

p. 178 © lilu1331 / 123RF Stock Photo

p. 188 © www.cosm.org

p. 198 en.wikipedia.org/wiki/Hippie_trail

p. 205 © static01.mediaite.com

p. 218 © rythmdance (Mia), www.deviantart.com

p. 232 www.fairfaxunderground.com/forum

p. 242 © depression by ajgiel, www.deviantart.com

p. 252 © rolffimages / 123RF Stock Photo

p. 259 © Lee Martin

p. 261 © Lee Martin

And the author?

Even at a very young age, Lee Martin demonstrated an independent nature. His outlook on life was to buck the trend, get away from the norm. People tend to settle for roles that are predetermined for them, either by their circumstances, their environment, their parents or their education. It wasn't like that for Lee, nobody made his decisions – except himself. When he grew into a teenager, he worked at many manual jobs to make a bit of money – kitchen porter and odd-job man and barrow-loader in a pottery. He went on the road and travelled to America and the Far East, leading a nomadic lifestyle and acquiring the ability to think for himself and try to understand the meaning of it all. He came back to the UK with ideas about writing this book, but events overtook him and he never got around to it until now. He mixed with New-Age travellers and got involved in events like the Beltane Bash at the Horse-Drawn Camp. With the spread of family-orientated music festivals in the new millennium, Lee was one of the organisers of the Lakefest happening in Gloucestershire, originally held at Croft Farm but now relocated to Eastnor Castle near Ledbury. He currently lives on Bredon Hill with his wife Becky and their two children.